D1827142

Algebra Teaching around the World

Algebra Teaching around the World

Edited by

Frederick K.S. Leung
The University of Hong Kong, Hong Kong

Kyungmee Park
Hongik University, Korea

Derek Holton
University of Melbourne, Australia

and

David Clarke
University of Melbourne, Australia

SENSE PUBLISHERS
ROTTERDAM/BOSTON/TAIPEI

A C.I.P. record for this book is available from the Library of Congress.

ISBN: 978-94-6209-705-6 (paperback)
ISBN: 978-94-6209-706-3 (hardback)
ISBN: 978-94-6209-707-0 (e-book)

Published by: Sense Publishers,
P.O. Box 21858,
3001 AW Rotterdam,
The Netherlands
https://www.sensepublishers.com/

Printed on acid-free paper

All Rights Reserved © 2014 Sense Publishers

No part of this work may be reproduced, stored in a retrieval system, or transmitted in any form or by any means, electronic, mechanical, photocopying, microfilming, recording or otherwise, without written permission from the Publisher, with the exception of any material supplied specifically for the purpose of being entered and executed on a computer system, for exclusive use by the purchaser of the work.

TABLE OF CONTENTS

SERIES PREFACE

The Learner's Perspective Study provides a vehicle for the work of an international community of classroom researchers. The work of this community is reported in a series of books of which this is the fifth. International comparative and cross-cultural research has the capacity to inform practice, shape policy and develop theory. Such research can reflect regional, national or global priorities. Cross-cultural comparisons of social practice in settings such as classrooms can lead us to question our assumptions about what constitutes desirable learning or effective instruction. International comparative research offers us more than insight into the novel, interesting and adaptable practices employed in other school systems. It also offers us a new perspective on the strange, invisible, and unquestioned routines and rituals of our own school system and our own classrooms. In addition, a cross-cultural perspective on classrooms can help us identify common values and shared assumptions across geographically disparate social settings, which in turn can facilitate the adaptation of practices from one classroom for use in a different cultural setting. The identification of structure and recurrence within cultural diversity can help us to distinguish between fundamental commonalities and local conventions. The topic of algebra provides a watershed in the school careers of many students and a common curricular referent for any comparisons of classroom practice in 8th grade mathematics classrooms. By focusing on a single mathematical domain: algebra, we allow other aspects of the mathematics classroom to become more visible through their variation. The chapters of this book document just how different are the forms in which algebra is employed, modeled, and experienced in mathematics classrooms around the world.

David Clarke
Series Editor

FREDERICK K.S. LEUNG, DAVID CLARKE, DEREK HOLTON &
KYUNGMEE PARK

CHAPTER 1

How is Algebra Taught around the World?

INTRODUCTION

Algebra is a major component of the mathematics curriculum in all countries around the world. There is ample research on the algebra curriculum and on algebra teaching reported in the literature, mainly on the importance of algebra (Edwards, 1990; Moses & Cobb, 2001; Kaput, Blanton & Moreno, 2008; National Mathematics Advisory Panel, 2008; Watson, 2009) and the difficulties students face in learning algebra (Van Ameron, 2002; Kieran, 2007; Harel, Fuller & Rabin, 2008; Linsell, 2009; Caglayan & Olive, 2010). However, research in international comparison of classroom algebra teaching is hampered by limits on comparability, due to differences in the grade levels of the classrooms studied. This book offers an opportunity to compare algebra teaching at eighth grade level across many countries that are both geographically and culturally distant. As a result this book will be of value to researchers with a focus on algebra, pedagogy or international comparisons of education. In addition, various research methods are on view that will be of value to young researchers and graduate students. Because of the pedagogical variations noted here, there is a great deal of material that will be of interest to both teachers and teacher educators.

THE LEARNER'S PERSPECTIVE STUDY (LPS)

The LPS provides a common platform for documenting eighth grade mathematics teaching in a large number of countries around the world. In addition to a standardized way of videotaping mathematics classrooms, the LPS collected data on the reflective accounts of participant students and teachers, adding 'complementarity' and richness to the data set (Clarke, 2000, 2006).

Not all of the LPS lessons are on algebra, but it is possible to select algebra lessons specifically and to study issues related to its teaching in eighth grade classrooms around the world. This is exactly what is being done in this book on algebra teaching based on the LPS data.

F.K.S. Leung et al. (eds.), Algebra Teaching around the World, 1–15.
© *2014 Sense Publishers. All rights reserved.*

What are algebra and algebraic activities?

In this book, we examine algebraic activities in classrooms from different countries. But what is algebra? According to Usiskin (1988), algebra is "generalized arithmetic; a way to solve certain types of problems; a study of relationships among quantities; and a study of structures" (Kaur uses this definition in chapter 5). Stacey, Chick and Kendal (2004), on the other hand, define algebra as "a way of expressing generality; a study of symbol manipulation and equation solving; a study of functions; a way to solve certain classes of problems; a way to model real situations; and a formal system involving set theory, logic, and operations on entities other than real numbers" (Novotná & Hošpesová use this definition in chapter 4). These definitions are not the same, but neither are they incompatible. Each emphasizes particular aspects of the mathematical domain of algebra.

Adopting an inclusive approach and accepting this multi-faceted characterization of algebra, algebraic activities can be understood as comprising three core activities: generational activity, transformational activity, and global/meta-level activity. "The generational activities involve the forming of expressions and equations that are the objects of algebra. The transformational activities include, for instance, collecting like terms, factoring, expanding, substituting, adding and multiplying polynomial expressions, solving equations, simplifying expressions, working with equivalent expressions and equations, etc. The global/meta-level mathematics activities refer to those for which algebra is used as a tool but which are not exclusive to algebra. They include problem solving, modeling, noticing structure, studying changes, generalizing, analyzing relationship, justifying, proving, and predicting, etc." (Kieran, 2004, quoted in Chapter 10 by Huang et al.).

In the definition of algebraic activities above, there seems to be an assumption that algebra is universal. But is it understood in the same way in different countries around the world? Do different countries expect students to learn the same knowledge and skills in algebra? And, more central to the focus of this book, are there differences in how algebra is taught in different countries? In this book, access to classroom data from several countries around the world allows us to address these related questions.

CONTENT OF THIS BOOK

Issues of concern pertaining to algebra teaching and learning may be different from country to country, and a number of different issues are discussed in this book. In Chapter 2, Anthony and Burgess describe how a New Zealand teacher used a "balance model" (Warren & Cooper, 2005) in teaching linear equations in order to occasion learning opportunities that support students' adjustments in the learning transition from arithmetic to algebra. The authors argue that the teacher's planning, instruction and interactions within the classroom are themselves a series of balancing acts that afford or constrain opportunities for students to make the necessary adjustments.

In Chapter 3, Pepin and Sør-Trøndelag report a Norwegian classroom where the concept of equality and the meanings and use of the equal sign were explored. The authors utilize the concept of "orchestration of signs" (Trouche, 2004) to explain the teacher's pedagogic practice in the algebra classroom, following a semiotic and 'instrumental' approach. In Chapter 4, Novotná and Hošpesová report two Czech teachers' approaches to teaching the topic of linear equations and their systems. The authors point out that the two teachers' approaches differed in terms of the pupils' expected output competencies and what is regarded as the most adequate tools for reaching them.

In Chapter 5, Kaur reports a case study of how a Singaporean teacher engaged her grade eight students in developing procedural fluency in algebraic structures through the use of varied learning tasks. In Chapter 6, Park and Leung report the perceptions of a Korean teacher and his students in relation to a series of algebra lessons. They show how the same lessons were perceived differently by the teacher and his students in terms of the lesson objectives and what is considered important in a lesson, because of their different levels of competence and their differing values with regard to mathematics.

In Chapters 7 and 8, Ohtani and Fujii report separately on algebra lessons in two different Japanese schools. Ohtani investigates factors which affect the connections among a series of lessons on simultaneous equations, and utilizes the construct of "Construction Zone" (Newman, Griffin & Cole, 1989) in analyzing students' progressive understanding of new mathematical concepts. He conceptualizes the "generic task" as a mediating tool between students and the teacher, which constitutes a construction zone where people with different levels of understanding can interact with each other, which in turn opens up a learning opportunity for deeper understanding. Fujii reports a series of seven algebra lessons, which were devoted to solving one mathematics problem in order to understand the concept of the range of variables. Fujii demonstrates how the Japanese teacher involved the students as a "community of mathematical inquiry" (Lewis, 1995) to deepen their understanding of mathematics concepts.

Chapters 9 to 11 are on algebra lessons in China. In Chapter 9, Huan et al. examine how algebra teaching in a Beijing classroom is aligned with the guiding principles of the official Mathematics Curriculum Standards in China. They report not only that the official curriculum standards exerted a strong influence on algebra teaching in this Beijing classroom, but also that the senior high school entrance examination in Beijing had a strong influence on the teaching. However, the authors point out that the spirit of the new curriculum was only followed superficially by the teacher. In Chapter 10, Mok shows a Shanghai teacher's pedagogical delineation of the graphical method of solving linear equations in two unknowns by an analysis of a series of algebra lessons. Through analysis of the lessons and interviews with the teacher, Mok characterizes both the teacher's beliefs and his instructional practice. In Chapter 11, Huang et al. utilize the theory of variation (Marton & Booth, 1997) to study the process of forming and developing algebraic concepts in algebra classrooms in Hong Kong, Macau and Shanghai. The authors report that the Chinese lessons followed a pattern of four phases, which provided learning opportunities for students to develop new concepts through exploring inductive/broadening variations of problems and to consolidate the concepts through practicing with deepening variations of problems and reflecting on the learning experiences.

In Chapter 12, Huang and Li compare algebra teaching in China and the USA, focusing on how the teaching promoted the understanding of algebraic concepts. The goals and contents of the algebraic lessons are compared, as well as the students' perceptions of the classroom instruction with regard to understanding in the two countries. In Chapter 13, Häggström utilizes the concept of "opportunity to learn" (Hiebert & Grouws, 2007) to analyse algebra teaching in Sweden and China (Shanghai and Hong Kong) based on the theory of variation. Häggström's purpose is to illustrate the methodological development in the field of research on mathematics teaching and the development of the concept "opportunity to learn" as a powerful tool to analyse and compare mathematics instruction.

ALGEBRA TEACHING IN DIFFERENT COUNTRIES

As can be seen from the description above, the intention of the authors in most of the chapters in this book is not just to describe how algebra is taught in their countries. Each chapter has a theme or focus of its own. Certainly each chapter offers a particular perspective on algebra teaching in a particular country and Chapters 12 and 13 make country-specific features explicit through the comparison of algebra teaching in classrooms in China and the USA and in China and Sweden respectively. But since the focus of all of the studies in all of the chapters is algebra and its teaching, the combination of sites and perspectives provides a rich and complex picture of similarity and variation in the teaching of algebra around the world.

The range of countries in which the LPS classrooms are situated is sufficient for us to make a comparison between two commonly-invoked cultural clusters: the Confucian-Heritage Culture (CHC) countries (Biggs & Watkins, 1996) and "Western" countries. For the sample of classrooms studied in this book, representatives of the CHC cluster of countries include China (Beijing, Shanghai, Hong Kong and Macau), Japan, Korea, and Singapore; while "Western" classrooms are represented by the Czech Republic, New Zealand, Norway, Sweden, and the USA. The significance of these two clusters of countries rests on the suggested cultural coherence within each cluster and the possibility that cultural coherence might translate into pedagogical coherence. While there may be substantial cultural differences between China and Japan and between the USA and the Czech Republic, the clustering of countries in this fashion has the capacity to provide insight into patterns of pedagogical similarity within a cluster and pedagogical distinctiveness between clusters. Such patterns are amenable to empirical investigation, given a data set such as that available within LPS. Equally, as will be seen, interesting differences are evident within clusters and even the designation of classrooms as "Chinese" can conceal interesting variations in practice between those as proximate as Hong Kong, Macau and Shanghai.

Naively, it might be asked, "How much difference can there be between one algebra class and another?" The chapters in this book demonstrate the variation possible in different classrooms around the world, even when the common focus is as specific as algebra.

Similarities and differences among countries

There are many commonalities in the ways in which algebra is taught among countries as revealed by the chapters in this book. But there are also striking differences. In discussing differences among countries, reference will be made to individual countries and to clusters such as the CHC countries and the Western countries. But we need to bear in mind that the LPS research design targeted sequences of at least ten lessons in the classrooms of three competent mathematics teachers in each city. The focus was the detailed documentation of competent practice, and the selected teachers and their classrooms should not be taken as representative of the countries concerned as a whole. Also, when discussing between-country differences, we should note that, even for this focused LPS sample, the detailed data set for each classroom revealed within-country differences in addition to the between-country differences being discussed.

Take the Czech Republic as an example. In chapter 4, Novotná and Hošpesová report two teachers teaching the same topic and trying to meet the same requirements of that country. Yet they taught in very different ways, one stressing more "how" while the other placed more emphasis on "why". Both linked new content to what students already knew, but the order of presentation of the content differed, the level of algorithmisation differed, the level of complexity and difficulty of the problems discussed differed, and the ways in which word problems were used differed. So even for a small sample of teachers in just one country, there are within-country differences in how algebra is taught. In the case of China, even greater differences were recorded between the classroom practices of the selected mathematics teachers in Hong Kong, Shanghai, Macau and Beijing. Notwithstanding these within-country differences, when we look at how algebra is taught in different countries, as revealed in this book, we can see that there are even wider between-country differences.

How is algebra taught differently in different countries?

Aims and objectives of the lesson. From the chapters in this book, when the aims of algebra lessons are described, it seems that what students are expected to learn in algebra (or in mathematics in general) is basically an understanding of algebraic concepts and procedural fluency in dealing with algebraic manipulations (Hiebert & Carpenter, 1992). But the ways in which these aims are formulated differ in different countries. The data reported in this book show that some teachers set very general and ambitious aims for algebra teaching, while other teachers tend to set concrete and detailed goals. For example, in Chapter 12, Huang and Li report a USA teacher setting very general goals, while a Chinese teacher set very specific and concrete aims for the lesson.

The content of the lesson. With respect to the content of the algebra lessons, the situations in the Western countries varied. Some lessons dealt with rather conceptual content, while the teaching in others was rather procedural. A common feature seemed to be a stress on everyday life problems, much more so than in CHC countries.

The lessons from these classrooms in the CHC cluster shared some common features, although the emphasis of the lessons varied from highly conceptual (Japan) to highly procedural (Hong Kong). A particular common feature among the CHC classrooms was the abundance of practice problems and exercises, which were generally of high cognitive demand. The problems were usually carefully planned: they varied systematically and the content of the problems was interconnected.

The way lessons are conducted. There is clear evidence from the descriptions in this book that there was a strong influence of public examination on the way in which algebra was taught in the classrooms in Beijing (see Huan et al., Chapter 9) and this seems characteristic of the CHC cluster in general. The way in which the lessons were conducted in the CHC classrooms suggests a prescribed syllabus that was followed closely, with a focus on the efficient delivery of mathematics content. Students in the CHC classrooms were, in general, serious about their learning. In contrast, the algebra lessons in the Western countries were more interactive (see also Kaur, Anthony, Ohtani, & Clarke, 2013), and the atmosphere was more relaxed.

Teachers in the classrooms from both clusters of countries said that it is important for students to participate in lessons, but the nature of that participation varied in interesting ways. For example, while small group work occurred in the classrooms in both clusters, collaboration among students during the group work was given greater emphasis in the Western classrooms. Group work, when it occurred, was monitored and controlled more closely by the teachers in the CHC classrooms than in the Western classrooms.

Conceptual understanding

Many lessons in the classrooms in both Western and CHC countries stressed conceptual understanding. For example, in Chapters 2 and 3, the New Zealand lessons (on solving linear equations based on the "balance" model, where the teacher's goal was to help the students eventually to solve equations detaching from the model) and the Norwegian lessons (on understanding the equality sign) both used the 'balance' or 'scale' model to discuss equality and linear equations. The concepts dealt with were fairly basic, but the approach was conceptual. Both series of lessons aimed at helping the students to understand important concepts in algebra.

The lessons from the CHC countries reported in this book also stressed conceptual understanding, and the lessons shared some similarities in structure. Huang et al. (Chapter 11) identify four phases of a typical Chinese lesson as follows:

1. Introducing the concept,
2. Explaining the meanings,
3. Discriminating the concept with varying exercises, and
4. Summarization.

Huang et al. illustrate this structure in Chapter 11 with a Shanghai lesson on systems of linear equations in two unknowns. The authors argue that a distinctive characteristic of Chinese lessons is teaching with variation. It is worth considering the implications of teaching with variation for the students' learning of algebra.

Theory of variation

In Chapter 13, Häggström draws on the theory of variation (Marton & Booth, 1997) and uses the concept of "opportunity to learn" to explain what students might learn in lessons taught with variation. Marton's and Booth's theory of variation is applicable to a wider field of learning, but since algebra is about generalization and transformation, it can certainly be argued that algebra can be learned effectively through teaching with variation. Variations of various components within a concept (for example, various components of the concept of system of linear equations in two unknowns) help students to understand the concept, and variations between different concepts (for example, the concepts of system of linear equations in two unknowns and system of other types of equations) help students to connect one concept to others (which will also help their understanding of the concept itself). Häggström compares six Swedish, Hong Kong and Shanghai lessons, and examines the different dimensions of variation opened in the lessons. The analysis of how the content was handled in the six classrooms shows a difference in students' 'opportunities to learn' in terms of the dimensions of variation (Marton & Pong, 2005).

VARIATIONS IN ALGEBRA TEACHING AMONG THE CLASSROOMS FROM THE CHC CLUSTER OF COUNTRIES

As pointed out above, in referring to the CHC or Western cluster of countries, we need to bear in mind within-cluster differences. But since nearly all of the CHC countries are represented in this book, the detail provided by the chapters reporting algebra teaching in these CHC classrooms is sufficient to justify a detailed discussion of the variations in practice among CHC mathematics classrooms.

Despite the identified similarities of the algebra lessons in the CHC countries, some major differences are evident. It is acknowledged widely that developing conceptual understanding and procedural fluency are important in mathematics learning (Hiebert & Carpenter, 1992; NCTM, 2000; NMAP, 2008), and the differences in algebra lessons among the CHC countries can be summarized in terms of the different emphases on these two aspects. Three different models can be identified: **The Procedural Model, the Conceptual Model and the Blended Model**. The classrooms in Korea, Singapore, Hong Kong and Macau seem to align most closely to the Procedural Model, while the Japanese classrooms exemplify the Conceptual Model. The classrooms in Shanghai and Beijing seem to implement a Blended Model that combines aspects of both procedural and conceptual emphases. The differences between these models illustrate how much variation is possible, even with those classrooms situated within the CHC cluster.

Similar distinct pedagogical differences have been discussed by Clarke, Xu and Wan (2013a and 2013b) from the perspective of patterns of classroom discourse. In fact, it can be argued that the differences in emphasis identified in the algebra lessons provide part of the rationale for the differences in discourse patterns. The emphasis on conceptual understanding corresponding to the promotion of fluency in the spoken use of mathematical terms is in contrast to an emphasis on procedural fluency, which does not necessarily require sophisticated mathematical language. Even where two classrooms appear to place the same emphasis on conceptual or procedural understanding, the instructional approach can still be quite different (for example, Korea compared with Singapore or the classrooms in Shanghai compared with those in Tokyo (see Xu and Clarke, 2013)).

Fujii (Chapter 8) points out that a typical Japanese problem-solving oriented lesson consists of four phases or components:

Phase 1: Presenting one problem for the day (understanding the problem),
Phase 2: Problem solving by students,
Phase 3: Comparing and discussing (students present solutions), and
Phase 4: Summing up by the teacher.

Fujii illustrates these four phases with a series of lessons on a paper-folding problem. It can be seen that there was a strong emphasis on conceptual understanding, as is evident from the fact that seven lessons were devoted to tackling just one mathematics problem. One might ask how, then, do the Japanese students attain their procedural fluency, given that so much lesson time is spent on the elaboration of mathematics concepts.

The answer may lie in the parallel *juku* system in Japan (Harnisch, 1994). So students acquire deep conceptual understanding through the classroom teaching in the regular schools, and then after school they attend *juku* schools and further practise their mathematics skills and consolidate their understanding (Leung, Park, Shimizu & Xu, 2012). This 'distribution of labour' in the Japanese system is an area of interest in itself, but is beyond the scope of this book. Such 'shadow education' systems are common across the cluster of CHC countries and are becoming more prominent in the Western cluster of countries as well. The Japanese example serves to illustrate the possibility that mathematics classroom practices in CHC countries may develop in symbiosis with the practices of the increasingly popular after-hours practice classes.

In Singapore, Hong Kong, Macau and Korea, content was typically covered relatively quickly, and students were given the opportunity to do a lot of practice exercises. This is quite a different pedagogy from that found in the LPS classrooms in Tokyo, Shanghai or Beijing. The other CHC countries also have a private tutorial school system that plays a similar role to the *juku* system in Japan (Kwok, 2004), but, based on the data reported in the chapters of this book, algebra teaching in the regular classrooms in these CHC countries seems to have a different emphasis from the regular classroom teaching in Japan. But this does not necessarily mean that the teaching of algebra in the classrooms in other CHC countries is not conceptual. As mentioned above, Huang et al. point out in Chapter 11 that the promotion of conceptual understanding in the Hong Kong, Macau and Shanghai classrooms was built into the varied examples practised by students. The difference between the Conceptual Model and the Procedural Model lies in whether the concepts are addressed explicitly (as in the case of the Tokyo classrooms and. to some extent, in the case of the classrooms in Shanghai and Beijing as well), or whether the concepts are embedded in well-designed, systematically varied exercises that students practice (as in the case of Singapore, Hong Kong and Korea). It can be argued that what we have called the Blended Model, as practised in Shanghai and Beijing, seems to capture both the emphasis on conceptual understanding of the Japanese model and the stress on procedural fluency identified in Singapore, Hong Kong and Korea. It is probably fair to say that the difference is best seen to be one of emphasis, with each classroom striking a different balance between conceptual understanding and procedural fluency.

COMPARING CHARACTERISTICS OF ALGEBRA TEACHING IN CHC AND WESTERN CLASSROOMS

From what is reported in this book, it seems that a common emphasis of algebra teaching in CHC countries is the 'linkage' or 'coherence' of mathematics concepts (Gu, Huang & Marton, 2004; Leung, 2001; Shimizu, 2007). This linkage of concepts is both within a topic (e.g., concepts within the topic of system of linear equations in two unknowns) and between topics (relation between system of linear equations in two unknowns and other topics).

Contemporary algebra teaching in many Western school systems places increasing emphasis on the use of algebra in mathematical modeling in 'real world' contexts (e.g., Czech Republic, Chapter 4). Other emphases in the teaching of algebra in Western classrooms include the instructional use of metaphors, such as "balance" (reported in both New Zealand and Norway, Chapters 2 and 3). These two examples can both be seen as being driven by a desire to assist students in the construction of meaning in relation to algebra, but the nature of that meaning is differently purposed. In each case, meaning construction is assisted by invoking contexts outside the domain of algebraic manipulation. The clear intention is to help students to form connections between algebra and other aspects of their experience.

9

Irrespective of whether they are classrooms akin to the Conceptual Model, the Procedural Model or the Blended Model, all of the algebra lessons in the CHC countries reported in this book look rather teacher-directed in comparison with the lessons from the Czech Republic, New Zealand, Norway, Sweden and the USA. As has been argued by Mok (2006), this appearance of teacher domination is misleading and it seems that conceptual understanding, as well as procedural fluency, can be achieved through teacher-directed lessons. These teacher-directed lessons include a lot of listening to explanations by the teacher and practice of mathematics problems. Of course, practising mathematics problems is an active learning experience, even when done under the dominating direction and close supervision of the teacher, but listening to the teacher's explanation can be an active mode of learning as well (refer to the notion of 'listening-oriented learning' proposed by Cortazzi and Jin, 2001, quoted in Chapter 11 by Huang et al.). However, the pre-requisite for listening to be an active learning experience is that there should be high quality content to be 'listened' to. It may also be advantageous for the content to be delivered in a manner that 'engages' the students' attention. Other research on the differences in the ethos of Asian and Western classrooms has suggested that a key difference is the location of responsibility: where Western practice requires the teacher to engage the student's attention, Asian practice places the responsibility for engagement with the student (Stevenson & Stigler, 1992). The phenomena of students listening to the teacher's explanation and engaging in a lot of practice may give the impression that the students are very passive. But the quality of the teacher's explanation, the strategic selection of the problems (with systematic variation) that students practise, and the informed use of worked examples are all essential aspects of competent practice in CHC classrooms and all have been connected by recent research to high quality learning (see Sweller & Cooper, 1985).

Contrasts such as implicit versus explicit, deep versus surface, or closed versus open may provide useful ways of characterising mathematics teaching in ways that reveal culturally-specific practices and beliefs. The contrasts point to the possibility of achieving effective teaching based on different philosophies and following different traditions (Clarke, 2013). In the final analysis, it is always the teacher who sets the agenda, and one may argue that the expression of student agency is a relatively infrequent occurrence. We always 'teach' students the teacher's version of mathematics or mathematics learning, be it the CHC 'didactic' mathematics and mathematics learning or the Western constructivist approach.

IS ALGEBRA "UNIVERSAL"?

Returning to a question posed at the beginning of this chapter, based on the different ways of teaching algebra reported in this book, and with reference to the discussion in the preceding sections, is algebra 'universal'? Is 'what algebra is' understood in the same way in different countries around the world? Further, there is the question of whether different countries expect students to learn the same knowledge and skills.

These are difficult questions to answer, partly because this book did not set out to address them specifically. It is worth noting, though, that in Chapter 4, Sutherland (2000), who has made a study of the curricula of 12 countries, is quoted as saying that "more research needs to be carried out in order to understand the implications of this [curriculum] on classroom practice". This research is not reported explicitly in this book.

It should also be noted that, in Chapter 8, Fujii makes the point that, in the Japanese Course of Study for elementary and lower secondary school mathematics, there is no specific mention of algebra. Fujii writes "instead of being an independent domain in the curriculum, algebra is included systematically in various parts of the mathematics curriculum, particularly at the elementary level" (p. 129). Fujii goes on to discuss the different conceptions of algebra proposed by Usiskin (1988) and the way in which these are aligned with algebra within the Japanese mathematics curriculum. It is clear that algebra is conceived, named and situated differently within mathematics curricula in different countries. These curricular differences are then compounded by differences in the ways in which algebra is taught. These differences in the teaching of algebra constitute the primary focus of the chapters in this book. However, it is clear that a number of countries see linear equations and their applications to be necessary (Chapters 2, 4, 5, 6, 7, 8, 9 and 11). There is a certain amount of prerequisite knowledge required for this topic. For instance, almost all of the material that is required for Year 8 students in Singapore, shown in Figure 1 of Chapter 5, must be needed by other countries too. It would be surprising if the Binomial Theorem and quadratic equations were omitted from that list. As has been said above, many countries also require understanding to support students' skill ability.

Given the different ways in which algebra is taught in different countries, it is reasonable to expect that students' conceptions of it might be different. The different ways algebra is taught reflect the fact that it is conceived of differently by teachers in different countries. But one may argue that algebra is algebra, no matter whether it is in China or Korea or Sweden or the USA! This touches on an absolutist versus a fallibilist view of mathematics. If we accept a fallibilist view, then the conceptions of algebra may indeed be different in different countries. The curricular encryption of algebra, as is evident from the Japanese example, mediates between algebra as a domain of mathematical knowledge and enquiry and algebra as a school subject and the object of classroom teaching and learning. The chapters of this book document just how different are the forms in which algebra is employed, modeled, and experienced in mathematics classrooms around the world.

Notwithstanding these different conceptions of algebra and algebra teaching, identifying good practices and explicitly formulating the practices and the reasons for their effectiveness systematically (in the form of a theory) should help reinforce and promulgate the effective practices and reduce the occurrence of the ineffective ones. This is a major aspect of what research in the field of comparative study in mathematics teaching and learning attempts to achieve. The chapters in this book are intended to support such comparisons by identifying key features in the practices of competent mathematics teachers in many different school systems.

CONCLUDING REMARKS

Different issues in algebra teaching are the primary focus of this book. They range from the question of the alignment between algebra teaching and the official mathematics curriculum; how procedural fluency is achieved through the use of varied tasks; a teacher's pedagogical delineation of a certain method in teaching an algebraic topic; to how students are involved as a 'community of inquiry' in algebra lessons. Different theories (including the construct of the 'construction zone'; the theory of variation; the notion of 'opportunity to learn'; and the concept of 'orchestration of signs') are used to characterize algebra lessons or to compare algebra teaching in different countries. Algebra teaching is perceived as a series of balancing acts for the teacher; discrepancies between students and their teacher in their perceptions of the algebra lessons are identified; how teachers in the same country approached the same algebraic topic differently is discussed; algebra teaching approaches in different countries are compared, and approached the same algebraic topic differently is discussed; and algebra teaching approaches in different countries are compared.

Many commonalities in algebra teaching around the world can be identified from what is reported in this book, but there are also striking and deep-rooted differences. The different ways algebra was taught in the mathematics classrooms of different countries points to how algebra teaching may be embedded in the culture and the general traditions of mathematics education of the countries concerned. The different classroom practices resulting from the different cultures may also help to explain the achievements of students from different countries in international studies of mathematics achievement. It is hoped that the following chapters provide useful insights into the classroom practices of mathematics teachers in different cultures and school systems and that the various accounts of the teaching of algebra enrich the didactical knowledge base of mathematics teachers and teacher educators internationally.

REFERENCES

Biggs, J. B., & Watkins, D. A. (1996). The Chinese learner in retrospect. In D. A. Watkins & J. B. Biggs (Eds.), *The Chinese learner: Cultural, psychological, and contextual influences* (pp. 269–285). Hong Kong: Comparative Educational Research Center, The University of Hong Kong.

Biggs, J. B., & Watkins, D. A. (1996). The Chinese learner in retrospect. In D. A. Watkins & J. B. Biggs (Eds.), *The Chinese learner: Cultural, psychological, and contextual influences* (pp. 269–285). Hong Kong: Comparative Educational Research Center, The University of Hong Kong.

Caglayan, G., & Olive, J. (2010). Eighth grade students' representations of linear equations based on a cups and tiles model. *Educational Studies in Mathematics, 74*(2), 143–162.

Clarke, D. (2000). *The Learner's perspective study*. Research design.: University of Melbourne.

Clarke, D. (2006). The LPS research design. In D. J. Clarke, C. Keitel, & Y. Shimizu (Eds.), *Mathematics classrooms in twelve countries* (pp. 15–29). Rotterdam, The Netherlands: Sense.

Clarke, D. J. (2013). International comparative research in educational interaction: Constructing and concealing difference. In K. Tirri & E. Kuusisto (Eds.), *Interaction in educational settings*. Rotterdam: Sense Publishers.

Clarke, D. J., Xu, L., & Wan, V. (2013a). Spoken mathematics as an instructional strategy: The public discourse of mathematics classrooms in different countries. In B. Kaur, G. Anthony & D. Clarke (Eds.), *Student voice in mathematics classrooms around the world* (pp. 13–32). Rotterdam: Sense Publishers.

Clarke, D. J., Xu, L., & Wan, M. E. V. (2013b). Students speaking mathematics: Practices and consequences for mathematics classrooms in different countries. In B. Kaur, G. Anthony, M. Ohtani, & D. J. Clarke (Eds.), *Student voice in mathematics classrooms around the world* (pp. 32–52). Rotterdam: Sense Publishers.

Cortazzi, M., & Jin, L. (2001). Large class in China: "Good" teachers and interaction, In D. A. Watkins & J. B. Biggs (Eds), *Teaching the Chinese learner: Psychological and pedagogical perspectives* (pp. 115–134). Hong Kong/Melbourne: Comparative Education Research Centre, the University of Hong Kong/Australian Council for Education Research.

Edwards, E. L. (Ed.). (1990). *Algebra for everyone*. Reston, VA: National Council of Teachers of Mathematics

Gu, L., Huang, R., & Marton, F. (2004). Teaching with variation: An effective way of mathematics teaching in China. In L. Fan, N. Y. Wong, J. Cai, & S. Li (Eds.), *How Chinese learn mathematics: Perspectives from insiders* (pp. 309–345). Singapore: World Scientific.

Harel, G., Fuller, E., & Rabin, J. M. (2008). Attention to meaning by algebra teachers. *Journal of Mathematical Behavior, 27*, 116–127.

Harnisch, D. L. (1994). Supplemental education in Japan: Juku schooling and its implication. *Journal of Curriculum Studies, 26*(3), 323–334.

Hiebert, J., & Carpenter, P. P. (1992). Learning and teaching with understanding. In D. A. Grouws (Ed.), *Handbook of research on mathematics teaching and learning* (pp. 65–97). New York, NY: Macmillan.

Hiebert, J., & Grouws, D. A. (2007). The effects of classroom mathematics teaching on students' learning. In F. K. Lester (Ed.), *Second handbook of research on mathematics teaching and learning* (pp. 371–404). Charlotte, NC: Information Age Publishers.

Kaput, J., Blanton, M., & Moreno, L. (2008). Algebra from a symbolization point of view. In J. Kaput, D. Carraher, & M. Blanton (Eds.), *Algebra in the early grades* (pp. 19–55). New York, NY: Lawrence Erlbaum Associates.

Kaur, B., Anthony, G., Ohtani, M. & Clarke, D. (Eds.) (2013). *Student voice in mathematics classrooms around the world*. Rotterdam: Sense Publishers.

Kieran, C. (2004). The core of algebra: Reflections on its main activities. In K. Stacey, H. Chick, & M. Kendal (Eds.), *The future of the teaching and learning of algebra: The 12th ICMI study* (pp. 21–34). Boston, MA: Kluwer.

Kieran, C. (2007). Learning and teaching algebra at the middle school from college levels: Building meaning for symbols and their manipulation. In F. K. Lester, Jr. (Ed.), *Second handbook of research on mathematics teaching and learning* (pp. 707–762). Charlotte, NC: Information Age.

Kwok, P. (2004). Examination-oriented knowledge and value transformation in East Asian cram schools. *Asia Pacific Education Review, 5*(1), 64–75.

Leung, F. K. S. (2001). In search of an East Asian identity in mathematics education. *Educational Studies in Mathematics, 47*, 35–51.

Leung, F. K. S., Park, K., Shimizu, Y., & Xu, B. (2012). *Mathematics education in East Asia*. Plenary panel presented at the 12th International Congress on Mathematics Education, Seoul, Korea.

Lewis, C. C.(1995). *Educating hearts and minds: Reflection on Japanese preschool and elementary education*. Cambridge: Cambridge University Press.

Li, S. (2006). Practice makes perfect: A Key belief in China. In Leung, Graf and Lopez-Real (eds.), *Mathematics Education in Different Cultural Traditions: A Comparative Study of East Asia and the West, The 13th ICMI Study* (pp. 129–138). New York, NY: Springer.

Li, Y., Huang, R., & Yang, Y. (1011). Characterizing expert teaching in school mathematics in China: A prototype of expertise in teaching mathematics. In Y. Li & G. Kaiser (Eds.), *Expertise in teaching mathematics: An international perspective* (pp. 168–196). New York, NY: Springer.

Linsell, C. (2009). Students' knowledge and strategies for solving equations. In *Findings from the New Zealand Secondary Numeracy Project 2008* (pp. 29–43). Wellington, New Zealand: Learning Media.

Marton, F., & Booth, S. (1997). *Learning and awareness*. Mahwah, NJ: Erlbaum.

Marton, F., & Pong, W. Y. (2005). On the unit of description in phenomenography. *Higher Education Research and Development, 24*(4), 335–348.

Mok, I. (2006). Teacher-dominating lessons in Shanghai: The Insiders' Story. In D. Clarke, C. Keitel, & Y. Shimizu (Eds.), *Mathematics Classrooms in Twelve Countries: The Insider's Perspective* (pp. 87–98). Rotterdam: Sense Publishers.

Moses, R. P., & Cobb, C. E., Jr. (2001). *Radical equations: math literacy and civil rights*. Boston, MA: Beacon.

National Council of Teachers of Mathematics. (2000). *Principles and standards for school mathematics*. Reston, VA: Author.

National Mathematics Advisory Panel. (2008). Foundations for success: The final report of the National Mathematics Advisory Panel. Washington, DC: U.S. Department of Education.

Newman, D., Griffin, P., & Cole, M. (1989). *The construction zone: Working for cognitive change in school*. NY: Cambridge University Press.

Shimizu, Y. (2007). Explicit linking in the sequence of consecutive lessons in mathematics classroom in Japan. In Jeong-Ho Woo et al. (eds.), *Proceedings of the 31st conference of the international group for the psychology of mathematics education* (Vol 4, pp. 177–184). Seoul: PME.

Stacey, K., & Chick, H. (2004). Solving the problem with algebra. In Stacey, K., Chick, H., & Kendal, M. (eds.). (2004). *The future of the teaching and learning of Algebra, The 12th ICMI Study* (p. 12). Boston, MA: Kluwer Academic Publishers.

Stacey, K., Chick, H., & Kendal, M. (eds.) (2004). *The future of the teaching and learning of Algebra, The 12th ICMI Study*. Boston, MA: Kluwer Academic Publishers.

Stevenson, H. W., & Stigler, J. W. (1992). *The learning gap: Why our schools are failing and what we can learn from Japanese and Chinese education*. New York, NY: Simon and Schuster.

Sweller, J., & Cooper, G. A. (1985). The use of worked examples as a substitute for problem solving in learning algebra. *Cognition and Instruction, 2*, 59–89.

Trouche, L. (2004) Managing complexity of human/machine interactions in computerized learning environments: guiding students' command process through instrumental orchestrations. *International Journal of Computers for Mathematical Learning, 9*, 281–307.

Usiskin, Z. (1988). Conceptions of school algebra. In Coxford, A. F., & Shuttle, A. P. (Eds.), *The ideas of algebra, K- 12* (pp. 8–19). VA: National Council of Teachers of Mathematics.

Van Ameron, B. A. (2002). *Reinvention of early algebra. Developmental research on the transition from arithmetic to algebra*. Utrecht: CD-β Press, Centre for Science and Mathematics education.

Warren, E., & Cooper, T. J. (2005). Young children's ability to use the balance strategy to solve for unknowns. *Mathematics Education Research Journal, 17*(1), 58–72.

Watson, A. (2009) Algebraic reasoning, in T. Nunez, P. Bryant & A. Watson (Eds.), *Key Understandings in mathematics learning*, London: Nuffield Foundation.

Xu, L., & Clarke, D. (2013). Meta-rules of discursive practice in mathematics classrooms from Seoul, Shanghai, and Tokyo. *ZDM–The International Journal on Mathematics Education, 45*(1), 61–72.

AFFILIATIONS

Frederick K. S. Leung
The University of Hong Kong
Hong Kong

David Clarke
University of Melbourne
Australia

Derek Holton
University of Melbourne
Australia

Kyungmee Park
Hongik University
Korea

GLENDA ANTHONY & TIM BURGESS[1]

CHAPTER 2

Solving Linear Equations: A Balanced Approach

INTRODUCTION

Concerted efforts at improving student performance in algebra demonstrate that "children throughout the elementary grades are capable of learning powerful unifying ideas of mathematics that are the foundation of both arithmetic and algebra" (Carpenter, Franke, & Levi, 2003, p. xi). In New Zealand, Britt and Irwin's (2005) investigation of the Numeracy Development Project found that those students who acquired flexibility in using a range of general arithmetical strategies also developed the ability to express the structure of those strategies in symbolic forms. Such a foundation should bode well for students learning about solving linear equations—a process that requires a sound understanding of mathematical equality, and the commutative, distributive and inverse properties. However, a large scale study by Linsell (2009) found that many New Zealand secondary students have limited facility with solving and understanding linear equations. In common with students across other countries (Chazan, 2008), these difficulties include "grasping the syntax or structure of algebraic expression" and understanding "procedures for transforming equations or why transformations are done the way they are" (National Mathematics Advisory Panel (NMAP), 2008, p. 32).

Some of the difficulties that arise when learning to solve equations are associated with the move to solving them algebraically as opposed to arithmetically. Kieran (2004) argued that, in negotiating this transition, a student must make a series of adjustments as follows:

A focus on relations and not merely on the calculation of numeric answers;
A focus on operations as well as their inverses and on the related ideas of doing and undoing;
A focus on both representing and solving a problem instead of merely solving it;
A focus on both numbers and letters rather than on numbers alone; and
A refocus on the meaning of the equal sign.

In this chapter, we look closely at one New Zealand teacher's sequence of lessons involving the solving of linear equations in a Year 9 (Grade 8) classroom. In focusing our attention on the lessons involving the shift from arithmetic linear equations—those with the unknown on one side only—to algebraic linear equations—those with

F.K.S. Leung et al. (eds.), Algebra Teaching around the World, 17–37.
© 2014 Sense Publishers. All rights reserved.

the unknown on both sides, we seek to understand the ways in which the teacher sought to occasion learning opportunities that support these adjustments. We argue that the teacher's planning for learning, his choice of instructional activities, and his in-the-moment (inter)actions within the classroom can be viewed as a series of balancing acts—acts that variously afforded or constrained opportunities for students to make the necessary adjustments and associated understandings concerning solving linear equations. Before turning our attention to the New Zealand data, we briefly review the research literature on teaching linear equations.

TEACHING LINEAR EQUATIONS

Over the years, researchers (e.g., Caglayan & Olive, 2010; Filloy & Rojano, 1989; Filloy & Sutherland, 1996; Johnson, 1989; Lima & Tall, 2008; Sfard & Linchevski, 1994; Vlassis, 2002) have experimented with various situations in which students learn to solve equations. Their studies highlight a range of teaching approaches and illustrate a variety of significant cognitive challenges associated with learning algebra. For example, we are aware from the work of Sfard and Linchevski that "algebraic symbols do not speak for themselves" (p. 191). In different contexts the expression $3(x + 5) + 1$ can be read as a computational process, a certain number, a function, or a mere string of symbols which represent nothing—an algebraic object in itself. Moreover, the one representation may sometimes be interpreted operationally and at other times structurally. Vlassis (2002) reported confusion with students' interpretations of the negative sign within an equation; was it to be viewed as an operation (to subtract) or as a negative quantity? Caglayan and Olive's (2010) study of the use of a representational metaphor (cups and tiles) for writing and solving equations of one unknown noted the existence of a disconnect between students' mental and physical operations. All of these studies concur that developing productive ways of thinking about algebraic symbols takes time and is one of the big goals of learning algebra (Kaput, Blanton, & Moreno, 2008).

Given the range of cognitive obstacles for symbolizations and representations, and the series of adaptations needed in thinking about solving equations algebraically, what teaching approaches are commonly available to the teacher? Pirie and Martin (1997) presented a useful summary of two general approaches that dominate classroom instruction:

> One method is to repeatedly change the equation, by 'doing the same to both sides' until one has an equation that directly gives the answer. Understanding is assumed to come through the notion of 'undoing' a series of operations to get back to the original value…an alternative approach is that of 'change sides, change signs' based on the concept of inverse operations. Here, understanding is built on the assumption that the integrity of the original equation is preserved. (p. 161)

Students do not, however, need to employ these formal methods of mathematical reasoning when solving one-step or two-step linear equations with 'x' on one side only. These equations can be solved intuitively using purely arithmetic means such as known facts, substitution, cover-up, or backtracking. However, when solving the likes of $ax \pm b = cx \pm d$, informal arithmetic methods do not suffice. Research has provided confirming evidence that students experience major difficulties in solving these 'non-arithmetical' equations (Linsell, 2009; Vlassis, 2002). Filloy and Rojano (1989) suggested that this type of equation demands teacher intervention, 'the didactic cut'. That is, they argued that the student requires assistance from the teacher in the form of some sort of device to negotiate access to the more complex domain of algebraic equations. Filloy and Sutherland (1996) summarised two extreme positions regarding a suitable device: (1) modelling the new operations and objects in some concrete context which is familiar to the students, so that they become endowed with meaning; and (2) beginning at the syntactic level, learning the appropriate syntactical rules and, later on, applying them to the resolution of problem solving and equations.

Herscovics and Linchevski (1994), in a similar exploration of the transition from arithmetic to algebra, introduced the notion of a 'cognitive gap' which "is characterized by the students' inability to operate with or on the unknown" (p. 75). Findings from further research (Linchevski & Herscovics, 1996) suggested ways to 'cross the gap', including specific instruction in 'grouping like terms', development of the balance model, and decomposing into a difference to facilitate cancelling subtracted terms.

A third perspective on the transition was offered by Pirie and Martin (1997). They argued that this 'cut', "this implied cognitive difficulty, is, in reality a notion imposed by the observer, with hindsight, to explain an artifact of particular methods of teaching" (p. 161). Their research described a teaching approach built on the metaphoric notion of equality as a 'fence'. Using this notion of equality, they researched an instructional sequence of activities that involved beginning with unknowns on each side. Despite the absence of formalization, or models, the students in their study built "a sound and secure basic image for the solution of linear equations from which they could work with confidence" (p. 177).

With all these approaches the underlying aim is for students to develop deep and conceptual understanding. As Kaput et al. (2008) suggest:

> If the algebraic system is not introduced via a well-grounded symbolization process in the context of both expressing generality and the lifting out of previously established actions, then it is based only in rules about itself and is symbolically and conceptually isolated from the foundations in what the student knows and can do. (p. 46)

19

THE BALANCE MODEL

Whilst Pirie and Martin (1997) used activities based on mathematical equations to provide images for the solution, a range of representations has been trialed in other studies. These include function machines, input-output tables, arrow diagrams, balance models, geometric models, and number lines (Vlassis, 2002). As the teacher in our study used a balance model we will provide some more details of this model. In the balance model, 'translation'— "moving from the state of things at a concrete level to the state of things at a more abstract level" (Warren & Cooper, 2005, p. 60)—involves the use of artifacts portrayed as weights. The 'equal sign' is taken to represent the pivot of the balance and the solution of the problem is achieved by adding or taking away the same things on both sides, to preserve the balance. Abstraction, according to Warren and Cooper entails:

> Recognising the important relational correspondence between the balance model, the weights as numbers, stating the identity of the two quantities or expression (i.e., the two sides of the balance scales), and applying this understanding to more abstract situations, such as, equations involving subtraction and unknowns as negative numbers. (p. 60)

Vlassis (2002) argued for the use of the balance model because of its power to convey the principle of transformations in equivalent equations through performing the same operation on both sides. In using the balance model, the difficulty of the didactic cut is avoided since the balance is not seen as 'directional' in any way, and it refocuses the role of the equal sign. Following a classroom intervention, Vlassis concluded that the scales provided students "with the principles they need to perform transformations, summarised in a single and self-evident image" (p. 355). The students in her study were able to retrieve this image easily, long after instruction involving the model had ceased.

However, the balance model is not without its limitations (Aczel, 1998). Intended to lead students through the method of 'doing the same to both sides', this model works best when the required operation involves 'taking away'. Significant limitations emerge including its inability to model subtraction equations and unknowns as negative quantities. It is here that the research argues that teacher intervention is crucial as students move from solving equations that are 'based on the model' to equations that are 'detached from the model'. The solving of equations that are 'detached from a model' requires further abstraction; "other activities are necessary that will allow students to distance themselves from the scales, while retaining the principles of the transformation that they introduce" (Vlassis, 2002, p. 357).

CONTEXTUALISING THE CASE

Since 2000 there has been a systemic implementation of a national *Numeracy Development Project* (NDP) in New Zealand. More recently the project has been extended into the secondary school, with the objective of building a strong foundation for algebraic thinking (Irwin & Britt, 2005). The secondary project shares many features of the NDP project (details are available at http://www.nzmaths.co.nz/node/1595). Most notable is a model for teaching strategic thinking in Number. The core feature of this teaching model—informed by the Pirie and Kieren (1994) theory for growth of mathematical understanding—is a recursive pattern that illustrates a dynamic relationship between the phases of 'Using Materials', 'Using Imaging', and 'Using Number Properties' (see Figure 1).

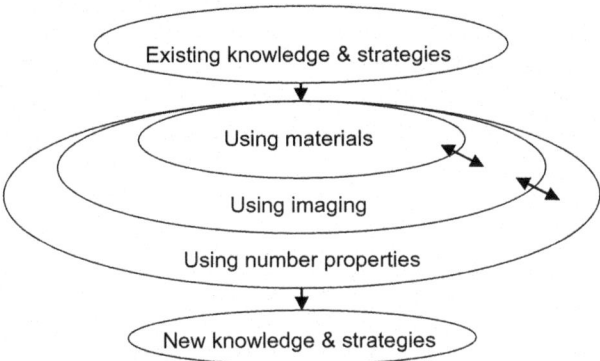

Figure 1. The Strategy Teaching Model (Ministry of Education, 2006, p. 5)

In addition to this teaching model the supporting documentation to the New Zealand curriculum offers the following guidelines for the teaching of equations:

> The beginning of 'real' algebra involves the generalisation of processes that are now well understood. For instance, in solving $2n + 7 = 35$, they should know: the idea of n as a variable that can take a particular value when constrained; understand the equality relation implied by the equal sign; 'undoing' the $+ 7$ by subtracting 7 from both sides; and 'undoing' the 2n by dividing both sides by 2.

Students should understand the equal sign as a statement of balance and know what operations to both sides of an equation preserve that balance, e.g. take off the same number from both sides...students should be able to find the required value using both sensible estimation and improvement, and by formal methods of applying inverse operations, e.g. $3p - 6 = 18$ so $3p = 24$ (adding six to both sides) so $p = 8$ (dividing both sides by three) (retrieved from http://www.nzmaths.co.nz/).

In this chapter we draw on data from a New Zealand Year 9 (Grade 8) classroom—one of three classrooms that are a part of the New Zealand component of the international Learner's Perspective Study (LPS). Dave, a teacher of 4 years' experience, was identified by the local mathematics community as an effective secondary school practitioner. Dave taught in a large coeducational urban school, catering for students from, in the main, the middle socioeconomic sector. His class of 30 students was one of two extension classes at the Year 9 level. This is a significant factor; students' competency with basic facts, fractions, negatives, and order of operations—a problem that is cited in the New Zealand literature (Linsell, 2009) as providing a major stumbling block to initial efforts to master linear equations—was a non-issue. Students in the research class demonstrated fluency and confidence in oral and written work involving the required calculations.

The teacher and his students agreed that our team could collect video, interview, and observation data across a sequence of 10 lessons that represented a unit on algebra—focused on solving linear equations (for a description of LPS research design see Clarke, 2006). In an interview following the sequence of lessons, Dave explained his teaching goals for the unit as twofold: (i) for students to be able to solve and understand linear equations of the form $ax \pm b = cx \pm d$ and (ii) for students to develop an understanding of the meaning of equality (=). The sequence of lessons is summarised as follows:

L1: Revisions of order of operations and algebraic notation and manipulation
L2: Solving 1-step linear equations of the form $x \pm b = c$ [using a working backwards model]
L3: Solving linear equations of form $ax \pm b = c$.
L4: Solving linear equations of form $ax \pm b = c$ using function boxes.
L5: Solving linear equations of form $ax \pm b = c$ [introduced fractions, decimals], forming equations and solving.
L6: Real world applications of solving linear equations.
L7: Review of definition of equations and refocus on the meaning of the equal sign, introduction of balance model to solve $3x + 4 = 2x + 9$.
L8: Use of balance model to solve $ax \pm b = cx \pm d$, including examples where $c < 0$.
L9: Solving equations of form $ax \pm b = cx \pm d$, including cases where fraction and decimals, and negative solutions occurred. Introduction to systems of equations with infinite or null solution sets.
L10: Real world applications of forming and solving equations.

Within the 10 lesson sequence, our interest is in those lessons that focused specifically on the transition from solving linear arithmetic equations to solving equations with 'x's on both sides (L7 and L8), with some reference to lessons that involved detachment from the balance model (L9 and L10). In examining the classroom data we take heed of the caution offered by Brown, Eade, and Wilson (1999): "We cannot easily define such an organisation of events which effects a transition to have happened. For, within any such event, there are multiple plots highlighting or implicating alternative phenomenological features" (p. 55). Thus, rather than looking to seek direct association between aspects of the teacher's instructions and the mathematics learning, we look to explore those aspects of the teacher's pedagogical practice that appear to have occasioned learning (Davis & Simmt, 2003). Although, on the surface, the instruction was in a large part centered on the use of a balance model, this was just one factor within the transition. We argue that the teacher's awareness that the tools used in solving simple linear equations should be able to be refined to "handle the subtleties and technicalities that arise later" (Cuoco, 2008, p. 51) was an overriding influence on the pedagogical process intended to support the transition. In order to focus on this goal, we illustrate how the teacher himself needed to engage in a balancing act in terms of pedagogical decisions and actions.

OCCASIONING THE TRANSITION

We have chosen to highlight significant classroom episodes, sometimes with student or teacher post-lesson commentary, to illustrate the nature of the tasks, tools, community interactions, and pedagogical practices that occasioned learning opportunities—for both students and teacher.

Anticipating future learning

A significant feature of Dave's pedagogical practice was to 'sow seeds' for students to think about and nurture in readiness for revisiting later in the instructional sequence. Thus it is important to mention that, prior to the transition lessons (L7 & L8), Dave had provided the students with a puzzle activity (L2) that involved three sets of scales with balancing icons that represented the four suits of a pack of cards. The task was to determine the value assigned to each of the represented icons by performing a series of equivalence transformations. Dave reflected in a post-lesson interview that:

> ...with the balancing of scales, I am trying to sow the seed for later on in terms of manipulating each side... I just wanted them to play around with it and see what they did with it and it was really open to them to see how they approached it...They got the idea that there were scales that needed to be balanced, and manipulating what goes on the sides of the scales was really what it was all about.

At this stage of his lesson sequence, Dave's purpose was guided by both an awareness of the students' current thinking and the need to refocus their thinking further down the track:

> Up until now most of them think the equal sign means 'works out to be', or 'I

23

get this', whereas later on I am going to have to adjust their view of what the equal sign means and think in terms of scales. And so later on when I talk about scales, they will have a reference point for it.

Early on Dave also anticipated "algebraic tools and habits of mind that fit into the larger landscape of algebra" (Cuoco. 2008, p. 51)—for when the problems became more challenging. For example, encouraging students to check answers by substitution, introduced at an early stage, had a dual role: to provide formative feedback on their learning and to transfer authority to the mathematics rather than the teacher/textbook:

> Later on when there are multiple steps like $3x - 1$ equals something then I want to get them doing substitution as part of their working…I want them to feel as though they don't need to rely on the back of the book, or me, to know that they got the right answer and some of them will get the wrong answer.

Refocusing on the meaning of the equal sign

The first six lessons principally involved forming and solving arithmetic equations using the 'undoing' strategy modeled with a 'function box'. Partway through L7 Dave indicated to the students that there was to be a change of focus: "We are going to take everything a little step further today." He challenged the class to stop and think about the equations that they had been solving—not in terms of how to solve them but in terms of 'what an equation is'. The question prompt—"What is an equation, what is important about an equation, how do we recognise an equation?"—resulted in the following discussion:

```
S:      Isn't it like two numbers, some numbers kind of
        like changing into other numbers, with pluses
        and times and minus and division.
Dave:   So how do we capture that change? What is the
        crucial thing that tells us that it is an equation?
S:      Numbers.
Dave:   Well we are probably going to have numbers in
        there somewhere. J?
J:      The operation like times, division.
Dave:   Right times, division. C?
C:      Has to have an equal sign in it.
Dave:   Equal sign. Do you reckon that equal sign is
        important; how important? Would we have an equation
        if there was no equal sign?
C:      No.
Dave:   No, so you've hit the nail on the head C, although
        J and S said you have to have something else other
```

```
than an equal sign don't we. Because if I just
put an equal sign on the board we don't have an
equation. So coming back to what you all said we
have to have something on both sides of the equal
sign, don't we. So what does it actually mean?
```

We see in this exchange that Dave was mindful to acknowledge and build on all student contributions. In teasing out "what does it actually mean?" the teacher then led a discussion about the EXECUTE button and the EQUAL button on his graphic calculator. This reference to the graphic calculator tool resulted in a student, J, offering the claim that 'equals' means "that side equals that side". Others revoiced this as "the left hand side of an equation is the 'same' as the right hand side".

Orientating students to more powerful ways of thinking

Whilst affirming the possibility that students may still want to regard equations to mean 'work it out—give me the answer', Dave reiterated several times during that lesson that they will need to "start changing the way [they] see equations". He stated that:

> It is very important that we have a strong understanding of what an equation is, of what it means. …. We need to clarify the meaning, so we are going to write some notes and then we are going to revisit this question and see if we know what this equal sign really, really means.

Later in L7 Dave again orientated the students' thinking though the use of a metaphor involving exploring and challenge:

> If you are exploring lakes, right, you go in your little boat and you are out there exploring some lake that hasn't been discovered yet. Does it really matter that the world is curved? If you are exploring a little lake, probably not. It is a bit like saying it doesn't matter if we think of equations as meaning 'work it out' if they are simply little equations like $5 + 3 = 8$…But if you start exploring oceans you are going to have a real problem if you think that the world is flat. You have to change how you look at things when you are exploring things on a larger scale. We are going to be exploring equations that are more difficult and more challenging than what you have faced so far. You are going to have to change the way you think about what equations mean.

In L8, we see more evidence that Dave orientated his students to the need to adopt practices and ways of thinking that would take their learning to the next stage. At the end of the first review of solving an equation, Dave commented on the power of the solution strategy proposed by a student:

> When you get to year 10, and year 11, and year 12, and year 13 and beyond, you are still going to be doing what J's done which is the same to both sides.

If you double one side, then double the other side, it is still equal. If you minus two from that side and minus two from that side it is still equal. You can do whatever you want to one side so long as you do the same to the other side it will still be equal.

Dave's exhortation of the power of the strategy was linked to his aim to consolidate more secure understanding of the equality, and move the students toward a structural rather than process view of equations. In L9, Dave again commended the new strategy, explicitly drawing students' attention to how the 'new' strategy can replace the earlier 'function box' undoing strategy:

Dave: Right question two [3x – 1.5 = 12.3] is one of
           those one we did earlier, remember the box? 'x'
           went in one side and something happened and out
           popped 12.3 and then we reversed that process to
           find x.
Chorus: Yes.
Dave: Does this new strategy still work for this, would
           someone like to talk us through question two?
H: Plus 1.5 to both sides.
Dave: Right, the strategy that we had was we don't want
           number constants on the left hand side, we know
           that to get rid of minus 1.5 we plus 1.5 and we
           have to do that to both sides otherwise it is not
           balanced and it is not equal.

From this exchange it appears that some student responses were more procedural than conceptual in nature. However, it is also apparent from the interviews that some students were aware of their obligations to provide conceptual explanations:

I like it at the end how he will go over it and doesn't just give us the answer; he will do the working to show us *how* to get to the answer and that is important that you don't just get the right answer. It's the working of how you got to the answer because some people will not do it the right way or the correct process so I think that is important.

INTRODUCING THE BALANCE MODEL

After the class concluded the initial discussion on the nature of equations and equality, Dave suggested that "a really good way to think of equations is like a set of balanced scales". However, rather than imposing his model on the students, Dave asked the students to draw a set of scales to represent the equation $5 + 3 = 2 + 6$. Wandering around the room, Dave commented that he was "seeing some great little designs". He then offered what he described as "a simple seesaw model", with $5 + 3$ on the left hand side and $2 + 6$ on the right hand side.

The first task with the balance model involved the students drawing a set of scales to represent and solve the problem $3x + 2 = 2x + 3$ with the hint that "work it out means what must x be". Having an attempt at a problem (before a teacher demonstration)—without the expectation that all students would necessarily be able to solve the problem in full—was a well established general obligation (Cobb, Gresalfi, & Hodge, 2009). Post lesson interviews confirmed that students expected to find these problems challenging, they expected to struggle sometimes, and they were aware that they may be called upon to contribute to a whole class resolution of the problem (Anthony, 2013). As one student remarked:

> The teacher will ask a range of different people for the answer or to explain so I think that is pretty good.

Following time to 'try' the problem on their own, the teacher then re-presented the problem $3x + 2 = 2x + 3$ using a projected computer applet involving a balance model with 'unit' and 'x' boxes. In response to Dave's request for a solution procedure the following exchange took place accompanied by the teacher's stepwise demonstration using the model:

```
J:       3x take away 2x equals x.
F:       Where did you get the 2x from?
Dave:    Hold on let's just go through what J is doing.
         So we have got 3x on the left hand side and you
         want to take away two of them. What is going to
         happen if I take away 2x?
S:       It's off balance.
Dave:    How are we going to keep it balanced, J?
J:       Well the 2x is going from that side as well.
Dave:    So what J is doing is taking 2x from both sides.
         It's going to keep it balanced, do you reckon?
         [Removes 2 boxes from each side]
Chorus:  Yes.
Dave:    Yes, that has worked okay, that's good.
F:       So x is 1.
Dave:    How do you get 1?
F:       Oh don't worry.
Dave:    Hang on J is on a roll, carry on J.
J:       Then you go x plus 2 equals 3 so then you go 3
         takeaway 2.
Dave:    So J took 2 away from the right hand side and now
         he has take 2 away from the left hand side. [Dave
         removes 2 units from each side] Is it balanced?
         Can we write this as an equation? So is the
         answer x = 1?
```

Chorus: Yes.

Building on the students' contribution and the model demonstration, the teacher then reworked the process symbolically. During this process Dave continued to revoice the 'do the same to both sides' strategy. Notably, he made no mathematical explanation as to why you would minus 2x from both sides, a concern raised earlier by student F. Devoid of any mathematical reference to inverse/identity properties, Dave continued to appeal to the embodiment (Lima & Tall, 2008) of removing 'things' to preserve the balance. Moreover, the image of the scales remaining balanced after each transformation was not linked at this stage to the mathematical equivalence of the transformed expressions— a key to advancing students' algebraic understanding (Watson, 2009).

In solving the next problem $4x + 2 = x + 11$, the students were asked to "try and *imagine* what we do". As well as giving a strong indication that the model was illustrative, rather than operational, Dave's request to the students to think about the aim of solving equations in terms of—"When we finish the job and we have x equals, have we got 'x's on the right hand side or just a number?"—appeared to be moving their thinking away from the 'non-directional' relational property of the balance model towards a more procedural approach to solving equations. The 'doing the same to both sides' strategy was now associated with 'getting rid' of the 'x's on the right hand side and 'getting rid' of the numbers on the left hand side:

Dave: Do we want numbers on the left hand side? [4x + 2 = x + 11 transformed to 3x + 2 = 11].

N: No.

Dave: We want to get rid of that plus 2. What can we do to get rid of that plus 2 S?

S: Minus 2.

Dave: We can minus 2, so in black I'm showing what I am doing. I am minusing 2. What must I do to this side? Must minus 2 to keep it balanced [3x + 2 -2 =11-2]. What do we get if we work this left hand side out?

P: 3x.

Dave: 3x, don't sound so cautious, you are perfectly right. We have taken away that 2 [points to 2 in Line 1] and all that is left is 3x.What is on the right hand side V?

V: 9.

Dave: 9, we are nearly there aren't we. Solving means x equals number. What can I do to get from 3x to x? P?

P: Nine divide by 3.

Dave: Divided by 3. If we divide 3x by 3 we have got x.
        If we divide 9 by 3 we have 3. I have done the same
        to both sides, keeping it balanced and we have
        finally worked out what is actually a challenging
        equation. How do we know it is right?

As before, the description of the steps suggested physically getting 'rid' of terms. However, while both students S and V described their actions in terms of acting on one side, Dave consistently took care to revoice their actions to include both sides. In doing so, Dave continued to reinforce the obligation that the students explain the choice of each step in terms of doing the same to both sides, as represented by the balance model.

Coping with the unexpected

In L8, Dave returned to the applet model of the balance. In class, he had stated that the reason was "so we are convincing ourselves exactly what is going on right through the whole solving process". In the post lesson interview Dave reported, "I was deliberately going through that process very slowly because I wanted them to get it and get it quite clearly what we were trying to do". In this lesson the model incorporated helium balloons that pulled the balance up for terms involving negative coefficients. The first step in solving the equation $3x - 3 = -2x + 7$ was achieved readily by *adding* three blocks to each side of the balance. Then, from the left hand side of the balance Dave removed 3 helium balloons and 3 blocks. He described this action as "simplifying…the 3 balloons and 3 blocks cancel each other out". In considering what to do next to the transformed equation $3x = -2x + 10$ the students were prompted "to take a close look at that -2x and get rid of it". Student N suggested "3x minus -2x". The suggestion to subtract the unwanted term rather than add the inverse was unexpected by the teacher. As noted in the post lesson interview:

> She surprised me when she said we take away -2x, which was good because she was thinking in terms of visual, we don't want -2x on that side. She looked at her strategy quite carefully and she knows we don't want any 'x's on the right hand side, she has seen the -2x on the right hand side and she said "we don't want its so let's take it away", the -2x, which isn't something that I taught them, but she has figured out that you can take away -2x and so that was interesting because it led me into this idea of taking away -2x like Miss N had done. Most of them [on inspection in walking around the room] had just plussed 2x to get rid of the -2x.

Here we see that student N's unanticipated response caused Dave to reflect on the role of the model per se. He alluded to an awareness that, in this case, the model invoked a visual, dynamic, approach associated with getting rid of terms and that this image may possibly be competing with the mathematical approach of 'do the

29

same (inverse) to both sides' that he is modelling with the written work. Within the lesson, Dave attended to N's response by first eliciting from the students that taking away -2x is the same as adding 2x mathematically, then rewriting the equation as $3x + 2x = -2x + 10 + 2x$. Then, as a precursor to solving the equation, he used the balance model to demonstrate that taking away -2x is the same as adding 2x by modelling the actions in two separate demonstrations:

> Are you happy N that taking away negative 2x is the same as plus 2x? Good. But notice that there is a slightly different thinking process going on because adding 2x is this [adding 2 blocks to the left hand side drops the balance down]. [Teacher removes the blocks to return to the original balance model of $3x = -2x + 10$.] But taking away a -2x, taking away the two balloons, [the right hand side goes down] has the same effect as if we put two plus 'x's on there [left hand side].

The implied equivalence was the action of the balance 'dropping down'. To complete the demonstration Dave then performed the actions of adding 2x (two blocks) to the left hand side and at the same time removing -2x (the balloons) from the right hand side [$3x + 2x = -2x + 10 - 2x$], explaining that this was "plus 2x to this side, and plus 2x to that side which is the same as taking away -2x". As observers in the lesson, we were concerned that the students may have found this justification difficult. In addition to the general concerns associated with the use of teacher-imposed concrete models (Caglayan & Olive, 2010), the actions in this case did not 'exactly' match with 'do the same to both sides' [i.e., 2 blocks were added in the left hand side and 2 balloons were removed from the right hand side]. However, Dave's remark in the post lesson interview shows that he did not share our perception:

> They could all picture if you had two balloons pulling one side up and you take them away the impact is going to be the same as if you put something on it to weigh it down.

Certainly, there was no evidence of students challenging the demonstration during the lesson. Moreover, in the post lesson interviews, the two focus students made no specific mention of this part of the demonstration. Student B, who was having trouble solving the problem prior to the demonstration, commented that "the model at the same time as the equation going up on the board made it really easy". Student J, who had successfully worked the problem using his own knowledge of negatives, commented that the model was not "hugely helpful".

Possibly this reflects the finding reported by Norton and Windsor (2008) concerning Australian Year 7 students' perceptions of concrete representations for solving equations. For students in that study, while most saw the initial value in material-based activities, once they "understood the structure they preferred more abstract methods" (p. 374).

Detaching from the model

Within this sequence of lessons, the aforementioned demonstration of equations involving negative coefficients was the last time the model was explicitly used. Had it served its purpose and what did the teacher deem that purpose to be? In the remaining two lessons, the general solution procedure was reinforced symbolically, with attention paid to the sequence of steps: getting rid of the numbers on the left hand side, and getting rid of the 'x's on the right hand side within the 'do the same to both sides' framework. Much attention was afforded to the need to check answers by substitution into the original equation, and 'proper' setting out of sequential transformed equations was reinforced by the teacher checking and modelling.

In detaching from the model, for some students the focus appeared to be dominated by procedural rules. For example, in the practice problems immediately following the final applet demonstration in L8 a student raised a query concerning the problem $3x - 8 = 2x + 10$. The student questioned whether he should start by taking away 3, as was the case in the earlier problem on the board. Dave, referring to the worked example in the 'notes', asked the student to "think what we are trying to do". He reminded the student that "we need to keep it balanced, so in this case here what are you going to do?" In the post lesson interview Dave confirmed that:

> [The student] wasn't really sure how to decide on that number so I had to direct him back to the notes and show him that the notes said add or subtract a number so that we end up with only a number on the right hand side. With that idea he thought about it and figured out why we had decided to minus the 3 from the equation $5x + 3 = 3x + 7$, then he figured out, "Oh! That is why we minused 3". And then when we looked at the following equation he picked up what we had to do and he made the link.

However, within the classroom discussions, Dave continued to reinforce the link to the model, as seen in L9 where he revoiced a student's suggestion to 'do the same to both sides':

> Yes, we have to do the same to both sides. That is really important because if we have a balanced set of scales the only way we are going to keep it balanced is by doing the same to both sides.

In the same lesson, when helping a student who wanted to 'get rid of' the -11x on the right hand side of the problem $13x + -2 = -11x + 6$, Dave again invoked the model to confirm the student's choice of operation:

```
T: You had -11x, you minus 11x, do you reckon that would
   get rid of the -11x?
S: No.
T: So what might you do differently so that you end up
   with no 'x's on the right hand side?
```

S: Plus it?

T: Plus it, yes, good.

S: So I go plus that and plus that as well [pointing to both sides of the equation].

T: That's right because that will keep it balanced and what you have done is imagine that -11x is the balloons pulling up and you have put eleven blocks on to make it perfectly balanced equals a zero.

S: -11x plus 11x equals zero.

The image of balance was invoked to significant effect on one further occasion. A game-type activity that involved playing cards to randomly generate equations provided opportunities for students to investigate null or infinite solution sets. In the whole class review Dave linked the justification of these 'new' types of solution sets back to the balance model. For example, with the null solution to $2x + -12 = 2x + 11$, the students were challenged to think about "if we had 2x and twelve helium balloons on the left and on the right we had 2x and eleven blocks would that ever be balanced?"

BALANCING ACTS

Recent investigations (e.g., Lima & Tall, 2008; Vlassis, 2002; Warren & Cooper, 2005) of the balance model have involved teaching experiments in which the teacher collaborated with the researchers, with a focus on assessing student learning outcomes. In contrast, this chapter has focused on the ways in which the case study teacher incorporated the balance model as part of his overall instructional design for teaching linear equations. Exploring Dave's use of the balance model in situ highlights the complexity of the *balancing acts* implicated in his pedagogical decision-making. Dave's planning and in-the-moment actions reflect a balancing of authority and agency, a balancing of caring for the student and caring for the mathematics, a balancing of presenting one way/model versus many ways/models, and a balancing of teaching for the moment versus teaching for the future. While not the main focus of the paper, our analysis of these actions provides insights—be they brief—into how the 'balancing' might be implicated with students' opportunities to develop algebraic understandings and habits of mind.

How did Dave manage such a balancing act? First, his planning was thorough. Because he was being videoed and felt some responsibility towards the research team (Walshaw, 2010), it was inevitable that his planning was more reflective than usual: "I put a lot of thought into it and it wasn't always intentional thought, it was just lying in bed at night thinking about these ideas". His planning was respectful of both his students and the algebra. From the first lesson, Dave wanted to build on from where his students were at; he noted, "I just really wanted to make sure they were comfortable with that [order of operations] before we started equations". In L3

Dave introduced the function box model to solve arithmetic equations. However, aware of the need to change direction eventually towards 'bigger ideas' to cope with more complex equations, he was careful to 'sow the seeds' for future learning. We noted earlier that he introduced puzzle problems involving balances and established checking procedures early on. Reflecting on L2, he also noted the importance of establishing 'setting-out' procedures:

> I am very fussy about them getting it set up properly. I notice the seniors, those that have developed those processes, they can solve any equation I give them no matter how complicated. It is because they just go step-by-step and they have that logical sequence…I ultimately want them all at that stage. …They haven't been approached with the idea of the balancing scales but once that comes in then they will understand, hopefully, why we are keeping the 'x' over to one side.

Focused on the 'big ideas' of algebra, Dave planned an instructional sequence that attempted to address the adjustments the students needed to make as they moved towards solving equations algebraically. In particular, he was aware of the need to provide opportunities for explicit attention to the meaning of an equation and the role of the equal sign. Several lessons were punctuated with considerable teacher effort to convince the students that they needed to 'change' the way they thought about equality. The existing classroom environment, marked by considerable trust and respect (Anthony, 2013), was likely to enhance the effectiveness of such exhortations.

In looking to support this call for a new understanding of equality and its role in solving equations, Dave introduced the balance model, complete with helium balloons. In talking about the value of the balance model in a post-lesson interview, Dave noted that:

> The idea of having a balanced scale, having them visually see what essentially works, visually step-by-step is really helpful. To be able to say "right, we are taking away three from this side" and then go to the software and "take three away" and see it is not balanced, and you need to keep it balanced, so what do we do? Step-by-step process, going from the working to visual really works very well.

Although Dave used the model to demonstrate specific 'steps' involving adding and subtracting terms, his end goal was that the model would evoke the image of both sides of the equation being in balance—an 'at one moment' image. In occasioning the shift in the students' thinking about equality, the perceived value of the balance model was that there was "no expectation of the equal sign conveying a notion of process, nor of it—at least at the initial stage of manipulation and simplification—adopting the meaning of 'gives the answer'" (Pirie & Martin, 1997, p. 165).

It appears that, as a group, these high achieving students were well aware that the balance model was just 'a model'—they appropriated what was useful, detached themselves from the model, and moved on. For some students, though expressing acceptance of the model, they chose to discard it and adopt a reliance on procedural steps associated with the symbolic representation. As they practised examples, their talk in groups quickly moved to references to the documented steps in their notes concerning getting rid of the numbers on the left hand side and the 'x' terms on the right hand side. Although Dave worked hard to press these students to make conceptual links, either these links were never made in the first place, or were too fragile to be sustained. Within the limitations of the data collected in this study such assertions must necessarily remain tentative.

In post-lesson interviews, Dave confirmed that students in this class varied in their motives and preferences for learning mathematics. Quite possibly, the in-class opportunities to recognise that an algebraic equation is a statement about relations between quantities were insufficient or ineffective to enable some learners to recognise the equivalence of transformations of equations (Sfard & Linchevski, 1994; Watson, 2009). For example, on occasions, there was evidence of confusion with the 'getting rid of' step. The goal of removing an unwanted term potentially focused some students' attention on taking away the term on one side of the equation. Although the teacher was careful to revoice each time that they would also need to 'do the same to the other side to keep it balanced', there were only passing references to a mathematical justification in terms of inverse operations. For those who continued to focus on the physical embodiment associated with 'removing terms' there was potential difficulty when 'getting rid of' was achieved by 'adding' to each side. Lima and Tall (2008) suggested that students who do not make the mathematical connections involving inverse operations are less likely to be able to justify when and how to 'remove' terms in the long term, and at a later date may revert to attempting the strategy of reversing, which Dave's students had met before with the function box model.

Strategy flexibility—be it operationalised as ease in switching between solution methods, or a person's tendency to select the most appropriate method in a given situation—is currently viewed as an outcome that is attainable and critical for mathematics students (Star & Newton, 2009). Balancing the teaching of one solution strategy or two, and balancing whether to set expectations that all students 'do the same' steps and 'setting out' of their thinking, were also considerations for Dave. In interacting with the students, for example, he was required to respond to challenges about which expression or term to simplify first. His reaction was always to be very positive about considering alternatives, commending the student for thinking about the problem and alternative ways of solving it.

In looking to develop positive learning outcomes for his students, Dave was critically aware that proficiency with algebra involves an integration of skill and understanding that "allows for flexible, adaptive, and appropriate use of algorithms" (Star & Newton, 2009, p. 557). Reflecting on his two-strategy instructional approach to solving linear equations, he remarked that:

Introducing a deeper idea of what equations is all about and letting them develop that and they will hopefully develop and pick up themselves both will work and if revising some of the simpler equations the strategy of undoing, going backwards, will work and manipulating both sides will work as well. ... I'm not sure if I will re-visit them [arithmetic equations] formally...I will prefer not to tell them, I want them to discover them on their own. Some will use this one method now for all their equations and others will think there are two possible ways of approaching it.

However, on completion of the unit Dave reflected critically on his approach as follows:

I'm not sure whether I would do that the same. I haven't quite decided whether that [the function box model] is helpful or whether that gets in the way of their understanding. I chose to do it because that is how they see the equal sign...a command that you ask them to work something out and you get the answers. So equals kind of means this is what I get, so I was trying to stay consistent with their understanding then develop the idea about balancing later on. It's possible next time I might introduce the scales earlier.

We surmise that this tension and wondering reflects Dave's awareness that some students were keen to adopt a more procedural approach to solving equations despite his press for them to adopt a more conceptual approach to solving equations.

CONCLUSION

In looking closely at Dave's pedagogical plans, actions, and reflections when teaching linear equations, we see he is highly aware of the importance of keeping an "eye on the mathematical horizon" (Ball, 1993). With specific reference to algebra, Dave's position affirms the stance "that a mathematical discipline like algebra, more than its collection of results, is the collage of methods and habits of mind used by its practitioners" (Cuoco, 2008, p. 51). His planning and his orientation of students to future learning were indicative of his assumption that these students will continue in mathematics, and as such, it is his responsibility to make sure that they establish appropriate mathematical practices and identities. The introduction of the balance model was one way that Dave chose to support the students' transition—not with the intent of hastening or easing the transition but with the intent of strengthening it. The model was intended to provide a thinking tool for students that afforded opportunities for them to make conceptual connections related to equality and equivalence of transformations of equations.

We argue that, although the model formed an implicit component of the mathematical ideas associated with solving algebraic linear equations, the device itself was just one of a multitude of parallel and competing practices and discourses within the classroom that occasioned learning. Dave was aware that, in some instances, student learning was procedurally orientated, and this caused him to question ways in which he might design a classroom system that afforded more forceful opportunities for students to make connections between ideas (Walshaw, 2010). For Dave, we see that, although he has been teaching for four years and is a highly regarded teacher, his teacher knowledge and pedagogical practices are, and are likely to remain, in a perpetual state of becoming. He is challenged by the need to balance competing demands within the classroom and is looking continually for new ways to achieve such a balance.

NOTE

[1] The authors acknowledge the valuable contribution of all of the New Zealand LPS research team members including Margaret Walshaw, Liping Ding, Anne Lawrence, and Peter Rawlins.

REFERENCES

Aczel, J. (1998). Learning algebraic strategies using a computerised balance model. In A. Oliver & K. Newstead (Eds.), *Proceedings of the 22nd conference of the International group for the Psychology of Mathematics Education* (Vol. 2, pp. 1–16). Stellenbosch: PME.

Anthony, G. (2013). Student perceptions of the 'good' teacher and 'good' learning in New Zealand mathematics classrooms In B. Kaur, G. Anthony, M. Otani & D. J. Clarke (Eds.), *Students' voice in mathematics classrooms around the world* (pp. 209–226). Rotterdam: Sense Publishers.

Ball, D. (1993). With an eye on the mathematical horizon: Dilemmas of teaching elementary school mathematics. *The Elementary School Journal, 93*(4), 373–397.

Britt, M. S., & Irwin, K. C. (2005). Algebraic thinking in the numeracy project: Year one of a three-year study. In P. Clarkson, S. Downton, D. Gronn, M. Horne, A. McDonough, R. Pierce, & A. Roche (Eds.), *Building connections: theory, research and practice.* (Proceedings of the 28th annual conference of Mathematics Education Research Group, pp. 169–176). Sydney: MERGA.

Brown, T., Eade, F., & Wilson, D. (1999). Semantic innovation: Arithmetical and algebraic metaphors with narratives of learning. *Educational Studies in Mathematics, 40*, 53–70.

Caglayan, G., & Olive, J. (2010). Eighth grade students' representations of linear equations based on a cups and tiles model. *Educational Studies in Mathematics, 74*(2), 143–162.

Carpenter, T., Franke, M., & Levi, L. (2003). *Thinking mathematically: Integrating arithmetic and algebra in elementary school.* Portsmouth, MH: Heinemann.

Chazan, D. (2008). The shifting landscape of school algebra in the United States. In C. E. Greenes (Ed.), *Algebra and algebraic thinking in school mathematics* (pp. 19–33). Reston, VA: National Council of Teachers of Mathematics.

Clarke, D. (2006). The LPS design. In D. J. Clarke, C. Keitel, & Y. Shimizu (Eds.), *Mathematics classrooms in twelve countries: The insider's perspective* (pp. 15–36). Rotterdam: Sense Publishers.

Cobb, P., Gresalfi, M., & Hodge, L. L. (2009). An interpretive scheme for analyzing the identities that students develop in mathematics classrooms. *Journal for Research in Mathematics Education, 40*(1), 40–68.

Cuoco, A. (2008). Introducing extensible tools in high school algebra. In C. E. Greenes (Ed.), *Algebra and algebraic thinking in school mathematics* (pp. 51–62). Reston, VA: National Council of Teachers of Mathematics.

Davis. B., & Simmt, E. (2003). Understanding learning systems: Mathematics education and complexity science. *Journal for Research in Mathematics Education, 34*(2), 137–167.

Filloy, E., & Rojano, T. (1989). Solving equations: the transition from arithmetic to algebra. *For the Learning of Mathematics, 9*(2), 19–25.

Filloy, E., & Sutherland, R. (1996). Designing curricula for teaching and learning algebra. In A. Bishop, K. Clements, C. Keitel, J. Kilpatrick, & C. Laborde (Eds.), *International handbook of mathematics education* (Vol. 1, pp. 139–160). Dordrecht: Kluwer.

Herscovics, N., & Linchevski, L. (1994). A cognitive gap between arithmetic and algebra. *Educational Studies in Mathematics, 27*, 59–78.

Johnson, D. (Ed.). (1989). *Children's mathematical frameworks 8-13: A study of classroom teaching.* Windsor: NFER -Nelson.

Irwin, K. C., & Britt, M. S. (2005). The algebraic nature of students' numerical manipulation in the New Zealand numeracy project. *Educational Studies in Mathematics, 58*, 169–188.

Kieran, C. (2004). Algebraic thinking in the early grades: What is it? *The Mathematics Educator, 8*, 139–151.

Kaput, J., Blanton, M., & Moreno, L. (2008). Algebra from a symbolization point of view. In J. Kaput, D. Carraher, & M. Blanton (Eds.), *Algebra in the early grades* (pp. 19–55). New York, NY: Lawrence Erlbaum Associates.

Lima, R. N., & Tall, D. (2008). Procedural embodiment and magic in linear equations. *Educational Studies in Mathematics, 67*, 3–18.

Linchevski, L., & Herscovics, N. (1996). Closing the cognitive gap between arithmetic and algebra: Operating on the unknown in the context of equations. *Educational Studies in Mathematics, 30*, 39–65.

Linsell, C. (2009). Students' knowledge and strategies for solving equations. In *Findings from the New Zealand Secondary Numeracy Project 2008* (pp. 29–43). Wellington, New Zealand: Learning Media.

National Mathematics Advisory Panel. (2008). *Foundations for success: The final report of the National Mathematics Advisory Panel.* Washington, DC: U.S. Department of Education.

Ministry of Education. (2006). *Numeracy Professional Development Projects 2006, Book 3 Getting Started.* Wellington, New Zealand: The Ministry of Education.

Norton, S., & Windsor, W. (2008). Students' attitude towards using materials to learn algebra: A year 7 case study. In M. Goos, R. Brown, & K. Makar (Eds.), *Navigating currents and carting directions* (Proceedings of the 31st annual conference of the Mathematics Education Research group of Australasia, pp. 369–376). Brisbane: MERGA.

Pirie, S., & Kieren, T. (1994). Growth in mathematical understanding: How can we characterise it and how can we represent it? *Educational Studies in Mathematics, 26*, 165–190.

Pirie, S., & Martin, L. (1997). The equation, the whole equation and nothing but the equation! One approach to the teaching of linear equations. *Educational Studies in Mathematics, 34*, 159–181.

Sfard, A., & Linchevski, L. (1994). The gains and the pitfalls of reification—the case of algebra. *Educational Studies in Mathematics, 26*, 191–228.

Star, J. R., & Newton, K. J. (2009). The nature and development of experts' strategy flexibility for solving equations. *ZDM Mathematics Education, 41*, 557–567.

Vlassis, J. (2002). The balance model: Hindrance or support for the solving of linear equations with one unknown. *Educational Studies in Mathematics, 49*, 341–359.

Walshaw, M. (2010). Pedagogical change: Rethinking identity and reflective practice. *Journal of Mathematics Teacher Education, 13*(6), 487–497.

Warren, E., & Cooper, T. J. (2005). Young children's ability to use the balance strategy to solve for unknowns. *Mathematics Education Research Journal, 17*(1), 58–72.

Watson, A. (2009). Algebraic reasoning. In *Key understandings in mathematics learning.* Oxford: Nuffield Foundation.

AFFILIATIONS

Glenda Anthony
Massey University
New Zealand

Tim Burgess
Massey University
New Zealand

37

BIRGIT PEPIN, OLE KRISTIAN BERGEM & KIRSTI KLETTE

CHAPTER 3

*Rethinking Algebra Teaching in the Light of 'Orchestration of Signs' –
Exploring the "Equal Sign" in a Norwegian Mathematics Classroom*

INTRODUCTION

Algebra continues to be the focus of reform efforts and research in mathematics education in many countries worldwide (e.g., Kieran, 1992 & 2006; National Council of Teachers of Mathematics (NCTM), 2000; Watson, 2009). There is a general concern (e.g., from policy makers, teachers and Higher Education councils) that students leave compulsory schooling with inadequate understandings of and preparation in algebra, and that they seem to be ill-prepared for future educational or professional opportunities (Moses & Cobb, 2001). Many universities (e.g., in the UK and the US) provide 'transition' or support courses for students who study mathematically demanding subjects in order to equip them with the relevant knowledge (see transition research, e.g., 'TransMaths' project at the University of Manchester[1]), also in algebra. In fact, there appears to be agreement that algebra reforms require a re-conceptualisation of algebra in school mathematics (e.g., NCTM, 2000).

A fundamental concept in algebra that has received considerable attention in mathematics education is that of equality and, connected to this, particularly the understanding of the equal sign (e.g., Kieran, 1981 & 2006; McNeil & Alibali, 2005). Knuth et al. (2006) claimed that 'the ubiquitous presence of the equal sign at all levels of mathematics highlights its importance' (p.298). It is generally acknowledged that the notion of 'equal' is complex and difficult for students to understand, and numerous studies have explored student understandings and use of equality and the equal sign (e.g. Alibali, 1999; Kieran, 1981).

Exploring *equivalence*, Gattegno (1974) stated that:

> We can see that *identity* is a very restrictive kind of relationship concerned with actual sameness, that *equality* points at an attribute which does not change, and that *equivalence* is concerned with a wider relationship where one agrees that for certain purposes it is possible to replace one item by another. Equivalence being the most comprehensive relationship, it will be the most flexible, and therefore the most useful. (p.83)

However, research into algebra tells us that the equal sign is not always interpreted by the learner, and presented by the mathematics teacher, in terms of equivalence.

F.K.S. Leung et al. (eds.), Algebra Teaching around the World, 39–57.
© *2014 Sense Publishers. All rights reserved.*

In this chapter we explore the meanings and use of the equal sign in a 9th grade Norwegian mathematics classroom from a cultural semiotic perspective, in order to develop deeper understandings of algebraic learning and teaching in classroom/ school environments.

UNDERSTANDINGS OF EQUALITY AND THE EQUAL SIGN

After decades of research to establish the importance of the equality concept (e.g., Baroody & Ginsberg, 1983; Falkner et al., 1999), the NCTM Standards (2000) reflected this importance by contending that "equality is an important algebraic concept that students must encounter and begin to understand in the lower grades" (p.94). Researchers have generally agreed on the important distinction between two understandings of equality: the 'operational'; and the 'relational' (e.g., Kieran, 1981; Filloy et al., 2003; Knuth et al., 2006). Kieran (1981) reported that:

> The equal sign is a 'do something signal', is a thread which seems to run through the interpretation of equality sentences throughout elementary school, high school, and even college. Early elementary school children ... view the equal sign as a symbol which separates a problem and its answer. (p.324)

Another important finding of algebraic research has been that pupils do not develop a more nuanced understanding of the equal sign 'by themselves' or as a matter of 'natural' mathematical maturation (Kieran, 1981). Saenz-Ludlow and Walgamuth (1998) reported a year-long study in which pupils were taught to use different meanings of the equal sign, for example to use the verb 'to be' instead of the equal sign in the tasks. This had implications for their view of the sign and there was an apparent shift from 'find the answer' to 'is the same as'.

In terms of difficulties with the development of relational meaning (typically in transition from arithmetic to algebra), different approaches have been used, in particular with respect to the symmetric and relational use of the equal sign (e.g., Kieran, 1981; Theis, 2005). These differences are exacerbated by the fact that relational meaning has different interpretations (e.g., Malle, 1993; Cortes et al., 1990); Prediger (2010) summarized six different meanings for equality (p.81):

1. Operational meaning: operation equals answer (e.g. $24:6-3=1$ or $f'(x)=(3x^2)'=6x$)
2. Relational meaning:
   a. Symmetric arithmetic identity, e.g. '$5+7=7+5$' or '$19=10^2-9^2$'
   b. Formal equivalence describing equivalent terms, e.g. '$x^2+x-6=(x-2)(x+3)$, '$(a-b)(a+b)=a^2-b^2$'
   c. Conditional equations characterizing unknowns, e.g. 'solve $x^2=x+6$'
   d. Contextual identities in formulae, e.g. volume formula for cone: '$V=\frac{1}{3}\cdot\pi\cdot r^2\cdot h$' or 'right angles with hypotenuse c and legs a, b satisfy $a^2+b^2=c^2$'
3. Specification, e.g. '$m:=\frac{1}{2}(a+b)$' or '$y=2x+52$'

This last category was introduced by Cortes et al. (1990); in this, identities are not described but are provided as in definitions. Many researchers have emphasised the context specificity of meanings of the equal sign, and they relate it to the long-term shift in meaning across age, for example in transition from arithmetic to algebra (e.g., Cortes et al., 1990; Kieran, 1981). However, for the student (even the older student) the problem remains if there are changes of meanings within one problem, and this is seen as a main obstacle in the learning process. At the same time, and in the mathematical problem-solving situation where students are expected to distinguish and switch, it also represents an important characteristic and strength of learning algebra.

Broadly speaking, there are at least three issues in terms of difficulties about the meaning of the equal sign. First, and as mentioned above, learners (and often teachers) continue to use the equal sign to mean 'calculate', because this is familiar and meaningful for them. Second, the equal sign is often used differently within mathematics, also by mathematics teachers. Students have to develop an understanding of equivalence, as compared to equality, when using the sign. For example, equivalence can mean that expressions give the same equal values for a range of input values of the variables, or that expressions are transformations of the same form. Kieran and Sfard (1999) used a graphical function approach, and hence the students in their study had the opportunity to recognize that equivalent algebraic representations of functions could generate the same graphs, and hence represent the same relationship between variables. Equality is seen as the intersection of graphs (as compared to equivalence when graphs coincide) (Watson, 2010). Third, using the equal sign differently may imply different meanings for letters which may be used as variables, parameters or hidden values, for example.

THEORETICAL FRAMEWORK

Radford (2010) introduced a typology of forms of algebraic thinking that rests on a semiotic theoretical approach which, in turn, is based on current research in the field (e.g., Kieran 2006). For him, "signs lose the representational and ancillary status with which they are usually endowed in classical cognitive theories in order to become the *material* counterpart of thought" (p.2). In this semiotic perspective algebraic signs and formulas can be seen in a different light. Whereas, traditionally, letters and signs, including the equal sign, have been regarded as *the* semiotic system, Radford included words and gestures, amongst others, in this system. Without challenging previous research on symbolic algebra, Radford, in principle, claimed that there are many semiotic ways other than (and along with) the symbolic one to express algebraic ideas (in his case the 'unknown'). This leaves room for a large conceptual zone which Radford termed the "zone of emergence of algebraic thinking". He and other colleagues, such as Arzarello and his team, Nunez and Edwards, Roth and his colleagues, and others, have paid attention to the "embodied nature of mathematical cognition" (Radford 2010, p.4).

In this theoretical framework 'signs' encompass and include the traditional meanings of the 'sign'. Radford outlined, first, that signs are "considered in a broad sense, as something encompassing written as well as oral linguistic terms, mathematical symbols, gestures, etc." (p.3), and, second, that they are considered as parts of algebraic thinking (and not mere indicators of thinking).

> In more precise terms, within this semiotic-cultural perspective, thinking is considered a sensuous and sign-mediated reflective activity embodied in the corporeality of actions, gestures, and artifacts. (Radford, 2010, p.3)

Moreover, Radford (2010) coined the term of *objectification* and, according to him, the processes of *objectification* are the social processes through which the student develops deeper understandings of the 'culturally' built in logic and becomes confident with forms and actions related and involved in these processes. Moreover, constructs such as the 'formula' develop different meanings: for example, the formula becomes a *narrative* (in a condensed manner) which tells about students' mathematical experiences.

In terms of narrative Bruner's notion of "narrative construction of reality" (1991) focuses on the idea of narrative as a 'cultural product' with which the mind structures its sense of reality - narrative operates as an instrument of mind in the construction of reality. He identified (at least) nine features of narrative (Bruner, 1991: narrative diachronicity; particularity; intentional state entailment; hermeneutic composability; canonicity and breach; referentiality; normativeness and the centrality of trouble; context sensitivity and negotiability; narrative accrual). For this purpose, that is to use narrative as a perspective that can inform algebraic thinking in teaching, we draw on one of the key themes reflected in Bruner's analysis, canonicity and breach or, in other words 'troubles' and how to overcome them.

The combination of these theoretical stances provides the basics of our 'semiotic' analysis of teacher pedagogic practice in an algebra lesson. More particularly, we will explore the following questions:

- What signs are used in this lesson, and how is the equal sign used by this teacher?
- How can we interpret this semiotically, and 'collectively'?
- What may this mean for algebra teaching, and more particularly for the use of the equal sign in mathematics classrooms?

THE STUDY

For this chapter we draw on data from the Learner's Perspective Study (LPS) (e.g Clarke et al., 2006) collected by the Norwegian LPS research team (see Klette, 2009; Bergem & Klette, 2010). The LPS aims to juxtapose observable classroom practices and the meanings attributed to those practices (e.g. by teachers and pupils). The LPS research design includes lesson sequences of about ten grade 8 lessons, using three video cameras and supplemented by the participants' accounts obtained in post-lesson Stimulated Recall interviews, and copies of classroom materials such as textbooks and other curricular materials. For this study one teacher's data, and in particular the early algebra lesson, were chosen for 'semiotic investigation'. The subsequent nine lessons and teacher and student interviews were analysed in terms of teachers' general pedagogic practices and pupils' perceptions of their learning practices, in addition to the analysis of the textbook used.

The theoretical framework for the semiotic analysis was provided in the previous section. More practically, a procedure involving the analysis of themes similar to that described by Woods (1986) and by Burgess (1984) was adopted. This included, at one level, the identification of the different 'signs' used by the teacher and the meanings attributed to them and, more generally, it meant using our knowledge of Radford's semiotics and testing the hypotheses offered by the literature, and building explanations and theorisations grounded in the data.

At another level, we tried to maintain the coherence of the teacher's case in terms of her pedagogic practice and with a holistic view (and respondent validated by the participant teacher interview), anchored in the teacher's own interview and the observations. The cursory analysis of textbooks helped here in identifying issues for examination. In addition, we could also draw on pupil interviews. More generally, it was important to locate and understand teacher pedagogic practices and the mathematics classroom cultures in Norway, and it was useful to draw on knowledge gained from earlier and ongoing research (e.g. Pepin, 1999; Pepin, 2011) which has highlighted the complex nature of teachers' work and classroom environments.

THE FINDINGS

Contexts-Mathematics classroom environments

Learners of mathematics at lower secondary level work in particular environments. In Norway most pupils go to comprehensive schools until the age of 16 and are taught in mixed-ability groups. In the Norwegian LPS there appeared to be particular 'customary ways' that most teachers in used in their teaching. For example, most teachers asked their pupils to work on exercises from textbooks for a considerable amount of time so that the pupils could practise what had been explained and the teachers could monitor their understanding. In Norwegian classrooms every pupil is provided with a textbook by the school to be used in school and at home: pupils are said to be 'entitled' to a common curriculum. However, the textbook used in the classes observed for this study differentiates between 'Blå'; 'Gul' and 'Rød' (which mean blue; golden and red) exercises, indicating that there are likely to be three tiers in each group, reflecting the pupils' perceived achievement levels.

All of the Norwegian teachers who were observed during this study drew on textbooks for exercises and sometimes for classwork. This practice was confirmed by the results of an 'attitude' survey of 13 grade 6-10 classes (see Pepin, 2011), in which the pupils said that, for much of their time in mathematics lessons they work on exercises from the textbooks. In fact, this was one of the reasons why many pupils disliked mathematics ("there is too little variation in maths").

However, evidence from this study shows that, in practice, the teachers found it hard to differentiate and provide exercises so that every pupil could access the mathematics. The pupils came to the lessons with different mathematics backgrounds (depending what they had been taught in previous years). In the Stimulated Recall interview, one teacher described her pedagogic practices and explained her efforts "to keep the whole class together" and at the same time attend to the mathematical needs of individual pupils.

> It's not always that easy to explain to students who haven't been taught equations before and who might not be that interested in mathematics and always requires the practical side of it... you'll get a lot of different answers. There's not a clear answer from all of the class. You'll get a mix of answers. (S4 T1)

She explained that she had developed pedagogic strategies to help her pupils cope with the variety of understandings (e.g. use peer assessment).

> I don't know, I don't always have the general overview. I have to admit that. But I knew I had a group of students who knew how to check the answers that I had checked on, and that I had given some explanations about. They had solved some exercises already. I saw it was working, when I talked to them. So I knew I had some students who could do the teaching for me in a way ... So I think the variation [of pedagogic strategies] is good. As a teaching method, to use students as teachers ... There is so much instruction from the blackboard in maths [lessons]. (S4 T1)

In terms of textbooks this school had chosen the above-mentioned textbook that differentiated between three levels of difficulties in terms of exercises: 'Blå'; 'Gul' and 'Rød', which in turn was perceived to provide opportunities, or not, for individual pupils to practise their developing understandings. In fact, this teacher did not mention the colours, but used the different level exercises for pupils to have more practice (at whichever level).

> ...sometimes the exercises on the plan don't suffice [to have enough practice]. Sometimes you have to do more. (S4 T1)

However, the testing system seemed to have an effect on the teachers' practice, and they used the grades to evaluate pupil performance on the work plan. This, in turn, provided a dilemma for them in terms of their support for those 'weak' students who invested a lot of effort, for apparently little effect.

> And then I have... I have sort of categorised them in accordance to where they're at ..., so that you can keep up with them. So I evaluate them according to their grades, the formal grade, and you have the running evaluation that takes place all the time. Then we have the formal tests, hand-ins and so on. Then I get a very...I think that...on their path to a summative assessment within a topic. (S4 T1)

One Norwegian teacher told us that she found it difficult to attend to individual pupils' problems and misconceptions in mathematics- there was too little time. However, she said that she had identified and used particular strategies to 'reach everyone'. One of these practices was the ½ hour teaching time when she had the whole class together. During this time she tried to "get students to reflect on their own", that is to step back as a teacher and encourage the pupils to think for themselves and initiate and encourage discussion in class. Often pupils who may generally have performed poorly in mathematics tests were encouraged to explain their answers at the blackboard; sometimes several pupils were taken to the board. This showed to the pupils that there are methods, "different ways of calculating".

In summary, the teachers found it difficult to attend to the needs of individual pupils. Although the textbook and individual 'work plans' supported individualistic pedagogic practices, the teachers mentioned that they had insufficient time and expertise to deal with every pupil's developing mathematical understandings.

Description of the lesson and identification/use of 'signs'

In the following we briefly outline and describe the early algebra lesson, identifying particular 'signs' (our bolding).

At the start of the lesson the teacher gave the pupils a text question:

Per and Kari have five **apples** jointly. Per has two apples. How many has Kari? Really simple, you know...yes, and then you laugh a little...But discuss in your groups, how can we calculate the answer and how would you put your calculations down in writing?

Photo 1

45

She explained that they would have to work in a particular way with these kinds of **text questions** ('read the text first', 'find the information', ...) . However, the pupils did not seem to be convinced that this was necessary:

> that's easy ... five minus two equals three ... that's easy ... [S4, P3]

The teacher insisted and tried to build up a structured approach, to introduce the problem algebraically:

> But, eh, how many apples Kari has is the **unknown**, what we are going to find, and that's the core of **equations.** When we work with equations we have something called the unknown, we are going to find an answer or something we don't know anything about. And the unknown...we name with a letter, usually it's **X**. ... If we are going to solve this as an equation...(writes on the board).

She used expressions such as 'known' and 'unknown', and wrote it on the board as an equation:

> How many apples Kari has, so, the unknown (**writes on the board while reading out load what she writes**), how...many...apples...Kari has. If we are going to write this as an equation ... (writes on the board) two, that's Per's apples ... and then I write X instead and that equals five. Do you all understand that we can write it down in this way? When X is the unknown, the answer we are going to find and it represents how many apples Kari has.

Photo 2

Some pupils appeared to be puzzled and a whole conversation developed about 'knowns' and 'unknowns':

P1: But what is the known?

T: What is the known? Yes, what is that? What is known in this? Nina?

P2: How many apples Per has and how many they have jointly?

T: How many apples Per has, because that is her (**points at the board**), and how many they have jointly ... ? That is five, and that is what we know and ... the unknown.

P1: Don't we have to have a **letter** for that?

T: No, we don't, because that is not something that is unknown. ... You are thinking like in algebra when we had **As and Bs and Cs** and so on. But now we have only one unknown and that is what we are working with all the time, that we have one unknown.

Although the pupils expressed their 'uneasiness'- they were not convinced that this question necessitated algebraic thinking - the teacher continued:

T: But what we, now we are demonstrating how to solve it and we start with very simple exercises to show you how you solve more difficult equation exercises. That is why we make use of such simple **numbers,** so that everyone will understand.

P: Why do we have this **X** anyway?

The teacher then proceeded to explain equations and introduced the equal sign:

T: ... we name all the unknowns X...then this is Per's apples (**writes below the arithmetic calculation on the board**) and here is the apples they have jointly. Kari plus Per (...) is Kari (**writes below the X**), that we don't know. And that is the unknown. This sign here, what sign is this? Iselin?

P: It is an **equal sign,** so should be just as much on the right side as on the left side.

T: This is an equal sign, and we use this in other situations as well when we calculate, and we say that it should be just as much on the left side as on the right side of the equal sign (**writes 'equal sign' below the sign and underlines the wording twice**).

She also moved directly to the concept of equivalence and the scale:

T: Just as much on the right side as on the left side
      ...always just as much on one side as the other
      in **numerical value**. ... Numerical value? The value
      of the numbers here, is just as much as the value
      there. ... what one often does with equations to
      make it, to make you learn from the ground up, it is
      often a good idea to...to use a gauge, or this **scale**.
      We draw a scale so that you get a visual image of
      equations...Now we will draw a balance, we will not
      calculate any further before we demonstrate it with
      a scale (she **draws a balance on the blackboard**).

      ... There is just as much **weight** on both sides,
      then we can say that the **midline here is the sign
      of equation seeing as it is in balance**. Here we
      have a **question mark (writes on one of the scales)**
      and that is Kari's apples, and then we have two
      apples which is...

      ... And they have the same weight, or there is just
      as much on both sides. It will always be so when it
      is an equation.

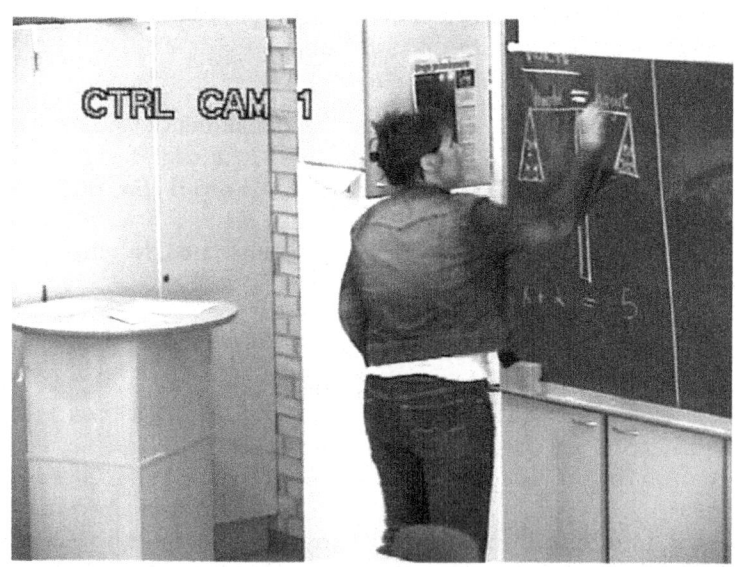

Photo 3

She subsequently used the scale to show equivalence:

> When we solve an equation we always want the X on the left side of the scale or the equal sign. It should always be on the left side alone. We want it all alone to find out what it equals.

> If I take away those two apples… What happens to the scale if I remove two apples? … The other side will go straight down. (**makes handsign**) … The other side will go straight down, because? What do I have to do so that the other side doesn't go straight down? What do I have to do with those five apples here? How many do I have to remove? Two. Do you get it? If I remove two here now…I remove the two apples…remove two apples…like…what do we call it when the scales are on the same horizontal line? Balance. .. What do we have left on the scales now? What do we have left on the left side when we have done this? …

Photo 4

Furthermore, she formalised the process:

> And then we have found out what X is…Now I am going to **show you on paper**, no, not on paper, how we write it out. … X plus two equals five (writes on the board). This is what we started with and on the scales we did X plus two and then minus two apples, to remove them so we were left with only X. And then I had to remember to subtract on the right side as well…Are you following me?…I am allowed to subtract or add on the left side, but then I have to do the same at the right side. And two minus two, how much is that? Iselin?

```
P:    Nought
T:    Is nought and I am left with X. And five minus two
      is? ...
P:    Three.
T:    Three. Now I have solved the equation. Then I have to
      write it in text because it is a text exercise. Kari
      has three apples.
```

Photo 5

We have described and followed this early part of the lesson in great detail, in order to see how the teacher introduced and developed the concepts, and used the different signs for her purpose. The lesson proceeded to solve another similar problem. The teacher then asked one pupil to come to the board to explain her answer and she then provided comments to the whole class about the solution:

When we solve an equation Iselin wants to get X alone. First she finds out what X is, you have to define what the unknown is in the task, and that is how old Olav is. Then she has used the information already given and writes it as an equation, because this is her equation, X plus seven equals 16. Then she starts to solve the equation…and she says she removes, why do you do this Iselin? Seven minus seven?.. Always when we solve an equation it is our job to get X by itself on the left side. And when we talk about the left side …it is the left side of the equation sign we talk about. We always want to get the X by itself like Iselin has tried to do here, remove the seven on one side and then we are allowed to remove seven on the other side, and then we have to do that in order for it to be correct, otherwise it wouldn't be balance, like Rino said, in our scales. ...When we have text exercises it is important that we write our answer in text. Another tip we will try to follow up on is to write the equal sign below one another throughout our calculations. It will bring order to our equations, in order to see what we are doing. That's a tip. Now we don't have time to go through any more. It wasn't much we did, but we had just half an hour today. We'll continue with equations on Wednesday...

In the following section we discuss the different 'signs' the teacher used in this particular algebra lesson (see bolded words), and the different sources of meanings she assigned to the equal sign.

DISCUSSION OF FINDINGS

One can identify different sources of meaning of the equal sign in this Norwegian mathematics classroom. Looking at the lesson description above, the teacher's use of the equal sign has implications for its meaning in the process of teaching. At a first level we could identify at least three ways that are outlined by the literature (e.g., Kieran, 1981): Firstly, the equal sign is seen as a 'do something' signal and separates the problem and its answers. The teacher mentioned that the equal sign is also used "when we calculate" and "in other situations".

> This is an equal sign, and we use this in other situations as well when we calculate, and we say that it should be just as much on the left side as on the right side of the equal sign (writes 'equal sign' below the sign and underlines the wording twice)

Second, the equal sign signifies that 'both sides yield the same value'. The teacher explicitly mentioned this when explaining the equation.

> ...always just as much on one side as the other in **numerical value**. ... Numerical value? The value of the numbers here, is just as much as the value there. ..

Third, the equal sign signifies equivalence relations when linked to when balance model.

> ... There is just as much **weight** on both sides, then we can say that the **midline here is the sign of equation seeing as it is in balance**.

Moreover, and looking through a slightly different lens, the equal sign can be regarded as sign or symbol within a semiotic system that is important for mathematical activity (e.g., Steinbring 2005) and where the sign is seen as part of a mathematical sign language. Steinbring (2005) drew on Otte's notion of *metaphor* (Otte 1984) to investigate the meaning of 'equation'. For him, algebra is a mathematical sign language, and he asked what the particularities of this language are, and in which ways meanings are attributed to the 'words' and 'phrases'. For this he used and analysed the 'equation'- equivalence- balance situation. In terms of results, he defined three levels of the relations between the 'object' and 'sign/symbol':

1. algebraic signs and symbols (ASS) serve as *names* for objects and as descriptors of reality;
2. ASS describe *relations* and *structures* within the context;
3. there is a *reciprocal action* between ASS, and structures and relations (Steinbring 2005, p.101).

Here it is important to identify and draw out the mathematical concept, in order not to confuse the sign with the concept (e.g., Duval, 1993). Duval claimed that mathematical signs do not represent empirical things, but embody relations:

> There is an important gap between mathematical knowledge and knowledge in other sciences ... we do not have any perceptive or instrumental access to mathematical objects, even the most elementary ... we cannot see them, study them through a microscope or take a picture of them. The only way of gaining access to them is using signs, words or symbols, expressions or drawings. But, at the same time, mathematical objects must not be confused with the used semiotic representations. This conflicting requirement makes the specific core of mathematical knowledge. (Duval, 2000, p.61)

For the equal sign and its use in this lesson, questions can be asked about when it is used as a 'sign', and when as a balancing 'tool', and when it signifies the process of balancing. The most noteworthy lesson episode here is when the teacher draws the equal sign above the centre of the scale (see photo 3), signifying the process of balancing the 'left' and 'right' hand side of the scale, which at this moment is 'in balance'.

Furthermore, and at a third level we take the semiotic perspective of Radford where 'signs' encompass and include linguistic terms, mathematical symbols and gestures as constituent parts of mathematical thinking.

In Radford's terms it can be said that the teacher uses a number of signs, and we can identify the following in this lesson sequence (see bolded words in last section):

- Words/expressions: 'apples'; 'unknown'; 'known'
- Gestures: underlining the equal sign; pulling the hand down signifying when the scale is pulled down on one side, gets 'out of balance'
- Algebraic signs and symbols: 'X'; 'A'
- Other signs: '?', underline
- Representations: scale/ balance
- Text: text/ question as relations
- Names: Kari; Per
- Numbers: 5 (and at times linked to names)

Radford's claim was that these signs become unique "by their mode of signifying" and help students to develop their "zone of emergence of algebraic thinking" (Radford, 2010).

Focussing on the equal sign, it is evident that this is used in several different semiotic ways, sometimes expressing 'doing', sometimes 'balancing', or 'unbalancing', for example. First, it is worth noticing which kind of text question the teacher has chosen for the topic of 'equations' and the use of the equal sign. Radford claimed that the mathematical problem at hand plays a crucial role. This is evident when pupils question the value of the test question with respect to the mathematical concepts they are meant to learn. Clearly, students did not see much sense in solving this problem algebraically: "it is easy ... why do we have this X anyway ... ?". It is also likely that pupils attach meanings in contexts, and when these contexts change, they have difficulties in establishing meanings for the symbol. "When do/can I use the scale model, when do I have to use the formal algebraic way of solving the problem?" In fact, several authors have investigated the affordances and constraints, and the usefulness of models, such as the balancing model, for particular problem situations (e.g., Vlassis, 2002). For example, Vlassis claims that the balance model can provide students with an 'operative' mental image containing principles to be applied, but it cannot overcome all obstacles linked to processes of abstraction in algebraic balancing (linked to negative numbers for example).

Second, we can identify different embodied and semiotic resources that are used to look at the problem in analytic ways. In the first stage the equal sign is used in the equation 'X+2=5' to tell the story of Per and Kari, and how many apples they each have. At the same time it is exploited for the explanation of the concept of 'unknown' and 'known' (photo 2) and the equal sign is written out in words and underlined twice - a strong gesture to emphasise the importance of the sign. In the second stage it is worked into the 'picture' of the balance, separating left and right with the labels 'left = right' above the scale, and explaining the process of balancing, whilst at the same time the equation (X+2=5) remains part of the 'story' (see photo 3). Here another gesture supports the meaning of the process: a sign of a hand pulling down as if the scale is being pulled down. In the third stage the equal sign is 'woven' into a more complicated balancing process (but principally in the same way as before) where apples and names are added (photo 4). At a fourth stage the sign is built into an algebraic equation which is meant to formalise the process of 'balancing': 'X+2-2=5-2' and, finally, linking a number to X ('X=3'). This then concludes the 'story' with a final answer written/elucidated in text (photo 5).

CONCLUSIONS AND IMPLICATIONS FOR THEORY AND PRACTICE

From the above, and considering the various uses of the equal sign and its meanings as reflected in teacher pedagogic practice, gestures and use of resources, we can develop a deeper understanding of teacher pedagogic practice, in particular with respect to the concept of 'balancing'. We propose the concept of *orchestration of signs* in the algebra classroom, to explain teacher pedagogic practice in terms of the use of signs and the meanings attached to them.

Leaning on the work of Trouche (2003; 2004), who developed this perspective to explain teacher pedagogic practice in technology-rich environments,

> ...*an instrumental orchestration* is defined as the teacher's intentional and systematic organisation and use of the various artefacts available in a -in this case computerised learning environment in a given mathematical task situation, in order to guide students' instrumental genesis (Trouche, 2004). (p. 214/15, Drijvers et al., 2010)

The metaphor of orchestration relates to teacher pedagogic practice, the didactical performance to the musical performance, where the interplay between the conductor (teacher) and the musicians (students) describes and is likened to the learning situation (in our case) in the mathematics classroom. We are aware that the metaphor has its limitations (see Drijvers et al., 2010), and moreover we do not adhere strictly to the construct as it was used by Trouche (2004) for the technology-rich classroom and the use of tools and artefacts. However, in terms of using *signs* (and in particular the different meanings of the equal sign) *orchestration* is a helpful construct.

If we see the sign at the level of an artefact, we can identify three different levels:

- As a primary artefact: the equal sign written on the board means 'is equal to';
- As a secondary artefact: the modes of action attached to the equal sign, e.g. 'calculate';
- As a tertiary artefact: as simulating 'balancing' and with the representation of the scale; hand sign signifying 'off-balance'.

This relates to Wartofsky's (1983) distinctions between three levels of artefacts. Building a system from and with these, and *orchestrating the signs* at these different levels in order for mathematical learning to emerge, can be said to be one of the main goals of teacher pedagogic practice.

However, how the teacher organises this is an individual 'enterprise' where every teacher uses his/her skills to weave their stories using the signs (and tools) in complex ways. In our case, the teacher told the story of Kari and Per, and the unequal distribution of apples between them. There are also more subtle, and unexpected, 'trouble' elements in the lesson; for example, why should one use equations to solve this 'easy' question?; the 'known' and the 'unknown'; etc. Seen in this way, the equal sign becomes more than a sign in the formula; the sign is part of the story that is told by the formula and it has a narrative character. The dilemma for students here is that if the context changes, the story changes, and this may shift meanings too- at least for students who have problems with algebraic understanding.

In conclusion, by bringing together a semiotic and 'instrumental' approach, we have been able to analyse algebra teaching in a different way. This has highlighted the complex relationships between the signs in particular the equal sign, as artefacts, and the meanings attached to and uses of signs by the teacher. We have claimed that *orchestration of signs* may be a useful construct to describe these processes. Furthermore, we have compared the sign in the 'context' of the formula, and in teacher *orchestration*, to a narrative told and given meaning by the teacher. This emphasises the highly individualised nature of teaching and of mathematics teachers' pedagogic practices; this individualism may not be a characteristic wished for by policy makers in their endeavour to standardise teaching.

In terms of the implications of these findings for teacher education, it can be argued that teacher educators may consider using frameworks such as 'orchestration of signs' in order to raise teacher awareness of the potential threats to mathematical learning when students move from one class to another, from one *orchestration* to another. However, the *orchestration of signs* highlights not only the results of the immediate activities, but the different shapes that these can take depending on the meanings attached to the signs. Trouche (2003) stressed the necessity for 'didactic management' of a system of what we would interpret as 'signs'. What signs should be proposed to learners, and how should teachers be guided in their *orchestration of signs*? What kinds of learner activities should be provided (in order to develop understandings of the different signs), and for what kinds of mathematical knowledge? Considering these questions, the following issues need to be addressed:

- New signs suggest new meanings in new environments which may require new sets of mathematical problems;
- It is important/essential to understand the constraints and potential of signs;
- It is important to understand and manage the orchestration process, and how the signs 'work together'.

In this respect the concept of *orchestration of signs* links issues of mathematics teacher pedagogic practices to teacher knowledge and pupil learning. Thus, and related to teacher education, we argue that the 'sign' can be regarded as a 'new' pedagogic resource to build competent teacher practice around its use; and that the *orchestration of signs* can be viewed as a creative pedagogic resource to develop an awareness of, or to notice, what constitutes important instructional moments.

Considering the theoretical implications, it is argued that the concept of *orchestration of signs* provides an analytic tool to investigate mathematics lessons in more detail by paying attention to the meanings of signs, and the role the different (algebraic) signs play in pedagogic practice whilst, at the same time, overseeing the 'whole', thus realising that, in the *orchestration of signs,* 'the whole equals more than the sum of its parts'.

NOTE

¹ http://www.education.manchester.ac.uk/research/centres/lta/LTAResearch/transmaths/into-he/`

REFERENCES

Alibali, M. W. (1999). How children change their minds: strategy change can be gradual or abrupt. *Developmental Psychology, 35*, 127–145.

Baroody, A. J., & Ginsburg, H. P. (1983). The effects of instruction on children's understanding of the 'equals' sign. *The Elementary School Journal, 84*(2), 198–212.

Bergem O. K., Klette, K. (2010). Mathematical tasks as catalysts for student talk: Analysing discourse in a Norwegian mathematics classroom. In Y Shimizu, B. Kaur, R. Huang, and D. Clark (Eds.), *Mathematical tasks in classrooms around the world* (pp. 35–62). Sense Publishers.

Burgess, R. G. (1984). *In the field: An introduction to field research.* London, UK: Allan & Unwin.

Cortes, A., Vergnaud, G., & Kavafian, N. (1990). From arithmetic to algebra: negotiating a jump in the learning process. In G. Brooker, P. Coob, & T. de Mendicuti (Eds), *Proceedings of the 14th Conference of the International Group for the Psychology of Mathematics Education*(Vol. 2, pp. 27–34). Oaxtepex, Mexico: PME.

Drijvers, P., Doorman, M., Boon, P., Reed, H., & Gravemeijer, K. (2010). The teacher and the tool: instrumental orchestrations in the technology-rich mathematics classroom. *Educational Studies in Mathematics, 75,* 213–234.

Duval, R. (2000). Basic issues for research in mathematics education. In T. Nakahara & M. Koyama (Eds.), *Proceedings of the 24th International Conference for the Psychology of Mathematics Education* (Vol. 1, pp. 55–69). Hiroshima, Japan: Nishiki Print Co. Ltd.

Duval, R. (1993). Registres de representation semiotique et fonctionnement cognitive de la pensee. In *Annales de Didactique et des Sciences cognitives, 5,* 37–65.

Falkner, K. P., Levi, L., & Carpenter, T. P. (1999). Children's understanding of equality: A foundation for algebra. *Teaching children mathematics, 6,* 56–60.

Filloy, E., Rojano, T., Solares, A. (2003). Two meanings of the 'equal' sign and senses of comparison and substitution methods. In N. Pateman, B. J. Dougherty, & J. T. Zilliox (Eds.), *Proceedings of the 27th conference of the international group for the psychology of mathematics education* (Vol. 4, pp. 223–230). Honululu, HI: CRDG.

Kieran, C. (1981). Concepts associated with the equality symbol. *Educational Studies in Mathematics, 12*(3), 317–326.

Kieran, C. (1992). The learning and teaching of school algebra. In D. Grouws (Ed.), *Handbook of Research on mathematics teaching and learning* (pp. 390–419). New York, NY: MacMillan.

Kieran, C. (2006). Research on the learning and the teaching of algebra: a broadening of sources of meaning. In A. Gutierrez & P. Boero (Eds.), *Handbook of research on the psychology of mathematics education: past, present, future* (pp. 23–49). Rotterdam: The Netherlands: Sense Publication.

Klette K. (2009). Challenges in Strategies for Complexity Reduction in Video Studies. Experiences from the PISA + Study: A video study of teaching and learning in Norway. In T. Janik & T. Seidel (Eds.), *The power of video studies in investigating teaching and learning in the classroom* (pp. 61–83). Waxmann Publishing.

Knuth, E. J., Stephens, A. C., McNeil, N. M., & Alibali, M. W. (2006). Does understanding the equal sign matter? Evidence from solving equations. *Journal for Research in Mathematics Education. 36*(4), 297–312.

Malle, G. (1993). *Didaktische Probleme der Elementaren Algebra.* Wiesbaden: Vieweg.

McNeil, N. M., & Alibali, M. W. (2005). Knowledge changes as a function of mathematics experience: all contexts are not created equal. *Journal of Cognition and Development, 6,* 285–306.

Moses, R., & Cobb, C. (2001). *Radical equations: math literacy and civil rights.* Boston, MA: Beacon Press.

National Council of Teachers of Mathematics- NCTM. (2000). *NCTM Standards 2000: Principles and standards for school mathematics.* Reston. Retrieved from http://standards.nctm.org/document/index.htm

Otte, M. (1984). *Was ist Mathematik? Occasional Paper 43 des.* IDM, Bielefeld: Universitaet Bielefeld.

Pepin, B. (2011) Pupils' attitudes towards mathematics: a comparative study of Norwegian and English secondary students. *ZDM—The International Journal on Mathematics Education, 43*(4), 535–546.

Pepin, B. (1999). The influence of national cultural traditions on pedagogy: classroom practices in England, France and Germany. In J. Leach & B. Moon (Eds.), *Learners and pedagogy* (pp. 124–139). London: Sage Publications.

Prediger, S. (2010). How to develop mathematics-for-teaching and for understanding: the case of meanings of the equal sign. *Journal of Mathematics Teacher Education, 13*, 73–93.

Radford, L. (2010). Algebraic thinking from a cultural semiotic perspective. *Research in Mathematics Education, 12*(1), 1–19.

Steinbring, H. (2005). Do mathematical symbols serve to describe or construct 'reality'? In M. H. G. Hoffmann, J. Lenhard, & F. Seeger (Eds.), *Activity and sign- grounding mathematics education* (pp. 91–104). New York, NY: Springer.

Theis, L. (2005). L'apprentissage du signe =: un obstacle cognitif important. *For the learning of Mathematics, 25*(3), 7–12.

Trouche, L. (2003). From artefact to instrument: mathematics teaching mediated by symbolic calculators. *Interacting with Computers, 15*, 783–800.

Trouche, L. (2004). Managing complexity of human/machine interactions in computerised learning environments: guiding students' command process through instrumental orchestrations. *International Journal of Computers for Mathematical Learning, 9*, 281–307.

Vlassis, J. (2002) The balance model: hindrance or support for the solving of linear equations with one unknown, *Educational Studies in Mathematics, 49*, 341–359.

Wartofsky, M. (1983). From genetic epistemology to historical epistemology: Kant, Marx and Piaget. In L. S. Liben (Ed.), *Piaget and the foundations of knowledges*. Hilseide, NJ: Lawrence Erlbaum.

Watson, A. (2009) Algebraic reasoning. In T. Nunez, P. Bryant & A. Watson (Eds.), *Key Understandings in mathematics learning*. London: Nuffield Foundation.

Woods, P. (1996). *Inside schools: Ethnography in educational research*. London: Routledge & Kegan Paul.

AFFILIATIONS

Birgit Pepin
Høgskolen i Sør-Trøndelag
Norway

Ole Kristian Bergem
Kirsti Klette
University of Oslo
Norway

JARMILA NOVOTNÁ & ALENA HOŠPESOVÁ

CHAPTER 4

Traditional Versus Investigative Approaches to Teaching Algebra at the Lower Secondary Level: The Case of Equations

"... These theoretical perspectives are to view algebra: (i) as a way of expressing generality; (ii) as a study of symbol manipulation and equation solving; (iii) as a study of functions; (iv) as a way to solve certain classes of problems; (v) as a way to model real situations; (vi) as a formal system involving set theory, logic, and operations on entities other than real numbers. Educational jurisdictions do not usually implement only one of these, but select from them within a given emphasis."

Kay Stacey and Helen Chick (Stacey, Chick & Kendal, 2004, p. 12)

INTRODUCTION

Van Ameron (2002, p. 3) stated that "Algebra is known to be a major stumbling block in school mathematics, both in the past and present. Historical studies on the developments of algebra education in the twentieth century show that the algebra studied in secondary school has not changed much over the years". Sutherland (2000) presented a comparative study of algebra curricula in twelve countries all over the world. She stated that "countries organize their algebra curriculum into different 'mathematical' categories and more research needs to be carried out in order to understand the implications of this on classroom practice".

School algebra is generally regarded as an extremely difficult part of the mathematics curriculum. Problems with algebra can be ascribed to external factors, with the teaching approach playing an important role in this respect. As van Ameron stated (2002, p. 3) "Traditional school algebra is primarily a very rigid, abstract branch of mathematics, having few interfaces with the real world. It is often presented to students as a pre-determined and fixed mathematical topic with strict rules, leaving no room for their own input. ... In other words, the mathematical context is taken as the starting-point, while the applications of algebra (like problem solving or generalizing relations) come in second place."

Traditionally algebra is conceived in school mathematics as the generalization of arithmetic. However, nowadays it covers a much broader spectrum, e.g. as a

F.K.S. Leung et al. (eds.), Algebra Teaching around the World, 59–79.
© 2014 Sense Publishers. All rights reserved.

language and/or as a tool for modeling (Herman, 2005; Broin, 2002); see also the motto of this chapter (Stacey et al., 2004, p. 12).

This chapter focuses mainly on the following components of algebraic competence: (a) the ability to understand equality and equations and to apply them in real world problem-solving settings[1]; (b) the ability to think in a symbolic language, to understand algebra as generalized arithmetic, and to understand it as the study of mathematical structures. The main topic discussed will be teaching linear equations and their systems.

ALGEBRA IN SCHOOL MATHEMATICS IN THE CZECH REPUBLIC

The results presented in this chapter are tied closely to the ways in which children meet and use algebraic elements in Czech school mathematics at pre-algebraic and algebraic levels. The following brief description of the main characteristics of teaching pre-algebra and algebra in the Czech Republic will give the reader an insight into the background (for more details see Novotná & Kubínová, 2001).

Traditionally, letters (or other symbols, e.g. *, □) are commonly used in school mathematics already from the first grade of primary school. The impulse for introducing letters comes from the teacher and is supported significantly by textbooks and pupils' work materials (workbooks, worksheets etc.) used in other subjects (pre-science, later physics, chemistry, science).

When solving some types of problems (word problems, calculations of perimeters, areas, volumes, etc., simple construction tasks in geometry, dependencies), pupils are asked to follow certain rules (given by the teacher, textbook etc.) to describe the solving process using letters. This is all followed even in cases when the problem can be solved much more simply, e.g. by insight, and when the strict use of letters makes the solution much more difficult.

While, in mathematics teaching, letters always represent variables, unknowns, constants or parameters (depending on the context) and are manipulated correspondingly, in science teaching (especially in physics) they are used only as 'labelled' numbers[2]. Because operating with letters is introduced later in mathematics than in other school subjects, there is a lack of interdisciplinary links.

Educational documents currently being used into practice in the Czech Republic give schools a lot of freedom in organizing their own curricula. The general document is called Framework Education Programme (FEP, http://www.vuppraha. cz/wp-content/uploads/2009/12/RVP_ZV_EN_final.pdf). This document fosters the decentralization of education, increases school autonomy and creates space for transformation of the teaching/learning processes. An important innovation is that the FEP enables different approaches to education to meet the individual needs of learners. It also defines all that is common and imperative in education.

The FEP for lower secondary level school mathematics includes linear equations and systems of two linear equations with two unknowns and the corresponding expected outcomes. According to the document:

The student (a) mathematizes simple real-life situations using variables; evaluates an expression, adds and multiplies polynomials, factorizes a polynomial using a formula or by pulling out the common factors together, (b) formulates and solves a real-life situation using equations and their systems, (c) analyses and solves simple problems, models specific situations in the domain of whole and rational numbers using mathematical apparatus. (FEP, 2007, p. 29).

The FEP is a binding fundamental pedagogical document. It is the common general frame of reference for the School Education Programme (SEP), the document elaborated by all schools according to their specific conditions. It is the responsibility of each school's head teacher to implement their SEP and all teachers participate in this implementation.

The SEP usually contains a detailed list of the expected outcomes in each domain of school mathematics. Below the example of algebra is used to illustrate how the SEP links subject matter to expected pupil competences.

Subject matter	Pupil's competences
Simple equations (6th grade)	Distinguishes between the concepts 'equality' and 'equation'.
	Solves simple linear equations using equivalent adjustments and verifies the validity of the result. ($2x - 6 = 8$, in the domain N, D)
Linear equations (8th grade)	Distinguishes between the concepts equality and equation.
	Solves linear equations using equivalent adjustments and verifies the validity of the result.
	Determines the value of an unknown from a formula
	Solves word problems from real-life situations leading to the solution of a linear equation.
Rational expressions, solution of linear equations with an unknown in the denominator (9th grade)	States under which conditions they exist.
	Reduces and multiplies out rational expressions.
	Adds and subtracts two or three rational expressions.
	Multiplies and divides two rational expressions.
	Transforms a compound rational expression to multiplication of two rational expressions.
	Solves simple linear equations with an unknown in the denominator.
	Solves word problems leading to the solution of simple linear equations with an unknown in the denominator.
Systems of linear equations with two unknowns (9th grade)	Solves a system of two linear equations with two unknowns using substitution method. Verifies the solution by substituting the result.
	Solves a system of two linear equations with two unknowns using the addition method in simple cases.
	Solves word problems from real-life situations using a system of two linear equations with two unknowns.

The SEP may incorporate a special programme for talented pupils as well as for pupils with special needs, as illustrated by the following example of an extension of the domain of linear equation:

- Discussion of the solution of a linear equation.
- Solution of more complicated word problems.
- Linear inequalities with one unknown.
- System of linear inequalities with one unknown.

Although the content and expected outcomes are similar, the teaching strategies differ considerably. In the following text two different teachers' approaches to teaching this topic will be presented. The similarities and differences will be compared from the perspectives of the teacher's competences and the learning outcomes.

DATA COLLECTION

In the research reported in this chapter we analyse the sequence of tasks and problems used by two teachers in ten consecutive lessons on the solution of linear equations and their systems in the 8th grade (students aged 14-15) of two lower secondary schools in the Czech Republic. In the following text, the schools will be referred to as CZ1 and CZ2. Both schools are located in a county town with approximately 100 000 inhabitants. The method of data collection was based on the Learner's Perspective Study (LPS) framework (Clarke, Keitel, Shimizu, 2006) and the lessons were video-recorded for later analysis. The two teachers are experienced and respected by parents, colleagues and educators.

THE ABILITY TO UNDERSTAND EQUALITY AND EQUATIONS

The traditional approach to teaching algebra is to drill the procedures for solving various types of equations and inequalities. It was clear from observing the two teachers that they were both influenced by this approach.

The CZ1 teacher had thoughtfully expanded her collection of equations to be solved. Gradually she introduced different types of equations that increased in difficulty. When solving the tasks, the pupils were asked to justify the respective stages of their procedures and were guided to see the inter-relationships between them (Novotná, Hošpesová, 2009). The following sample problems will help to illustrate this approach:

- Equivalent adjustments to both sides of the equation (already known to the pupils) (e.g. $2y - \dfrac{2y+3}{2} = 1 - y$); followed by a whole class discussion: What about squaring or taking the square roots on both sides of the equation? Are these adjustments equivalent?

- Explanation of concepts (equivalent, root of an equation, number sets, set theory notation, difference of sets) and their mathematical notation. Whole class discussion: How do we recognize that an equation has infinitely many roots? Has no solution? Equations with the unknown in the denominator together with the discussion of the conditions of existence, e.g. $\dfrac{3}{x-3} - \dfrac{7}{x+3} = \dfrac{10}{x^2-9}$.

- Non-equivalent adjustments, e.g. $\sqrt{4x+6} = -4$.
- Equivalent adjustments of systems of two linear equations with two unknowns (e.g. $\begin{array}{l} \dfrac{2a-3b+5}{2} + \dfrac{4a-1}{5} = 5 \\ \dfrac{a+b+2}{3} - \dfrac{a+b+1}{4} = 1 \end{array}$). Whole class discussion about linear functions and their equation, graphs and their intersections with axes, direct and indirect proportionality, hyperbola.

- Discussion of the equation with parameter $d \cdot x + 1 = 2(4x+1) - 5x$; for homework, pupils chose one real number for the parameter and solved the equation without the parameter. The teacher presented on the blackboard what was said in the discussion.

- Word problem mathematized by a system of equations or one equation.

- Solving procedure of linear inequalities (e.g. $(y-2).3 - \dfrac{y+3}{2} < 0$). Whole class discussion: What happens when we multiply both sides by a negative number, and zero? What equivalent adjustments for inequalities exist?

- Systems of inequalities (e.g. $\begin{array}{l} 3 - x \le \dfrac{1}{2} + 2x \\ 2 + x > 7x + \dfrac{3}{2} \end{array}$) and discussion on differences between systems of equations and inequalities.

- Test:

1. $\begin{array}{l} (x+1)^2 + 7 > (x-4)^2 \\ (1+x)^2 + 3x^2 \le (2x-1)^2 + 7 \end{array}$

2. $\dfrac{x+1}{2x-3} - \dfrac{7}{4x^2-9} = -\dfrac{4-x}{2x+3}$

3. What will the temperature of water be if we mix 5 litres of 15°C water and 4 litres of 25°C water?

- Whole class discussion: summary of the types of word problems that pupils can solve (with trajectory, time and velocity; with collaboration[3]; with mixtures[4]).

- Discussion of topics that will be taught at a later stage: equations with parameters, with absolute value, quadratic equations.

The CZ2 teacher also prepared a set of tasks of an increasing difficulty for her pupils. However, while the pupils were working on the solutions, she kept emphasizing a set of rules already known to them, called the rule of '5Z'(= order of steps when solving linear equations: 1. simplify, 2. bracket, 3. fraction, 4. calculate, 5. verification) [The use of Z in the acronym is based on Czech terminology.] These rules were recalled repeatedly in the whole 10-lesson sequence. In some cases, the pupils solved several problems that needed the use of one rule, which was supposed to give them sufficient practice. Much attention was also paid to the written recording of the solution. The teacher tried to persuade the children that the accumulation of several operations in one notation would decrease the danger of making a mistake (both authors of this article doubt this conjecture).

The sequence used by the teacher to revise concepts, with examples of the solved problems are as follows :

- Brainstorming about where the pupils have already come across equations.
- Whole-class discussion: Different ways of finding the unknown. What does it mean to evaluate the unknown? What do the pupils understand by equivalent adjustments?
- The teacher recalled the model of a balance and employed it to justify the use of the 'inverse operation rule'[5] and the application of adjustments to both sides of the equation (e.g. $y + 7 = 15$; $2y - 1 = 0$; $2(y - 1) = 0$).
- Examples of simple non-linear equations: $|y| = -3$ (0 roots); $y^2 = 9$ (2 roots); $\sqrt{y} = 5$ (1 root).
- Solving equations (e.g. $(5x - 4) \times 7 = 182$).
- Searching for linear equations with infinitely many roots (e.g. $x + 5 = x + ?$).
- Searching for linear equations with no root (e.g. $x + 5 = x + ?$).
- Multiplication of both sides of an equation by 0 is not an equivalent adjustment.
- Practising equivalent adjustments and equations with infinitely many roots and with no root, e.g. $x + 8 = 3x + 8$, $2a - 5 = 2a - 4$.
- Different ways of recording of the calculations – types of equations: $ax = b$, $ax + b = c$, $a, b, c \in Q$.
- Examples of non-linear equations (quadratic, with more than one solution, with absolute value); e.g. $x^2 = 9$; $(y - 1)^2 = 16$; $(4 + x)^2 = 0$; $|z + 1| = 5$; $|x - 1| = 0$.
- Preparation for equations with fractions (e.g. $\frac{x}{9} + 7 = 1$).
- Rule 2 of "5Z" (solution of equations such as $8(u - 3) = 2u$; $7 - (y + 1) = -2(3 - 3y)$.
- Rule 3 of "5Z" (solution of equations such as $\frac{1}{3}y + \frac{3}{2}y - 1 = 0$).

- The test assignment follows.

  1. $4(2x-5)+1 = x+2$

  2. $\dfrac{x-3}{2} + 2x = 3x - 4$

- Practising equivalent adjustments $1 - \dfrac{1}{6}(2z-6) = \dfrac{1}{4}(3-z)$.

- Expressing in mathematical symbols (e.g. the difference between the number 8 and the double of 9; Record what distance will be covered by a car in 2 hours, 1 minute, 17 minutes if the car is going at the speed r km/h.).

- Word problems—solution from the 2nd grade (graphical), judgment/reasoning, by equation.

- Word problem solved by an equation.

- Solution of several word problems introduced as types: with trajectory, velocity and time. Whole class discussion on ways of determining the unknown.

- Solution of word problems with percentages; starts with the discussion recalling what a percent is, how it can be calculated (via 1 percent, by the rule of three)

- Solution of word problems with collaboration.

Note: For the 11th lesson, word problems about mixtures were planned.

THE ABILITY TO APPLY EQUALITY AND EQUATIONS IN REAL WORLD PROBLEM-SOLVING SETTINGS

What we could observe in both classes was a continuous inclusion of word problems in the algebraic subject matter. However, the approaches of the two teachers were diametrically different.

The CZ1teacher used word problems for application of the taught equations and their systems and of inequalities. It seemed to us that she selected word problems of high difficulty and focused on making the pupils understand how to use equations to mathematize the situations. Let us illustrate her approach by presenting her selection of word problems (they appeared in the lessons in the given order; the number of the lesson in which they were used is in the brackets):

- Plane Il 18 took off from the airport at the speed 630 km/h. 10 min later TU 134 took off and is flying at the speed 840 km/h. How long will it take before both planes are at the same distance from the airport? Calculate this distance. (Lesson 2)

- A steamboat connects two ports. The return journey takes 2h 30 min. Travelling down the river it goes at the speed of 12 km/h, and travelling up the river it goes at 8 km/h. Calculate the distance between the two ports. (Lesson 3)

- A 95 m long train is crossing a bridge at the speed of 45 km/h. It takes 12 seconds from the moment when the locomotive drives onto the bridge until the moment when the last carriage leaves the bridge. How long is the bridge? (Lesson 3)

- One vessel contains 40°C warm water and another vessel contains 20°C warm water. How many litres of water from the respective vessels do we have to mix to get 10 litres of water with a temperature of 24°C? (Lesson 7)
- The following holds for two numbers: Their sum is 44, and the quotient is 2 and remainder 5. What are these numbers? (Lesson 7)
- We have acids of 40% and 70% concentrations. How many portions of each of the acids do we have to mix to get 3 litres of acid of concentration 50%?
- A company produced 52 bicycles in 4 months. Two more bicycles were produced in the first month than in the fourth. In the second month they produced twice as many bicycles as in the first month and in the third month half of the first month's production was produced. How many bicycles were produced in each of the months? (Lesson 8)
- 12 workers needed 7.5 hours to unload 7 wagons. However, after 3 hours of work four of them were transferred to different work. How long did the unloading of the wagons take? (Lesson 10)
- How much chemical substance of 40% concentration do we have to add to 90 ml of a substance with 55% concentration in order to get a 50% concentration of the substance? (Lesson 10)
- The sum of two consecutive natural numbers and their triples equals 92. What are these numbers? (Lesson 10)
- It takes 12 hours to mow a lawn with one lawn mower, and 8 hours with another one. (a) How long will it take to mow the lawn if both mowers are used? (b) How long will the mowing take if only the first mower is used in the first two hours? (Lesson 10)

The following sample from Lesson 2 illustrates the method by which the CZ1 teacher managed her pupils during the mathematization of word problems:

```
Teacher (from now on T): First everybody read it for
        themselves … And now read it out, Klárka.
Klárka: Plane Il 18 took off from the airport at the speed
        630 km/h. 10 minutes later TU 134 took off and is
        flying at the speed 840 km/h. How long will it
        take before both planes are at the same distance
        from the airport? Calculate this distance.
T:      Well, the reflection of reality in this word
        problem is slightly distorted. In real life the
        planes wouldn't be flying in the same direction,
        would they? Probably. Because that would be
        complicated. And each of them has a different
        flight level. However, for this calculation we'll
        simplify it and will suppose that they're flying
        like this. Well, prepare your exercise books and
        let's make a written record of this word problem.
```

What kind of a word problem is it? You should be able to say. Jirka?

Jirka: [*Mumbles something that is not comprehensible.*]

T: Speak up.

Jirka: With movement.

T: With movement. Well, then it's a good idea to record it using a simple drawing. OK. So let's suppose that both planes took off from the airport [*she starts making the diagram with data on the blackboard, see the diagram below*] even though it's highly unlikely, in the same direction. Well. And now all we know about the first plane. Its name, its type aren't important but which piece of information is important, Michal?

Michal: It's the speeds.

T: So dictate them to me.

Michal: The first plane flies at the speed 630 km/h and the other 840

T: I couldn't understand, eight hundred...

Michal: 840 km/h.

T: Then there's some other important piece of information, in the assignment. Luboš?Luboš:That the second plane took off 10 minutes later.

T: Yes, after 10 minutes [*records into the schema created on the blackboard*] or 10 minutes later. And now yet another piece of information hidden in the text. Formulate it for me. David.

David: -

T: Read it again.

David: -

T: Well, they already know it here. So, David, you can't calculate it without it, you must formulate it. Formulate a question, will you? What are we supposed to calculate?

David: We are to calculate how long it'll take before both planes are at the same distance.

T: Yes. So how could you say this in other words? Michal?

Michal: That they'll meet.

T: That they'll meet? That they'll catch up? Or even like this. That they'll have covered ...

Pupil: the same distance.

T: That's it. Yes, that they'll be at the same distance. And what data are we to calculate? How long will it take, David has already mentioned this, and there's still something else, isn't there?

Pupil: How far.

T: Yes. And how far it'll be from the airport. So how many kilometres and in what time, in how many hours for example or minutes will this occur, the situation?

The following diagram is on the blackboard:

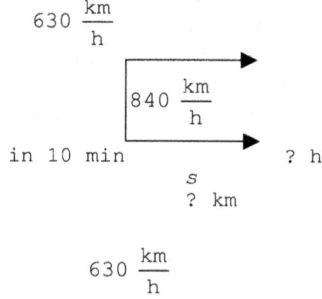

So, a problem with movement. It always includes what quantities? Jirka?

Jirka: Trajectory, velocity, time.

T: Yes. So you recall, the, as I always told you, the simplest formula $s =$ Many pupils: v times t.

T: Yes, velocity times time. All right. And we'll solve this using an equation, to get some practice of what we're doing now; it means we need to know what will be the same in there, what will equal what. Dominika?

Dominika: Trajectories.

T: Yes, the covered distances. And how is trajectory computed? Well?

Pupil: Speed times time.

T: All right, velocity times time. Well, we have the velocities here [*pointing at the diagram on the blackboard*] but what's missing there?

Pupil: Time.

T:	Time. Yes. So how long did the first plane fly, Vítek?
Vítek:	*x*.
T:	what?
Vítek:	*x* minutes.
T:	*x* minutes. So you will have to convert this here [*pointing at the velocities in the diagram on the blackboard*]. My advice for you is that you do it in hours.
Vítek:	So *x* hours.
T:	OK, *x* hours. That'll be easier. And now here, the other plane. How long did it fly, Petr?
Petr:	*x* minus one sixth of an hour.
T:	Well done. 10 minutes, one sixth, so *x* minus one sixth of an hour. OK. So we have there the velocities, the time, so we should be able to make the equations. You said what would be equal?
Pupil:	The trajectories.
T:	The trajectories. So who'll dictate it to me? Michal?
Michal:	*x* plus *x minus* one sixth.
T:	How is trajectory calculated, Michal?
Michal:	We multiply velocity times time.
T:	Say it again. Speak up.
Michal:	Velocity times time.
T:	So dictate it to me. Velocity?
Michal:	Hmm, *x*.
T:	In what units is velocity measured?
Michal:	Kilometres per hour.
T:	So why are you dictating *x*? So the speed of the first plane?

Michal:	630.

[T *gradually constructs an equation on the blackboard*].

T:	Times time
M:	Times *x*.
T:	You see. It is the same as the trajectory of the second plane.
Michal:	840
T:	So…
Michal:	*x minus* one sixth, all that in a bracket.
T:	Well, you see. *x minus* one sixth.

69

The following equation is written on the blackboard
$$630x = 840\left(x - \frac{1}{6}\right)$$

T: And now let's solve it.

The CZ2 teacher included word problems considerably more often. They were always presented as a sequence of problems of the one type, but gradually increasing in difficulty. The teacher obviously focused on drilling the solving process of the different types of problems. Let us illustrate this observation by considering the following selected tasks. The problems are presented in the order in which they appeared in the lessons. The lessons are labelled.

Lesson 7 (mostly devoted to symbolic notation of verbal statements)
Express in mathematical symbols:

- How do we show the difference between the numbers 2 and 9; the difference between the number 8 and the double of the number 9;
- One ticket costs 12 CZK. How is the price of three tickets recorded? How do we record the price of fifteen tickets? How is the price of n tickets recorded?
- Record the sum of number d and number 2; the difference between number d and number 2, the double of number d, one half of number d, ... ;
- A full fare is 36 CZK, and the reduced fare is 24 CZK. Record: 5 passengers paid full fare, 12 passengers paid reduced fare; m passengers paid full fare, n paid reduced fare.
- An average speed is r km/h. Record what distance they will have covered in: 2 hours, 1 minute, 17 minutes.
- Show how to record the quintuple[6] of the sum of numbers 13 and 17, sum of quintuples of numbers 13 and 17, double of number 6, triple of number 6, triple of a number reduced by 6 is 6, sextuple of number 6
- The sum of three consecutive numbers is double the last of the numbers. Which numbers are they?
- The greengrocer sells two different kinds of apples, Jonathan and Golden Delicious. Zuzana bought 3 kilograms of Jonathan apples. A kilogram of Golden Delicious apples is 3 CZK cheaper and Zuzana bought 2 kg of them. In total she paid 109 CZK for her apples. How much was one kilogram of Jonathan apples and how much did the Golden Delicious cost?

Lesson 8 (Procedure *"scheme → table → equation"* was stressed.)

- Pavlína sets off on a trip and was walking at an average speed of 4 km/h. One hour later Libor sets off in the same direction at an average speed of 7 km/h. How long will it take before Libor catches up Pavlína and what distance will he have covered?
- The road from Adam's house to Eve's is 5 km long. Adam set off to meet Eve at the speed of 6 km/h. Eve set off in the opposite direction at the same moment

at the speed of 4 km/h. How long did it take before they met and how many kilometres had Adam covered to reach the place where he met Eve?

- Modified version: Identical situation but Eva set off 15 minutes later than Adam.

Lesson 9 (Solving word problems with percentages)

- A bricklayer and his labourer are together paid 6 600 CZK for their work. The bricklayer gets 40 % more than his labourer. How many crowns does each of them earn?
- There are 79 pupils in three eighth grade classes. There are 12% more pupils in 8.A then in 8.B; there are 8% pupils fewer in 8.C than in 8.B. How many pupils are there in each of the classes?
- An agricultural cooperative owns some land. 55% of this land is arable; the remaining 270 hectares are covered with forest. How many hectares of land does the cooperative own?
- The material needed to construct a building was transported by three lorries of different sizes. The load weight on the second lorry was 20% greater than the load weight on the first lorry. The load weight on the third lorry was 20% greater than the load weight on the second lorry. The load weight on all three lorries together was 18.2 t. How many tonnes of material were loaded on each of the lorries?

Lesson 10 (Solving word problems with collaboration)

- In a gardening center Ondřej and Jakub are digging a patch. Ondřej finishes one patch in 20 minutes, Jakub in 30 minutes. How long will it take them to dig one patch if they work on it together?
- It takes 12 hours to drain a flooded building pit with the first pump and 4 hours with the second pump. (a) Pepa's estimate is that both pumps together will need 6 hours to drain the pit. Do you think this estimate is correct? (b) Verify your conjecture. How long will it take if both pumps work simultaneously?
- It takes 2 hours to fill up the swimming pool by the first pipeline, 3 hours by the second pipeline, 4 hours by the third pipeline. How long will it take to fill up the swimming pool by all three pipelines simultaneously?
- The coal reserves will last 12 weeks when heating a bigger room and 18 weeks when heating a smaller room. How long will it take before the reserves are consumed if, for the first 4 weeks, both rooms are heated and, afterwards, only the smaller one is heated?
- A farmer has two seeding machines of different capacities. The first one needs 12 hours to sow one field, the second needs 10 hours. How many hours will it take to sow one field if both seeding machines are used simultaneously? If the farmer owns two equal-sized fields, how long will it take him to sow both fields using both seeding machines simultaneously?

The following sample from Lesson 10 illustrates how the CZ2 teacher manipulated her pupils to copy her solving procedure without thinking about the order of the single steps. The pupils were solving the first task from this lesson (see "gardening centre" above).

```
T:          And now let's show how very simply we'll record
            these problems. We won't be using a table but as
            if it were a table, but without lines. Leave the
            first row of that as if it is an empty table,
            write a bit lower. What will we record first?
            Honzík?
Honzík:     Names.
T:          Names, well done. So first I write down page 90,
            exercise 8, then I imagine I leave the first
            row empty and then I record the names Ondřej
            and Jakub. So. And what is there now in the
            following step? … Ondřej, Jakub are working on
            patches. In the next line, Lucka, read it. Or
            in the following sentence, sorry.
```

[*T gradually adds data to her record on the blackboard.*]

```
Lucka:      Ondřej finishes a patch in 20 minutes
T:          Fine. Stop reading. With whom will it take him
            20 minutes?
Lucka:      On his own.
T:          On his own, excellent. So I record here, into
            the first row 'on his own' and we record the
            data for the situation when the boys are doing
            it on their own. So, Ondřej, how long would it
            take you?
Ondřej:     20 minutes.
T:          Well done. 20 minutes. And you, Jakub?
Jakub:      30.
T:          Yes. So. I suppose you're more vigorous, not
            slower. To make it possible to compare the boys
            somehow, Michal, we need some common unit.
Michal:     Minutes.
T:          Careful here, they both have minutes, that's
            not the unit, but some common unit of time. What
            would that be, the common unit? … How much they
            do in … in
Pupil:      One minute.
T:          And why not in one hour? OK, one minute, fine.
            And be careful here. What will Ondřej do in 1
```

minute? What will it be in 1 minute? What in fact will we find out?

Pupil: How much of the patch he's finished.

T: Excellent, well done. What part of the patch will have been dug. If it were, for example, a metre, then he would have dug 1/20 metre. So, be careful here. So I write into the first row in 1 minute. If it were hours here I would write it in hours. If it were weeks, I'd write it in weeks. In one unit of time. And now there'll be no minutes, nothing, because they're parts of the dug patch. Ondřej does one twentieth and the other boy one thirtieth of the new patch. It's clear, isn't it? And we're asked at the end, Viktor, what?

Viktor: How long will it take them to dig the patch if they work together?

T: Do we know it or do we not? Well. So, how long will it take them? In x minutes, I could write in a minutes, y minutes, so. How much of the patch will Ondřej have dug e.g. in 3 minutes, Marta? In three minutes.

Marta: -

T: Ondřej.

Marta: Three twentieths.

T: Excellent. In 5 minutes?

Marta: Five twentieths.

T: And in x minutes?

Marta: x twentieths.

T: Wonderful. So $x/20$ and $x/30$. I already wrote it down here myself. I hope you don't mind.… And what will they have dug? What will they've dug, Petr?

The teacher finishes her record on the blackboard:

	on his own	x min
	1 min	
Ondřej 20 min	$\dfrac{1}{20}$	$\dfrac{x}{20}$
Jakub 30 min	$\dfrac{1}{30}$	$\dfrac{x}{30}$

Petr: Patches.

T: Patch. How many do we have, of the patches?

Petr: One.

T: One. They complete together the one collaborative task. Try to make the equation when they've dug one patch. Try to construct it on your own. We already have: in x minutes he finishes $x/20$, the other one $x/30$. What does it equal? Try it on your own. … I've just asked about this, so try to can manage it yourself.

All pupils write in their exercise books: $\dfrac{x}{20} = \dfrac{x}{30}$.

T: So let me begin as I think … Because Ondřej and Jakub will have dug $x/20$ and $x/30$. They've dug … And, Ondřej, what do you think you'll have dug?

Ondra: A patch.

T: How many patches?

Ondra: One.

T: So what does it equal?

Ondra: A patch.

T: one finished job done together. *She writes down:* $\dfrac{x}{20} + \dfrac{x}{30} = 1$.

THE ABILITY TO THINK IN A SYMBOLIC LANGUAGE, TO UNDERSTAND ALGEBRA AS GENERALIZED ARITHMETIC, AND TO UNDERSTAND ALGEBRA AS THE STUDY OF MATHEMATICAL STRUCTURES

The effort to approach algebra in this way can be observed in the work of both teachers. The reader must have been aware of this at many different stages of the previous text. However, we found parts of lessons in which the teachers unequivocally (be it consciously or unconsciously) focused on fostering relationships between arithmetic and algebra. It was more apparent in the approach used by the CZ2 teacher.

The CZ2 teacher began the whole sequence of the recorded lessons by a discussion about the relationship between arithmetic and algebra. This discussion had the form of a brainstorming activity on aspects of equations that the pupils had already come across in their earlier school years (already mentioned above). She reminded them that they were taught to solve problems (such as: Honzík has 3 cars. How many more does he need to have 5 cars?) using equations ($3 + x = 5$) already in the 1st grade. In the 2nd grade they solved equations such as: $70 - x = 40$, $x + 20 = 60$. In the 6th grade they solved simple linear equations (e.g. $(x + 7):6 = 8$). She also reminded the pupils that, in the past, they had solved equations with the use of diagrams; they were able to rewrite a diagram into an equation and vice versa. To illustrate this, the following example

$$\boxed{x} \xrightarrow{+8} \boxed{} \xrightarrow{-6} \boxed{} \xrightarrow{-12} \boxed{} \xrightarrow{-15} \boxed{0}$$

was rewritten in symbols: $x + 8 - 6 - 12 - 15 = 0$, transformed to $x - 25 = 0$ and then solved using the "inverse calculation" $(+ 25)$.

Also sequences described above (Lesson 7), in which the pupils used mathematical symbols to describe given relations verbally, were motivated by the effort to cultivate and develop the skill to mathematize the problem assignment.

In the case of the CZ1 teacher it was more difficult to pinpoint the moments in which the relationship between arithmetic and algebra would be shown unequivocally. However, this teacher often used arithmetic to support her pupils' comprehension. The following teaching episode, from Lesson 8, might be regarded as an example of this. At the end of Lesson 7, the pupils had been asked to solve the following problem: Determine 2 numbers whose sum is 44 and whose quotient is 2 and remainder 5. The teacher realized that her pupils had failed to understand the problem. That is why she returned to it at the beginning of Lesson 8:

Teacher: It seems that yesterday, at the end of the lesson, not everybody understood the problem with the remainder. Is it so? Well, Adam, I'm not asking you. If even you did not, then it would be really serious. So, once again, OK? Don't write anything yet. Look. Who understands how it was with the remainder?

A few pupils put up their hands to show they have understood.

Teacher: You see, so it's not everybody. Well, look, twenty thirds, twenty thirds [*she writes* $\frac{20}{3}$ *on the blackboard*] is clearly a concrete real number. And now I want to transfer it to a whole number, or a mixed or a decimal number. So first a mixed number, how do I proceed?

Pupils + teacher together: Well, we divide the numerator by the denominator.

Teacher: 20 divided by 3 is

Pupils: 6 [*The teacher writes on the blackboard = 6, i.e. the record:* $\frac{20}{3} = 6$]

75

Teacher: 3 times 6 =

Pupils: 18

Teacher: So the remainder is 2. Some time ago, when you were much younger, you used a bracket here [*pointing behind number 6 on the blackboard*] during the process of division and you wrote the two in the brackets. But that was just an aid, mathematically it's not correct. What is it, the two in the brackets? It should mean times 2, shouldn't it? So how do we proceed? There are two left and these two are still waiting to be divided by the three. Am I right? So we write $\frac{2}{3}$. [*The teacher writes on the blackboard* $\frac{2}{3}$, *i.e. record:* $\frac{20}{3} = 6\frac{2}{3}$.] Well, and it was the same in the exercise yesterday. It was, how was it? Take the textbook, page, I think, 88.

Pupils: 89.

Teacher: 89, yes 89, exercise 36, 36. Vítek. Read it out.

Vítek: Determine two numbers whose sum is 44...

Teacher: I'll interrupt you here. So the first number was x and the other number was consequently 44 − x, that's clear. [*The teacher writes on the blackboard* $\frac{x}{44-x}$.] And now, well.

Vítek: ...and whose quotient is 2 and remainder 5.

Teacher: Yes. So. And now we recorded it with an equation, their division. What should it be, Lucka?

Lucka: x over 44 − x. [*Teacher writes on the blackboard* $\frac{x}{44-x}$.]

Teacher: Yes. And could it also be recorded the other way round, as 44 − x over x? I could have written it like that, too. Yes, but we chose the first way. What's the result of this division?

Student: 2.

Teacher: 2. Yes. And the remainder?

Student: 5

Teacher: The remainder is 5. So that is the remainder 5 but its value is not the same as the two, as this two here, [*pointing at* $\frac{20}{3} = 6\frac{2}{3}$], it's waiting to be divided by that 44 − x. That's why it was like this [*writing on the blackboard*

$$\frac{x}{44-x} = 2 + \frac{5}{44-x}.\,]$$

EQUATIONS IN CZ1 AND CZ2

Both teachers shared the common objective of finding an efficient way to teach linear equations and their applications. The result of their work should be pupils able to comprehend this part of school algebra and to apply this knowledge to other situations. As already mentioned above, school algebra is a traditional part of school mathematics. Its teaching has been subject to much research, and many of the research findings have been implemented in the classroom. Therefore, one would expect that the approaches used in schools (at least in the same geographical and historical setting, which was the case of CZ1 and CZ2) would be similar and would be based on the experimental and theoretical findings.

However, we have demonstrated in the previous text that this is not the case. There is an obvious difference in the two described approaches; it has not been the intention of this chapter to criticize either of them. The similarities and differences that were identified here will be used to analyze the students' motivation and their approaches to solving new problems.

The difficulty level of the mathematics used to teach the topic was much higher in the case of the CZ1 teacher than in that of the CZ2 teacher. The CZ2 teacher started by recalling concepts and procedures from primary school, while the CZ1 teacher built onto lower secondary mathematics. This is the first difference that can be detected easily from a glance at the activities in both classes. We do not regard this difference as very important; what is crucial is that both teachers tried to link the new subject matter to what should already have been known to their pupils.

The levels of algorithms used in the activities were not the same in the two cases. The CZ1 teacher concentrated a lot on the development strategies in relation to each of the problems. The order of the presented problems was not strictly from simpler to more complicated tasks; they were mixed. The CZ2 teacher adhered to the traditional way, "from simpler to more complex" tasks, and assigned the pupils a lot of drill tasks in order to ensure that they had grasped the algorithmic skills securely. She insisted that they should follow the presented procedures accurately. She introduced shorter, more "economical" procedures with the aim of minimizing the number of mistakes that her pupils made.

There is an important difference to be seen in the levels of complexity and difficulty of the problems dealt with. The CZ2 teacher presented a considerable number of very simple tasks. The reason was to automate the algorithms that could serve her pupils as scaffolding when solving non-algorithmic problems. In the programme proposed by the CZ1 teacher, such activities were very scarce. Despite this, her pupils did not seem to face too many difficulties in standard procedures.

The differences between the CZ1 and CZ2 teachers' approaches are in the competences expected of the pupils and in what the two teachers regarded as the most adequate tools for reaching them. In an earlier paper (Novotná, Hošpesová, 2007) we characterized the two teachers as follows: "The CZ2 teacher was mostly concentrating on the question 'How?'; she developed problem-solving strategies in the relationship with each problem. The CZ1 teacher paid more attention to the question 'Why?' and tried to plant the new knowledge on top of her students' previous knowledge." This can be seen when we look at the target knowledge the teachers expected their students to gain and what they considered as the target knowledge. The analyses of the series of the 10 consecutive lessons clearly show that the CZ1 teacher saw the target as her pupils' ability to apply the learned knowledge to new situations, whereas the CZ2 teacher was concerned with the successful application of the taught algorithms.

ACKNOWLEDGEMENTS

The data analysed in this chapter were gathered by the team from the Pedagogical Faculty of the University of South Bohemia in České Budějovice chaired by Helena Binterová. The authors want to thank all the team members for providing us with the rich source of data.

This research was partially supported by projects GAČR 14-01417S and GACR P407/12/1939.

NOTES

[1]   Other abilities, belonging to Crawford's definition of algebraic competence (Crawford, 2001, p. 192) will not be analysed.

[2]   The student uses a letter but works with it as if it were a specific number used as a cryptogram.

[3]   Problems where two or more subjects of different productivity levels are working together on a task/ activity.

[4]   Problems where we look for the optimal composition of mixtures (temperatures, concentrations, prices, …) or their individual components.

[5]   It is a rule often used by pupils without knowing why they apply it. They say: "We will transfer the term to the other side of the equation and give it the opposite sign".

[6]   Czech words for quintuple and sextuple, unlike their English equivalents, are common and easily understandable words.

REFERENCES

Broin, D. (2002). *Arithmétique et Algèbre élémentaires scolaires*. [Doctoral thesis.] Bordeaux: Université Bordeaux I.

Crawford, A. (2001). Developing algebraic thinking: Past, present, and future. In H. Chick, K. Stacey, J. Vincent & J. Vincent (Eds.), *The future of the teaching and learning of algebra. Proceedings of the 12th ICMI Study Conference* (pp. 192–193). Melbourne: The University of Melbourne.

Framework Education Programme for Elementary Education FEP EE (with amendments as of 1st September 2007). Retrived at 23. 10. 2013 from http://www.vuppraha.cz/wp-content/uploads/2009/12/RVP_ZV_EN_final.pdf

Herman, J. (2005). What the concept "school algebra" includes. In: Researching the Teaching and Learning of Mathematics. In: *Proceedings MATHED Intensive Programme 2003*. Linz.

Novotná, J., & Hošpesová, A. (2007). What is the Price of Topaze? In J. H. Woo, H. C. Lew, K. S. Park & D. Y. Seo (Eds.), *Proceedings of the 31st Conference of the International Group for the Psychology of Mathematics Education* (Vol. 4, pp. 25–32). Seoul : PME.

Novotná, J., & Hošpesová, A. (2009). Linking in Teaching Linear Equations—Forms and Purposes: The case of the Czech Republic. In Y. Shimizu (Ed.), *Mathematical Tasks in Twelve Countries*. Sense Publishers.

Novotná, J., & Kubínová, M. (2001). The influence of symbolic algebraic descriptions in word problem assignments on grasping process and on solving strategies. In H. Chick, K. Stacey, J. Vincent & J. Vincent (Eds.), *The future of the teaching and learning of algebra. Proceedings of the 12th ICMI Study Conference* (pp. 495–500). Melbourne: The University of Melbourne.

Stacey, K., Chick, H., & Kendal, M. (Eds.). (2004). *The Future of the teaching and learning of Algbera. The 12th ICMI Study*. Boston/Dordrecht/New York/London: Kluwer Academic Publishers.

Sutherland, R. (2000). *A Comparative Study of Algebra Curricula*. [Report prepared for the Qualifications and Curriculum Authority]. Bristol: University of Bristol.

Van Ameron, B. A. (2002). *Reinvention of early algebra. Developmental research on the transition from arithmetic to algebra*. Utrecht: CD-β Press, Centre for Science and Mathematics education.

AFFILIATIONS

Jarmila Novotná
Charles University in Prague
Faculty of Education
Czech Republic

Alena Hošpesová
University of South Bohemia České Budějovice
Faculty of Education
Czech Republic

BERINDERJEET KAUR

CHAPTER 5

Developing Procedural Fluency in Algebraic Structures – A Case Study of a Mathematics Classroom in Singapore

INTRODUCTION

Algebra is an integral part of the school mathematics curriculum in Singapore schools. Pupils are introduced to algebraic thinking in the early grades of elementary school through a representational method known as "The Model Approach" (Ferrucci, Kaur, Carter & Yeap, 2008, pp. 195–210). They are first introduced to the formal idea of using algebra as generalized arithmetic in grade six. In the following grades from seven to ten, the study of algebra revolves around all of the four conceptions of school algebra, as outlined by Usiskin (1988), i.e.

- algebra as generalised arithmetic;
- algebra as a way to solve certain types of problems;
- algebra as a study of relationships among quantities; and
- algebra as a study of structures

In grade eight, Algebra is a significant component of the school mathematics curriculum and the topics, in particular, expansion and factorization of algebraic expressions, solving quadratic equations by factorization, algebraic manipulation and formulae, and simultaneous equations lay the foundation for the subsequent study of more advanced topics such as functions and problem solving and modelling in mathematics.

Figure 1 shows how the different algebra topics are developed in the Singapore mathematics curriculum. From the figure it is apparent that the main activities of school algebra, as stated by Kieran (1996), are:

- generational involving the forming of expressions and equations that are the objects of algebra;
- transformational, based on rules such as collecting like terms, factoring, expanding, adding and multiplying polynomial expressions, etc.; and
- global/meta-level where algebra is used as a tool, such as problem solving, modelling, and analysing relationships.

Much of the algebra curriculum at the grade 8 level in Singapore centres around the study of structures (Usiskin, 1988) and involves transformational activity

F.K.S. Leung et al. (eds.), Algebra Teaching around the World, 81–98.
© *2014 Sense Publishers. All rights reserved.*

(Kieran, 1996) which requires pupils to carry out rule-based operations on algebraic expressions. This chapter focuses on how a mathematics teacher in a Singapore school mathematics classroom engaged her grade eight students in developing procedural fluency in algebraic structures. Procedural fluency entails skill in carrying out procedures flexibly, accurately, efficiently, and appropriately (Kilpatrick, Swafford & Findell, 2001).

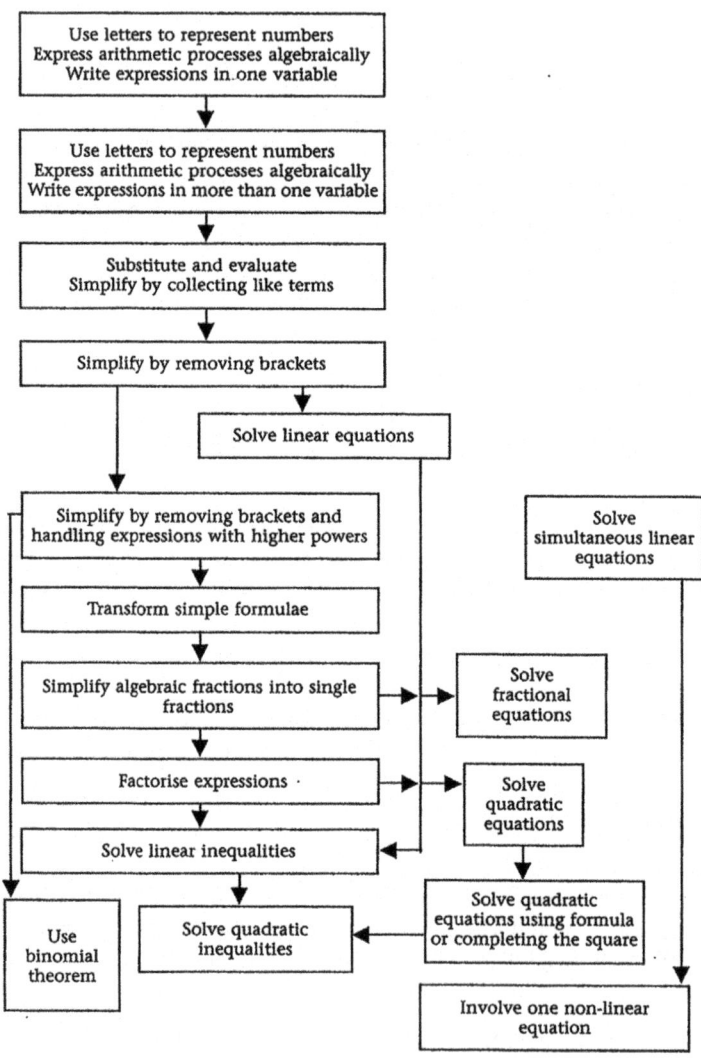

Figure 1. Development of topics (Yeap, 2008)

THE CASE STUDY

From the corpus of data collected in Singapore, in accordance with the protocol set out in the Learner's Persective Study (LPS) (Clarke, 2006), the video records and lesson tables of one teacher (Teacher 2) and the interview transcripts of two of her students were the main source of data for this case study. A lesson table is a chronological narrative account of activities that take place during the lesson. This table also details all the tasks (learning, review, practice and assessment) that the teacher used during the lesson, and their source. After each lesson, the two focus students were interviewed separately. During the interview, a video record of the lesson was used as a stimulus for students to reconstruct accounts of classroom events.

Teacher 2, from School 2, was a female with 27 years of teaching experience. She taught a class of 40 students. In this chapter her first lesson (L1) is studied to document teacher actions that aided the development of procedural fluency in factorisation, namely the difference of two squares. In addition, the interview transcripts of the two focus students, conducted in their L1, are studied, to ascertain what their personal goals for the lesson were, what they attached importance to in the lesson and their procedural fluency to factorise the difference of two squares.

Teacher Data

The teacher data comprise the sequence and content of the first lesson of Teacher 2. The sequence of the lesson comprised seven stages. The stages and details were as follows.

Stage 1:   Introduction of factorisation involving difference of two squares

Teacher [T]:   Alright, factorization of expression in the form of difference of two... squares. So this factorization we are making use of...this formula...okay.

T: Right, difference of two squares ... you must make sure that you have this pattern, a square minus b square.

Teacher wrote on the board:

$a^2 - b^2 = (a + b)(a - b)$

Stage 2:   Demonstration of how to apply $a^2 - b^2 = (a + b)(a - b)$

Teacher wrote on the board:

$Q1(a)\ x^2 - 9 =$

B. KAUR

T: And here given to you X square minus nine. Nine, is it a perfect square number?

T: Yes. So you can make it to…X square minus what number square?

T: Three square. So you can apply the formula there. You will get X plus three, X minus three. Okay?

Teacher completed factorisation on the board

$Q1(a)\ x^2 - 9 \quad a^2 - b^2 = (a+b)(a-b)$

$= x^2 - 3^2$

$= (x+3)(x-3)$

Teacher wrote on the board:

$Q1(b)\ y^2 - 1/16$

T: What about the next one? …Y square minus one over sixteen. How do you change it?

T: Y square minus…

T: Ya… one over four, whole thing square…you will get Y plus one quarter, Y minus one quarter. Very simple, right?

Teacher completes factorisation on the board

$Q1(b)\ y^2 - 1/16$

$= y^2 - (\frac{1}{4})^2$

$= (y + \frac{1}{4})(y - \frac{1}{4})$

Teacher wrote on the board

$Q2(a)\ 9y^2 - 4z^2$

T: Now, what about this one… how do you change it? Nine Y square is actually? …

T: Yes, three Y whole thing square. The other side?

T: Ya, two Z square. So what's the final answer?

T: Three Y plus two Z and then…

T: three Y minus two Z

Teacher completed factorisation on the board

$Q2\ (a)\ 9y^2 - 4z^2$

$= (3y)^2 - (2z)^2$

$= (3y + 2z)(3y - 2z)$

84

Stage 3:   *Students assigned seatwork*

T: Okay, I let you try 2(b) and 2(c).

T: Try out these two. [Teacher walks around the classroom.]

2(b) $a^2x^2 - 16y^2$

2(c) $50x^2 - 2p^2$

T: Ah, how do you do 2c? Think about it. Fifty, is it a perfect square number?

T: No. Two, is it a perfect square number?

T: And then what should you do?

Stage 4:   *Presentation of solutions*

T elicited the solution for Q 2(b) from the students and wrote on the board:

T: A X ….whole thing square….

T: And? Four Y…whole thing square. So will be A X…plus four Y//

Teacher wrote on the board

2(b) $a^2x^2 - 16y^2$

$= (ax)^2 - (4y)^2$

$= (ax + 4y)(ax - 4y)$

The teacher asked Jacinta to present her solution to Q 2(c):
Jacinta wrote on the board:

2(c) $50x^2 - 2p^2$ $a^2 - b^2 = (a + b)(a - b)$

$= 2(25x^2) - 2(p^2)$

$= 2(5x)^2 - 2(p)^2$

$= 2(5x + p)(5x - p)$

T: Right…because fifty is not (a) perfect square, two is not a perfect square. So what you do is…this is factorization, right? So you do by…taking out the common factor. Taking out the common factor… you will get ah the…this one will become a perfect square number, twenty-five. Okay. Actually the second step…if you want, you can do it like that…

85

The teacher demonstrated an alternative to the second step of Jacintha's solution
She wrote on the board:

$50x^2 - 2p^2$

$= 2(25x^2 - p^2)$

$= 2(5x + p)(5x - p)$

T: Alright. You can take out the common factor. Okay. And
   then if you are familiar, straightaway you can write
   down the answer. No need to put the, this pattern
   again, okay. …

T: So not necessary every time you can form. So sometime
   you need to do something about it. Okay...ah...more
   challenging one.

Stage 5: Students assigned more work (challenging tasks)

The teacher wrote on the board:
Factorise the following:

3 (a) $18m^2 - 8n^4$

(b) $(x - 1)^2 - (2x + 3)^2$

The teacher promised to reward the first student to come up with the correct solution
with a lollipop. The students worked on Q3(a) and (b), while the teacher walked
around the class and provided individual guidance to those who needed help.

The following is an excerpt of individual guidance provided by the teacher to one
student:

T: Difficulties?

S: Hm….

T: What is the common factor of 18 and 8?

S: Two

T: Two. Then take out the two lah. What is inside the
   bracket? Ah...then don't forget about the square.

T: The next step, two and two common right? Take out
   the two lor. You follow this. Two and two common,
   take out the two.

T: So A plus B, A minus B lor. So this is actually your
   A right. This is actually your B square right. So
   according to the formula will be... A plus B, A minus
   B... okay? The same, you take out the two. You take
   out the two, so it becomes like that, right? Same
   power you can put together correct? Ah... Then this

one is two, then this one is two squared… So it's two N lah square, square[1].

Several students managed to do Q3(a) with the guidance the teacher provided as she walked around the class. The teacher guided the whole class to factorise Q3(b) on the board. None of the students managed to get the lollipop.

T: This is a difference of two squares. Instead of one term, I give two terms here. This is actually your A square… this is actually your B square. Can you see the pattern?

T: The A is actually X minus one, B is actually X, ah, two X plus three. So…

T: So… You make use of the formula, it will be A. This is A ah…plus B… A minus B. Can you see the pattern?

The teacher wrote on the board:

$3(b)\ (x-1)^2 - (2x+3)^2$

$= [(x-1) + (2x+3)][(x-1) - (2x+3)]$ $a = x-1$

$= (x - 1 + 2x + 3)(x - 1 - 2x - 3)$ $b = 2x+3$

$= (3x + 2)(-x - 4)$

T: Because your A is actually… X minus one. Your B is actually… two X plus three. So you apply the formula, A plus B, A minus B. This is not the final answer yet. You have to simplify whatever is inside the bracket. So you open the bracket… the other side you open it… remember to change the sign… and you group the like terms together. X plus two X, you will get three X. And how many?

T: Plus two, right… and this one? What do you get?

T: X minus two X, what do you get?

T: Minus X. And minus one minus three?

A student asked the teacher to show the factoring of 3(a).
She went through the steps for 3(a).

T: What is the common factor, eighteen and eight?

T: Two. What do you get?

T: N to the power of four. So nine and four are perfect squares. Can you do it straightaway? What is the answer?

T: … it will be three M whole thing square… minus… two…

The teacher wrote on the board:

$3(a)$ $18m^2 - 8n^4$

$= 2(9m^2 - 4n^4)$

$= 2[(3m)^2 - (2n^2)^2]$

$= 2(3m + 2n^2)(3m - 2n^2)$

Stage 6: Group Quiz (a mode of continual assessment)

The teacher gave the class a group quiz after every lesson. Members of the group took turns to answer the questions and, if they were unable to do so, group members were allowed to help them, which resulted in the group scoring a partial score. Otherwise, the group received a full score. The teacher asked the first member of each of the groups A to D to come forward. She wrote $4x^2 - 25$ on the board for them to factorise.

For group A: Mei Yi wrote:

$= 4x^2 - 5^2$

$= (4x - 5)(4x + 5)$

For group B: Edwin wrote:

$= 2x^2 - 5^2$

$= (2x + 5)(2x - 5)$

For group C: Benjamin wrote:

$= (2^2x^2) - (5^2)$

$= (2x - 5)(2x + 5)$

For group D: Dalilah wrote:

$= (2x)^2 - 5^2$

$= (2x + 5)(2x - 5)$

The teacher engaged the whole class in examining the solutions and highlighted the mistakes. The groups were also given their scores. Next, the teacher asked the first member of each of the groups E to H to come to the board. She wrote $121 - 36x^2$ for them to factorise.

For group E: Pavitra wrote:

$= 11^2 - (6x)^2$

$= (11 + 6x)(11 - 6x)$

For group F: Zhiling wrote:

$= 11^2 - (6x)^2$

$= (11 + 6x)(11 - 6x)$

For group G: Ming Han wrote:

$= 11^2 - 6^2x^2$

$= (11 + 6x)(11 - 6x)$

For group H: Priyanka wrote:

$= 121 - (6x)^2$

The teacher engaged the whole class in examining the solutions and highlighted the mistakes. The groups were also given their scores. Another round was carried out and this time the second member of each group was asked to come to the board and do the factorisation. For groups A to D, they had to factorise: $49x^2 - 1$, and for groups E to H, they had to factorise $\pi R^2 - \pi r^2$. Once again the teacher engaged the whole class in examining the solutions, highlighted the mistakes and awarded the groups their scores.

Stage 7(Part I):   Homework

The students were assigned the following tasks for practice as homework. These tasks were to be reviewed at the beginning of the next lesson.

Factorise the following:

1. $36d^2 - 1$

2. $n^2 - 100\,m^2$

3. $p^2 - 81q^4$

4. $a^2b^2 - 1$

5. $121 - y^2$

6. $36x^2 - y^8$

7. $49c^2 - d^2e^2$

8. $c^2 - (d + 2)^2$

9. $9(x - 3y)^2 - 16(2x + y)^2$

10. $4(6a - 5b)^2 - (3a - b)^2$

11. $1 - 25\,x^2y^2$

12. $x^2y^2 - 36z^2$

13. $49x^4y^4 - 25z^4$

14. $225\,x^3 - 169\,xy^2$

15. $a^4 - b^4$

16. $(a^2/25) - (4b^2/9)$

17. $50\,a^3 - 8\,ab^2$

18. $(x^2/9) - (y^2z^2/16)$

19. $4x^2 - (9/25)$

20. $27a^2 - 3$

21. $32\,a^2b - 2b^3$

22. $a^2b^2 - (c^4/64)$

Stage 7(Part II):   Written assignment (a mode of continual assessment)

The students were given the following assignment as part of their continual assessment. This assignment had to submitted to the teacher by a due date, to be graded and contribute a fraction of the overall percentage towards the overall mathematics grade.

Factorise completely:	
1a) $2 - 18x^2$	1g) $242y^3 - 8y$
1b) $32 - 50a^2$	1h) $x^4 - 1$
1c) $98x^2 - 162$	2a) $2p^4 - 18p^2q^2$
1d) $8x^2 - 72$	2b) $x^4y^2 - 4x^2y^4$
1e) $5y - 20y^3$	2c) $64a^4 - 4b^4$
1f) $y^3 - 64y$	2d) $m^8 - 81$

3. Evaluate with the help of algebraic rules $999^2 - 998^2$

4. Use algebraic rules to evaluate $86.25^2 - 13.75^2$

5. Evaluate $\dfrac{58^2 - 12^2}{29^2 - 6^2}$

6. With the help of algebraic rules, evaluate $2400^2 - 2402^2$

7. Given that $(2x)^2 - (2y)^2 = 36$ and $x + y = 2$,

calculate the value of $(x - y)^2$

Student Data

During the interview the focus students, S1 and S2 were asked what their personal goals for the lesson were. Their responses were as follows:

Interviewer (Int): So what were your personal goals for that lesson?
S1:   ...Understanding the topic well.
Int: Mm-hm.
S1:   By - yeah - memorizing all the fac - er all the formulas.
Int: What do you mean by formulas?
S1:   Like... er example A plus B squared,... equals to A squared plus two AB plus B squared... Something like this.

```
Int:   Okay. So how do you know you have understood the
       topic?
S1:    By looking at que... at the question and I… know
       which formula I should use.
Int:   So any other goals that you actually want to achieve,
       beside understanding and memorizing the formula?
S1:    … No.
Int:   Do you have similar goals for every lesson?
S1:    Yes.


Int:   What were your personal goals for this lesson?
S2:    To learn more, to get prepared for tests and…
       future.
Int:   Mm-hm.
S2:    Also to build up a…better relationship with the
       teachers and friends ah.
Int:   Mm…okay. What do you mean by that?
S2:    Um…through…er like discussion like that then we'll
       understand more about our friends and teachers.
Int:   Oh…okay. So do you have similar goals for every
       lesson?
S2:    About the same ah.
```

During the interview, the students were given the remote control for the video player and asked to play the lesson and find sections of it that they thought were important and explain why they thought so. Table 1 shows the segments of the lesson to which the students attached importance.

At the end of the interviews the students were asked to factorise the following expressions:

> 3c) $x^4y^2 - 4x^2y^4$
> 3d) $32xy^4 - 2x^5$

Figures 2 and 3, show the work of students S1 and S2 respectively. Both made some mistakes. The following transcripts show that S1 was able to self correct her mistake when alerted to it.

```
Int:  Alright. But er…I noticed that there's a X square Y here
      [poining to the second line of Q3c] but then how come you er
      ended up with XY [pointing to the third line of Q3c]?
S1:   [amends answer]
Int:  Oh so it's a...
S1:   Careless mistake
```

Table 1. Segments of the lesson that were important for the two focus students

S1

Episode	What the teacher was doing	Why this was important to the student
1	Teacher demonstrated how to factorise $a^2 - b^2$ [Stage 2 of Teacher data]	Student got to know a new formula. Increased student's list of formulae for use.
2	Teacher demonstrated how to factorise Q *3(b) $(x-1)^2 - (2x+3)^2$*. [Stage 5 of Teacher data]	This was a learning point for the student. It demonstrated the variations that $a^2 - b^2$ may take on.
3	Teacher asked students to get ready for group quiz. [Stage 6 of Teacher data]	This made sure that the students understood all the things the teacher taught.

S2

Episode	What the teacher was doing	Why this was important to the student
1	Teacher assigned seatwork. [Stage 3 of Teacher data]	The tasks were challenging. The exercise was good for speed training and preparation for tests and examinations.
2	Teacher asked a student to show working on the board. [Stage 4 of Teacher data]	Gives student an opportunity to learn from mistakes of classmates.
3	Teacher asked students to get ready for group quiz. [Stage 6 of Teacher data]	This provides students with the opportunity to test understanding, discuss and work with peers.

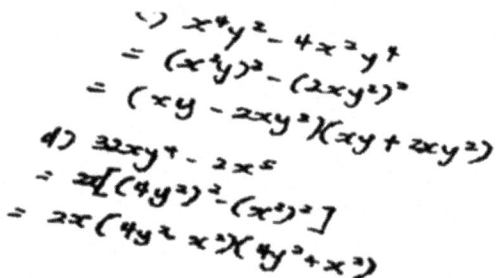

Figure 2. S1's solutions (screen shot from video record of interview)

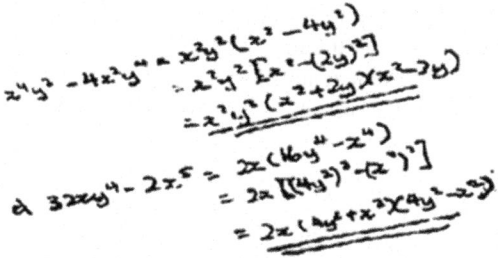

Figure 3. S2's solutions (screen shot from video record of interview)

FINDINGS AND DISCUSSION

Nature of classroom discourse

The teacher simply told the students what the factorisation of an expression in the form of difference of two squares was, i.e. $a^2 - b^2 = (a + b)(a - b)$ and subsequently referred to the identity as a "formula". She made no attempt to verify it or give it any form of geometrical or other meaning. She placed emphasis on recognising the pattern, $a^2 - b^2$ and use of the formula "$a^2 - b^2 = (a + b)(a - b)$" to factorise expressions that were of the type "difference of two squares". Through the many subsequent examples the teacher engaged her students in factoring the difference of two squares with many variations of the squares, often eliciting responses from the students, revoicing their responses and thinking aloud to make her thinking visible to them. The examples used were selected carefully and increased systematically in complexity. The discourse pattern adopted by the teacher was of the initiation-response-feedback (IRF) discourse format (Sinclair and Coulthard, 1992). From the public talk of the students in the class it was apparent that, apart from the occasions when students asked the teacher to show them the solution to the task "$18m^2 - 8n^4 =$", they almost never raised any questions to clarify their thinking.

The learning tasks—Patterns of variation

For this lesson, the object of learning was factoring the difference of two squares, i.e. $a^2 - b^2 = (a + b)(a - b)$; this falls into the category of transformational school algebra activities (Kieran, 1996). Through variation of examples that were structurally similar to $a^2 - b^2 = (a + b)(a - b)$, the teacher engaged the students in mental gymnastics with the goal of developing procedural fluency. Table 2 shows the learning tasks.

The first and second learning tasks were used by the teacher to introduce a new concept directly, while the third and fourth were used to stimulate the students' thinking to make links with the knowledge that was introduced via the first and second tasks. The teacher's prompts were spontaneous when the students showed signs of 'difficulty' working with the third and fourth learning tasks. Throughout the entire classroom discourse, the teacher placed a lot of emphasis on recognising the pattern: "$a^2 - b^2$" and hence factoring $a^2 - b^2 = (a + b)(a - b)$.

Table 2. Learning Tasks

Position	Learning Task	Comments
First	$x^2 - 9 =$	This learning task was used to introduce the students to the factoring of two squares and the introduction of the identity: $a^2 - b^2 = (a + b)(a - b)$
	$y^2 - 1/16 =$	This task was used by the teacher to reinforce the use of the identity: $a^2 - b^2 = (a + b)(a - b)$
Second	$9y^2 - 4z^2 =$	This task was used by the teacher to show the students a variation of the forms of a^2 and b^2
Third	$50x^2 - 2p^2 =$	The teacher gave the students this task for practice. During the review of student work she seized the opportunity to introduce the students to the factoring of a multiple of the difference of two squares; i.e. $c\,a^2 - c\,b^2 = c(a + b)(a - b)$.
Fourth	$(x-1)^2 - (2x + 3)^2 =$	The teacher gave the students this task for practice. However none of them were able to do it. The teacher showed the students that, in this task, 'a^2' was $(x - 1)^2$ and 'b^2' was $(2x + 3)^2$; the factors $(a + b)$ and $(a - b)$ were linear combinations of $(x - 1) + (2x + 3)$ and $(x - 1) - (2x + 3)$ respectively. This task was used by the teacher to demonstrate to the students yet another variation of the forms of a^2 and b^2.

The practice tasks and assessment tasks

Throughout the lesson there was emphasis on both practice and assessment. Both practice and assessment tasks were given to the students during the instructional period as well as out-of-class work. The practice tasks given to the students during the instructional period were similar to the learning tasks. The assessment tasks given during the 'quiz' were also similar to the learning tasks. Table 3 shows the practice and assessment tasks used by the teacher during the lesson. The homework tasks, shown in Table 4, mainly provided the students with more practice. Only seven tasks may be considered challenging, as they required the students to integrate their knowledge or go beyond what was done during the lesson.

Table 3. Practice and assessment tasks used during the instructional period

Practice Task	Assessment Task	Comments
$a^2x^2 - 16y^2 =$	$4x^2 - 25 =$ $121 - 36x^2 =$ $49x^2 - 1 =$	These tasks were similar to the learning task: $9y^2 - 4z^2 =$
$18m^2 - 8n^4 =$	$\neq R^2 - \neq r^2 =$	These tasks were similar to the learning task: $50x^2 - 2p^2 =$

Table 4. Homework tasks

Homework Tasks		Comments
Routine	Challenging	
$(a^2/25) - (4b^2/9) =$ $(x^2/9) - (y^2z^2/16) =$ $4x^2 - (9/25) =$ $36d^2 - 1 =$ $n^2 - 100m^2 =$ $a^2b^2 - 1 =$ $121 - y^2 =$ $49c^2 - d^2e^2 =$ $1 - 25x^2y^2 =$ $x^2y^2 - 36z^2 =$	$a^4 - b^4 =$ $49x^4y^4 - 25z^4 =$ $a^2b^2 - (c^4/64) =$ $p^2 - 81q^4 =$ $36x^2 - y^8 =$	These tasks were similar to the learning task: $9y^2 - 4z^2 =$
$27a^2 - 3 =$ $225x^3 - 169\,xy^2 =$	$50a^3 - 8\,ab^2 =$ $32a^2b - 2b^3 =$	These tasks were similar to the learning task: $50x^2 - 2p^2 =$
$c^2 - (d + 2)^2 =$	$9(x - 3y)^2 - 16(2x + y)^2 =$ $4(6a - 5b)^2 - (3a - b)^2 =$	These tasks were similar to the learning task: $(x - 1)^2 - (2x + 3)^2 =$

The assessment tasks, which were a part of the written assignment, were of two types. The first type was similar to the practice tasks that the teacher gave the students to work on in class and do as homework after the lesson. The second type required the students to apply their knowledge to compute statements of arithmetic without the use of calculators or tedious calculations. These tasks are shown in Table 5.

Table 5. Written assignment tasks

Factorisations		
Factorise completely:		Application of Algebraic Rules

1a) $2 - 18x^2$	2a) $2p^4 - 18p^2q^2$	3. Evaluate with the help of algebraic rules
1b) $32 - 50a^2$	2b) $x^4y^2 - 4x^2y^4$	$\quad 999^2 - 998^2$
1c) $98x^2 - 162$	2c) $64a^4 - 4b^4$	4. Use algebraic rules to *evaluate 86.25² –*
1d) $8x^2 - 72$	2d) $m^8 - 81$	*13.75²*
1e) $5y - 20y^3$		5. Evaluate $\underline{582 - 122}$
1f) $y^3 - 64y$		$\quad\quad 29^2 - 6^2$
1g) $242y^3 - 8y$		6. With the help of algebraic rules,
1h) $x^4 - 1$		$\quad$ evaluate $2400^2 - 2402^2$
		7. Given that $(2x)^2 - (2y)^2 = 36$ and
		$\quad x + y = 2$, calculate the value of $(x - y)^2$

It is apparent from the tasks in Table 5 that the students were expected to have the fluency to factorise the difference of two squares, which may appear in various forms, as well as apply the basic algebraic rule: $a^2 - b^2 = (a + b)(a - b)$ to compute statements of arithmetic without the use of calculators or tedious computations. However, to the extent to which the students may have conceptualised algebra as "the general arithmetic" (Saul, 2008, p.65) and used the algebraic rule in non-routine situations such as "factor 4899" (cited by Saul, 2008) is left unanswered.

Student perspective of the lesson

From the responses of S1 and S2 to the interview prompt about their personal goals for the lesson, it is apparent that both students had goals with regards to learning. S1 wanted *to understand the topic well, memorise* the *formulas well* and apply them appropriately. She claimed to have similar goals for every lesson. S2 had cognitive and social goals. Her cognitive goal was to *learn more*, get *prepared for tests* and also *future* needs. Her social goal was to work with friends and teachers and understand them better through discussions. She too claimed that her goals were almost similar for every lesson.

S1 identified three segments of the lesson that to which she attached importance. The segments occurred in Stage 2 of the lesson, when the teacher demonstrated how to factorise $a^2 - b^2$, Stage 5 of the lesson, when the teacher showed how to factorise Q3(b) i.e. *3(b) $(x-1)^2 - (2x+3)^2$*, and Stage 6 of the lesson, she asked the students to get ready for the group quiz. The demonstration of how to factorise $a^2 - b^2$ introduced S1 to a new 'formula' and this increased her repertoire of formulae. The step by step factorisation of Q3(b) by the teacher on the board enlightened S1 about the variations that $a^2 - b^2$ may take on. S1 attached importance to the group quiz as the activity provided an avenue for the students to assess their learning.

S2 also identified three segments of the lesson to which she attached importance. These segments occurred in Stage 3 of the lesson, when the teacher assigned seat work, Stage 4 of the lesson when she asked a student to present her solution on the board and Stage 6 of the lesson when she asked students to get ready for the group quiz. S2 attached importance to seatwork, as the tasks were challenging and it was a good opportunity to prepare for tests and examinations. The presentation of solutions on the board by fellow classmate gave S2 an opportunity to learn from the mistakes of her peers. S2 attached importance to group quiz as the activity provided her with the opportunity to test her understanding, discuss and work with peers.

It is evident, from Figures 2 and 3, that both students demonstrated satisfactory procedural fluency of the use of the identity: $a^2 - b^2 = (a + b)(a - b)$, at the end of the instructional period.

CONCLUSION

Procedural fluency entails skill in carrying out procedures flexibly, accurately, efficiently, and appropriately (Kilpatrick, Swafford & Findell, 2001). In the lesson described in detail in this chapter it may be said that, through the use of learning tasks that varied in the forms of the structure $a^2 - b^2 = (a + b)(a - b)$ together with the practice tasks and assessment tasks, the teacher has attempted to develop procedural fluency in algebraic structures in the grade eight students in her class. According to Marton's and Booth's (1997) theory of variation in teaching, the teacher used the structure $a^2 - b^2 = (a + b)(a - b)$ as the object of learning and through the variation of the a^2 and b^2 provided her students with the necessary experience to factorise the difference of any two squares.

According to Gu's, Huang's and Marton's (2004) classification of patterns of variation / invariance, the nature of variation adopted by the teacher was one which may be called "generalisation" (p. 336), as the invariant was the algebraic structure and the variants were the different forms of the algebraic structure. Finally, through the numerous practice and assessment tasks, she also engaged her students in mental gymnastics to develop their fluency in using the structure.

ACKNOWLEDGEMENTS

This paper makes use of data from the research project "Student perspective on effective mathematics pedagogy: Stimulated recall approach" (CRP 3/04 BK), funded by the Centre for Research in Pedagogy and Practice, National Institute of Education, Singapore. The views expressed in this paper are the author's and do not necessarily represent the views of the Centre or the Institute.

NOTE

[1] i.e., $(2n^2)^2$

REFERENCES

Clarke, D. (2006). The LPS research design. In D. Clarke, C. Keitel, & Y. Shimizu, (Eds.), *Mathematics classrooms in twelve countries* (pp. 15–29). Rotterdam, The Netherlands: Sense Publishers.

Ferrucci, J. B., Kaur, B. Carter, J. A., & Yeap, B. H. (2008). Using a model approach to enhance algebraic thinking in the elementary school mathematics classroom. In C. E. Greenes & R. Rubenstein (Eds.), *Algebra and algebraic thinking in school mathematics* (pp. 195–210). VA: National Council of Teachers of Mathematics.

Gu, L., Huang, R., & Marton, F. (2004). Teaching with variation: An effective way of mathematics teaching in China. In L. Fan, N. Y. Wong, J. Cai, & S. Li (Eds.), *How Chinese learn mathematics: Perspectives from insiders* (pp. 309–345). Singapore: World Scientific.

Kieran, C. (1996). The changing face of school algebra. In C. Alsina, J. Alvarez, B. Hodgson, C. Laborde, & A. Perez (Eds.), *8th International Congress on Mathematical Education: Selected lectures* (pp. 271–290). Sevilla, Spain: S.A.E.M. Thales.

Kilpatrick, J. Swafford, J., & Findell, B. (2001). *Adding it up.* Washington, DC: National Academy Press.

Marton, F., & Booth, S. (1997). *Learning and awareness.* NJ: Lawrence Erlbaum.

Saul, M. (2008). Algebra: The mathematics and the pedagogy. In C. E. Greenes & R. Rubenstein (Eds.), *Algebra and algebraic thinking in school mathematics* (pp. 63–79). VA: National Council of Teachers of Mathematics.

Sinclair, J., & Coulthard, M. (1992). Towards an analysis of discourse. In M. Coulthard (Ed.), *Advances in spoken discourse analysis* (pp. 1–34). London: Routledge.

Usiskin, Z. (1988). Conceptions of school algebra. In A. F. Coxford & A. P. Shuttle (Eds.), *The ideas of algebra, K- 12* (pp. 8–19). VA: National Council of Teachers of Mathematics.

Yeap, B. H. (2000). The teaching of algebra. In P. Y. Lee (Ed.), *Teaching secondary school mathematics—A resource book* (pp. 25–50). Singapore: McGraw Hill Education.

AFFILIATION

Berinderjeet Kaur
National Institute of Education
Nanyang Technological University
Singapore

KYUNGMEE PARK & FREDERICK K. S. LEUNG

CHAPTER 6

*Eye of the Beholder: The Discrepancy Between the Teacher's
Perspectives and Students' Perspectives on Algebra Lessons in Korea*

INTRODUCTION

The didactic triangle in which the student, the teacher and the content (mathematics) form the vertices of a triangle has been a 'trivium' (Goodchild and Sriraman, 2012) used to conceptualize teaching and learning in the mathematics classroom (National Research Council, 2001). Under this conceptualization, the didactic relationship is a ternary one among the student, the teacher, and the pieces of knowledge at stake (Sensevy, et al, 2005). In the mathematics classroom, the teacher interacts with students, where mathematics content constitutes the major substance of the interaction. For effective learning to take place, the students and the teacher should ideally share a common understanding of the lesson. But do the students and the teacher evaluate the same lesson they have experienced in similar ways?

In the TIMSS 2007 survey of students and teachers, substantial differences between students' perceptions and teachers' perceptions of mathematics lessons were found. For example, eighth grade students reported more 'memorizing formulae and procedures' than did their teachers. In the Korean data, forty-eight percent the students reported memorizing how to work on problems in at least half of their mathematics lessons, compared to 62 percent reported by their teachers. The teachers also reported more emphasis on 'working problems on their own', 'explaining answers', 'relating what was being learned in mathematics to their daily lives', and 'deciding procedures for solving complex problems' than did their students (Mullis, Martin, and Foy, 2009). The results from this large scale international comparative study indicate a potential discrepancy between teachers' and students' perceptions of mathematics lessons in general.

In most mathematics classroom studies, the teacher's perspective tends to be the focus of analysis while the students' perspectives tend to be neglected. Since a good understanding of students' perspectives is a necessary condition for effective teaching, it is important to include this in classroom studies. In this regard, this study documents the teacher's perspectives and students' perspectives of the same algebra lessons, compares the two perspectives, and identifies the differences, if any, between the two. Specifically, this study attempted to find out whether there are discrepancies between the teacher's and students' perspectives in terms of:

F.K.S. Leung et al. (eds.), Algebra Teaching around the World, 99–112.
© *2014 Sense Publishers. All rights reserved.*

1. the objectives of a lesson,
2. what is considered important in a lesson, and
3. how mistakes made by the teacher in a lesson are perceived by the students and the teacher.

PREVIOUS STUDIES

This study analyzed the Korean data of the Learner's Perspective Study (LPS), including the videotaped lessons and their transcripts, the post-lesson video-stimulated interview data, and the post-lesson questionnaires. There have been several studies which used videotaped lessons as stimuli in the interview. For example, Jacobs and Morita (2002) conducted an interview using videotaped lessons to examine American and Japanese teachers' ideas about what constitute effective mathematics pedagogy. Goos (2004) conducted a video-stimulated recall interview with the teacher and a group of students in grades 11 and 12 to find out how the teacher established norms and practices that emphasized mathematical sense-making and justification of ideas and arguments. These two studies conducted interviews incorporating lesson videos, but did not attempt to compare and contrast the teacher's and the students' perceptions.

As mentioned earlier, most classroom studies in the past have focused on the teacher's perspectives. However, there have also been several attempts to explore the students' views on mathematics learning. One of these attempts was a longitudinal study conducted by Francisco (2005), who characterized the views of mathematical learning of five high school students, based on their mathematical experiences. Francisco presented the students' views according to five themes about learning: the nature of knowledge and what it means to know, the source of knowledge, the students' motivation to engage in learning, their certainty in knowing, and how their views vary with particular areas of mathematical activity.

In terms of the discrepancies between the teacher's and the students' perspectives of mathematics lessons, one of the few studies was conducted by Shimizu (Shimizu, 2006). Shimizu juxtaposed the lesson videos and the post-lesson interviews with the teacher and the students, and then identified the teacher's and the students' perceptions of the events in the same lesson. The numbers and times of elements in each lesson identified as being significant by the teacher and the students were compared, and interview excerpts were provided to show the conformities and discrepancies between the teacher and the students in their perceptions of classroom events. The present study also juxtaposed the teacher and the student perspectives, as reflected in the lesson videos and the post-lesson interviews, but instead of comparing the numbers and times of elements identified significant by the teacher and the students, the videos and interview transcripts were reviewed to identify salient discrepancies between the perspectives of the teacher and the students. How this was done is explained below.

RESEARCH METHODOLOGY AND DATA COLLECTION

As mentioned above, this study is based on the Korean data of LPS. LPS implemented a Complementary Accounts Methodology, which was distinguished from other approaches to classroom research by the nature of the data collection procedures leading to the construction of 'integrated data sets' and the inclusion of the reflective voices of the participant students and teachers in the data set (Clarke, 1998, 2001). The essence of LPS was 'complementarity' in terms of both participants' accounts (the teacher and the students) and the integrated data set (classroom video and interview). This study made full use of the strength of the research methodology adopted by LPS. By juxtaposing the teacher's and the students' reconstructive accounts of the mathematics lesson that they had just experienced, it was possible to explore the differences in their perceptions. Capitalizing on the richness and potential of the collected data as well as the strength of the methodology, the teacher's and the students' perceptions of the salient features of the lessons were investigated as were the discrepancies between the two perceptions.

Characteristics of the school, the class, and the teacher

Data collection was conducted for the 8th grade mathematics lessons in three middle schools located in Seoul, Korea. Ten consecutive lessons were videotaped in each school; the topics covered in the three schools were 'Systems of linear equations in two unknowns', 'Similarities of geometric figures', and 'Probability' respectively. Since algebra is the theme of this book, only the algebra-related lessons, i.e., from only one of the three schools, were selected for this study. The school under study was a junior high school for girls, a mid-sized urban school in which each grade was composed of 5 classes and the number of students per class was about 36. The teacher, who was responsible for all of the algebra lessons studied, was a male teacher in his mid 40s, who had 18 years of teaching experience.

Videotaping of lessons

Videotaping a classroom phenomenon is likely to be "the least intrusive, yet most inclusive, way of studying the phenomenon" (Pirie, 1996, p. 554). In this study, the videotaping was done using three cameras—a teacher camera, a student camera (four focus students in each class) and a whole-class camera. An audio-video mixer was used to combine the teacher camera and student camera images in a split-screen arrangement, to form the 'learner practice composite image'. This integrated image was used to prompt the teacher's and students' re-constructive accounts in the interviews (Clarke, Keitel, & Shimizu, 2006).

Teacher and student interview

Two out of the four focused students who were videotaped in each lesson were interviewed right after the lesson through being asked to watch the lesson video-clip just recorded in the classroom. The teacher was also offered the opportunity to provide retrospective reconstructive accounts of classroom events, through video-stimulated post-lesson interviews. In the interviews, the teacher and the students were given control of the video replay and asked to identify and comment upon classroom events that they thought were important. By juxtaposing the teacher's and students' reconstructive accounts of the same lesson, it was possible to find clues to identify any discrepancies between the teacher's and students' perceptions of the lesson.

The interviews were conducted in a semi-structured way following a partly open framework which allowed for focused, conversational, two-way communication. The sequential interview questions included "What do you think that lesson content and lesson objectives were about?", and "After watching the videotape, is there anything you would like to comment on the lesson?" But not all questions were designed and phrased ahead of time. Impromptu follow-up questions were created during the interviews, allowing both the interviewer and the interviewees the flexibility to probe into the details of the lesson events.

DATA ANALYSIS

In order to answer the research questions, the students' and the teacher's interview transcripts were reviewed, and the relevant lesson videos were watched. To identify what was considered important in the lesson, the post-lesson teacher questionnaires were also reviewed. In sum, the interview transcripts were the primary source for finding the differences or discrepancies between the students' and the teacher's perceptions, and the lesson videos and post-lesson teacher questionnaires were used to support the findings.

RESULTS

1. The objectives of the lesson

During the interview, the teacher was asked what the objectives of the lesson were. In the interview after the 5th lesson, he mentioned that one of the main objectives of the lesson was to guide the students to understand that different methods of solving a system of linear equations resulted in the same solution.

```
[Teacher interview after the 5th lesson]
Interviewer: What do you think the lesson content and
        lesson objectives were about?
T:      In this lesson the objective was to let students
        solve systems of linear equations. There are two
        ways: the method of substitution and the method
        of elimination by adding and subtracting. But the
        results are the same.
```

In fact, the teacher's intention was clearly reflected in his teaching. The following excerpts show that, during the videotaped lessons, his focus was on the mathematical property that the same solution was arrived at both from the method of elimination by adding and subtracting and the method of substitution. Indeed, he repeatedly emphasized this property in the 4th and 5th lessons.

[4th lesson]
T: We are not supposed to get different answers depending
      on whether we use the method of elimination by adding
      and subtracting or the method of substitution,
      right? We must get the same answers.
[5th lesson]
T: So, whether we use the method of elimination by adding
      and subtracting or the method of substitution, the
      answers need to come out the same.
...
T: Of course, example 2 tells us to use the method of
      elimination by adding and subtracting to solve the
      problem, but we could rearrange part 1 and plug part
      1 into part 2 and use the method of substitution to
      solve the problem and there would be no difference.

Despite the teacher's emphasis on the mathematical property of getting the same solution from the two different methods, the students' attention seemed to be focused elsewhere. According to the forms of the given linear equations, there is usually a simpler method to solve the system of linear equations. The students wanted to know how to choose a more efficient method of solving systems of linear equations. In other words, they were more interested in acquiring a practical recipe for choosing a more convenient method to solve the systems of linear equations. In response to the question "what was the objective of this lesson?" in the interviews, the students' answers were as follows:

[Student interviews after the 4th lesson]
S7:   When the teacher explained about the method of
      substitution, he should have explained why we apply
      the method of substitution.

S8:   I want the teacher to explain how to choose the
      method of solving systems of linear equations. I
      just want the teacher to explain how to solve the
      problems in an easy way.

[Student interview after the 5th lesson]
S10: I want to know which way is easier. I continue
      to use the method of elimination by adding and
      subtracting. Sometimes, the computation is

```
complicated. I want to know when I have to use the
method of substitution.
```
. . .
```
In this part, the teacher said this problem should
be solved by the method of elimination by adding and
subtracting and this problem should be solved by
the method of substitution. But the teacher didn't
tell us why. ... I mean, it would be better if the
teacher tells us why using the method of elimination
by adding and subtracting is convenient here.
```

As can be seen above, three out of the four students interviewed after the 4th and the 5th lesson wanted to get practical information about how to choose the method of solving systems of linear equations. In particular, one student was interested in the method of selecting a variable to be isolated when using the method of substitution.

```
[Student interview after the 4th lesson]
S8:    When   the    teacher    explained    the    method    of
       substitution, he put x or y on one side. I wanted
       to know how to do that.
Interviewer: You mean that you want to know how to choose
       the variable to be isolated.
S8:    Yes, I want to know which variable is better to be
       isolated.
```

For the teacher who has complete mastery of the knowledge of systems of linear equations, the more important fact worth emphasizing in the lesson was the uniqueness of the solution regardless of the method adopted. In the two lessons, the teacher stressed that the two methods produced the same solution. However, for the students who were in the process of learning systems of linear equations, the two methods looked different. Since both methods gave the same solution, the obvious question to ask is 'which method should be used under different circumstances?' Thus, as far as the objectives of the lessons or what the teacher and students wanted to get out of the lessons were concerned, there was a mismatch between the teacher's intention to teach and the students' expectation to learn.

2. What is considered important in the lesson

What did the teacher and the students consider to be important in the lessons in this study? One of the important components of the introduction part of systems of linear equations is the fact that the ordered pairs which satisfy a linear equation with two unknowns (indeterminate equation) lie on a line when they are marked on the coordinate plane. Conversely, all the points on the line satisfy the linear equation with two unknowns. Did the teacher consider this content to be important?

In the post-lesson questionnaire, the teacher was asked, "What was the main thing that you wanted students to learn from today's lesson?" and, "Why do you think it is important for students to learn this?" The teacher's answers to these questions reflect that he did consider these contents to be important:

> The main thing was to find the solutions of a linear equation with 2 unknowns. Also they were supposed to know that the graph of that equation is a line when the domain is real numbers. This is important because a linear equation with 2 unknowns is a foundation for systems of linear equations. [Teacher's answer to the questionnaire after the 1st lesson]

What the teacher considered as important was also reflected in his teaching. In the 1st lesson, these key ideas were explained clearly and efficiently.

```
[1st lesson]
T:    But, if x and y are not natural numbers, but real
      numbers, we would get many many points. Right? It
      would work when x is 1 and x is 2 and x is 3 because
      we can solve for y.
T:    If we were to graph all of those points, we'd get
      all of the points in between, like this. We would
      have to keep on plotting points. What would happen
      then? ... Our graph would be a line.
...
T:    2x plus 3y minus 20 equals 0. This is the form
      of linear equations; ax plus by plus c equals 0.
      Right? Right.
T:    In that case, there are many potential solutions.
      Know that when graphed, a straight line results.
      All of the coordinate values of the points on this
      line are - what - of linear equations?
T:    They are all potential solutions...
```

However, it is not easy for students to understand this content unless they have a clear understanding connecting the solutions of an indeterminate equation and representing the ordered pairs on the coordinate plane. What then did the students consider to be important in the lessons?

During the post-lesson interviews, the focus students could not answer the question, "What do you think that lesson content and lesson purpose were about?" at all. When going over the lesson video, instead of pointing out important things in the lesson, they commented on rather irrelevant facts about it.

```
[Student interview after the 1st lesson]
Interviewer: Do you have anything to say?
```

```
[S1 stopped the lesson video]
S1:    There was an empty space there, so it would be
       better to make a chart over there with enough
       space, not here. The blackboard was too crowded.

[S2 stopped the lesson video]
S2:    Here, when drawing the graph, I got confused because
       the teacher didn't erase the previous one, and drew
       another graph just using a different color.
```

This discrepancy between what the teacher and the students considered as important continued in the 2nd lesson. The teacher's answer in the post-lesson questionnaire and transcripts of part of his teaching are shown below:

> The main thing was to understand what does the solution of a system of linear equations mean. The solution satisfies the two equations, and also this is the intersection of two lines representing the two linear equations.[Teacher's answer to the questionnaire after the 2nd lesson]

```
[2nd lesson]
T:     At that one point, it solves the equation for
       this line as well as for this line, right? In
       other words, this is the point that satisfies the
       requirements for both of the systems of linear
       equations.
T:     When we don't have parallel lines, our two straight
       lines will intersect at exactly one point. The
       point where our lines meet is where both parts of
       our linear equations are satisfied.
```

Again, in the post-lesson interview, the two focus students, instead of alluding to the key ideas of the lesson, mentioned trivial aspects of the lesson such as the colors of the chalk.

```
[Student interview after the 2nd lesson]
Interviewer: What do you think that lesson content and
       lesson objectives were about? ... Do you have anything
       to say?
[S4 stopped the lesson video]]
S4:    Here, when the teacher used colored chalk, he should
       consider which color is invisible for students in
       the back row.
```

When we just consider the teacher's responses in the questionnaire and his teaching, it is clear that the teacher had a good idea of what was important in the lessons. The lesson seemed to be well presented, but the student interview data paint a different picture. Somehow the students failed to point out what was important in the lesson, and their attention was diverted from its main points. Instead, the students' attention was drawn to irrelevant aspects.

3. How mistakes made by the teacher in a lesson were perceived by the students and the teacher

In the course of teaching, teachers inevitably make mistakes such as accidentally writing down wrong numerical values or making computational errors. Teacher error was not one of the research questions of the study, however in the process of analyzing the data, the students' and teacher's perceptions of the teacher's errors emerged. Throughout the ten lessons videotaped, the teacher made mistakes 3 times, in the 2nd, 3rd and 9th lessons.

[2nd lesson]
(The teacher was discussing the problem: 'Find the number of adults and teenagers if the sum of adults and teenagers is 6, and the total entrance fees is 7000 won[1] when the entrance fee for adults is 1500 won and that for teenagers is 1000 won'. The teacher mistook the entrance fee for teenagers to be 1200 won, and wrote down a wrong equation, 15x+12y=70.)

T: ... What if we plug in 3. If we plug in 3, this becomes 45 and this becomes 25, so is there anything that works? ... Yes or no? What if we plug in 4 for x?
Numerous students: The equation is wrong.
T: Oh, the entrance fee for teenagers is 1000 won. This should be 1000 won. [teacher corrects 12y to 10y on the board]
T: So what happens here? 15x plus 10y equals 70. Let's take a look at equation 2 again. ...

[3rd lesson]
(The teacher was discussing the problem: 'Find the values of m and n when (2, 1) is the solution of the system of linear equations mx+ny=4 and x+y=m'. If we plug in x=2 and y=1, then m=3. But the teacher was mixed up and thought that n=3.)
T: Now, since we have the value for n, we can solve for m, right? When we plug in 3, 2m plus 3 equals 4, 2m equals 1. Then the value of m is 1 over 2. This is how we get the value of m, right?

107

T: Right. Is this supposed to be m? Yes, this is
        supposed to be m.
Numerous students: [mumbling in order to correct the
teacher] The value being solved for is not m, but n.
T: Is this supposed to be m? n? ... Ok, m equals 3.
        ... That means that n equals minus 2.

[9th lesson]
[The teacher was discussing the problem: 'A school went
to the park for a picnic. They collected 100 won per
student to pay for the entrance fee and found out that
they were 1600 won short. When they collected 200 won
per student instead, they found out that they went over
by 2400 won. Find the number of students as well as the
entrance fee per student.' The teacher set up the system
of linear equations, and found the number of students
(40) and the total fee (5600 won). In the next segment
the teacher is finding the fee for each student.]

T: We're solving for the fee of each student. How do
        we find the entrance fee? We can calculate it by
        dividing 5600 by 40. Right?
S: Yes.
T: This simplifies into ... Four one is four, four and
        four is forty? How much is this?
S: [students murmuring calculations] 140 won.
T: 400.
S: 140. 140
T: 400. Right? ... Oh, we get 140 won, 140 won.

What did the teacher think about his own mistakes, and what did the students think
about such mistakes? During the interviews, the teacher did not mention the mistakes
he had made in the lessons, although the interviews were conducted in the context of
his viewing his own recorded teaching. On the other hand, in the interviews with the
students, 5 out of 20 made unsolicited mentions of the teacher's mistakes.

[Student interview after the 2nd lesson]
S3:   Here, the teacher said 1200. But it was supposed
        to be 1000. The teacher made a mistake and I got
        confused.

[Student interview after the 3rd lesson]
S6:   In this part, the teacher made a mistake. It was fun
        though. Still I hope that he should have explicitly
        corrected his mistakes.
[Student interview after the 9th lesson]

S16:   Unlike the other time, the teacher paid attention to the students and the explanation was in detail, I like that. But he made a computational mistake, it spoiled the lesson.

S17:   I wish that he didn't make any mistakes in the lesson. At least he should have corrected his mistakes.

Even for the interview conducted after the 4th lesson, in which no mistake was made by the teacher, one student still commented about the mistakes. The student seemed to remember the mistakes in the 2nd and the 3rd lesson.

[Student interview after the 4th lesson]
S7:   The teacher makes mistakes sometimes. The teacher should reduce the chances of making mistakes.
Interviewer: The teacher may make mistakes because he is also a human being.
S7:   But the teacher makes mistakes often.

The excerpts from transcriptions of the post-lesson interviews suggest that the teacher tended to disregard the mistakes he made during the lessons, yet the students were annoyed by these mistakes and wanted the teacher to rectify the errors explicitly. The mistakes were not seen by the teacher to be significant since, in his view, they did not affect the main flow of the explanation seriously. But for the students, who gradually understood the contents based on the teacher's explanation one by one, the errors seemed to have hindered their understanding. The teacher was unaware of the fact that his mistakes mattered to the students. Thus, the students and the teacher attributed different meanings and importance to the teacher's mistakes.

DISCUSSION

The nature of classroom learning and teaching is multifaceted and complex. One of the students interviewed mentioned that she perceived the lesson she experienced during the class differently from the same lesson as viewed from the video-clip. Her evaluations of the lesson were different before and after watching the video.

[Student interview after the 3rd lesson]
S6:   At that moment, I thought the teacher didn't explain well, but after watching the video-clip, I realized that the teacher did it quite well. He delivered the content in a well-ordered manner.

Considering the fact that even the same lesson was evaluated differently by the same person (before and after the lesson), it is not surprising that the same episodes of the lesson were interpreted differently by the teacher and by different students.

For the teacher, who knew the systems of linear equations well, the two methods for solving systems of linear equations were essentially the same, and the intention of introducing the two methods was to show that the same solution was arrived at. However, for the students who were in the process of acquiring the competency to solve systems of linear equations, it was more important to know how to select the method. Thus they interpreted the objectives of the same lesson from completely different perspectives.

Similarly, since the teacher had planned and designed the lesson, it was clear to him what the important points were. But the students had to decode the rich and complex array of activities in the lesson in order to be able to tell what the important points of the lessons were, unless the teacher organized the teaching and learning activities explicitly and effectively to impress upon the students what the important points were. To achieve this, the teacher needed not only to have a clear idea about the important points of the lesson in his own mind, he also needed to be able to "see" the lesson from the eyes of the students, and design the teaching and learning activities based on this understanding of their perspectives so that they may achieve a shared understanding of the important points of the lesson as designed by the teacher. In a word, while we may not expect students to have been able to detect and understand the discrepancies between the teacher's and the students' perspectives of the lesson, it was the teacher's duty to be aware of such discrepancies and introduce measures to close the gap between the teacher's and the students' perspectives. To make the teacher more familiar with the students' views, some suggestions can be made, for example try to secure more opportunities to talk to students, do frequent interviews with students, and ask students to write a journal and carefully read them.

This discrepancy in perspectives was also the cause of the different attitudes towards interpreting the teacher's mistakes. For the knowledgeable teacher, when he realized that he had made a mistake, he was of course 100% sure that it was a mistake, and that this careless mistake should not affect the general flow of the mathematical argument of the lesson. So, in this sense, the mistakes were not important. But for the students who were in the process of learning a new mathematics concept, every step in the process was a building block for the concept. When the students encountered something which, in their view, may have been a mistake, it was important for them to know for sure whether or not it was indeed a mistake or whether it was because of their lack of understanding that they thought it was. Seen from this light, their expectation that the teacher should explicitly correct the mistake is understandable. This result raises the need to pay attention to the different meaning constructed by the teacher and the students as participants in the same lesson. For the competent teacher, the mathematics he teaches is "ready-made mathematics", but for students the mathematics they are learning is always "mathematics in the process of making" (Freudenthal, 1983). The different 'mathematics' in the eyes of the teacher and in the eyes of the students is the cause for their different attributions of what is important in mathematics teaching and learning, including how important are the mistakes made by the teacher in the lesson.

CONCLUSION

In this chapter, we have shown that the teacher and the students have different perspectives of the same algebra lessons because their mathematics competences and their mathematics-related values are different, and consequently what they consider as important as well as their intentions are different. Teachers usually try hard to have their students understand their perspectives, but the lesson we have learned from the results presented in this chapter is that it is more important for the teacher to understand mathematics and mathematics learning from the students' perspectives, and to adjust his teaching to address their concerns from their perspectives. As the examples quoted in this chapter show, very often the teacher sees his own lesson as a well-taught one, perhaps with minor imperfections, but nevertheless a good lesson. In contrast, the students see a lesson with mistakes uncorrected, with some points stressed but for reasons that they do not know, and a lesson which does not address their concerns and interests. The implication is that the teacher has the responsibility to try to see his lessons in the eyes of the most important beholders—the students— and to make the lessons good not only from his own perspectives, but from the students' perspectives as well.

This study was a preliminary attempt to identify the discrepancies between the teacher's perspectives and the students' perspectives, based on a limited number of algebra lessons in Korea. It would be interesting to investigate whether these discrepancies are content-specific and country-specific, or they are general phenomena which can be expanded in other content areas, and in countries other than Korea. Further studies are needed in order to arrive at a more mature understanding of the discrepancies between the teacher's perspectives and the students' perspectives and the implications of these discrepancies for teaching practice.

NOTE

[1] "Won" is the currency used in Korea

REFERENCES

Clarke, D. J. (1998). Studying the classroom negotiation of meaning: Complementary accounts methodology. In A. Teppo (Ed.), *Qualitative research methods in mathematics education. Journal for Research in Mathematics Education, Monograph No 9* (pp. 98–111). Reston, VA: NCTM.

Clarke, D. J. (Ed.). (2001). *Perspectives on practice and meaning in mathematics and science classrooms.* Dordrecht: Kluwer Academic Publishers.

Clarke, D. J., Shimizu, Y., & Keitel, C. (2006). *Mathematics classrooms in twelve countries: The insider's perspective.* Rotterdam: Sense Publishers.

Francisco, J. M. (2005). Students' reflections on their learning experiences: lessons from a longitudinal study on the development of mathematical ideas and reasoning. *Journal of Mathematical Behavior, 24,* 51–71.

Freudenthal, H. (197). *Mathematics as an educational task.* Dordrecht-Holland: Reidel Publishing Company.

Goodchild, S., & Sriraman, B. (2012). Revisiting the didactic triangle: from the particular to the general. *ZDM, 44*(5), 581–585.

Goos, J. (2004). Learning mathematics in a classroom community of inquiry. *Journal for Research in Mathematics Education, 35*(4), 258–291.

Jacobs, J., & Morita, E. (2002). Japanese and American teachers' evaluations of videotaped mathematics lessons. *Journal for Research in Mathematics Education, 33*(3), 154–175.

Kang, W., & Kilpatrick, J. (1992). Didactic Transposition in Mathematics Textbooks. *For the Learning of Mathematics, 12*(1), 2–7.

Mullis, I. V. S., Martin, M. O., Gonzalez, E. J., & Chrostowki, S. J. (2004). *TIMSS 2003 International Mathematics Report.* International Study Center, Lynch School of Education, Boston College, Boston.

Mullis, I. V. S., Martin, M. O., & Foy, P. (2009). *TIMSS 2007 International Mathematics Report.* TIMSS & PIRLS International Study Center, Lynch School of Education, Boston College, Boston.

National Research Council. (2001). *Adding it up: Helping children learn mathematics.* Washington, DC: National Academy Press.

Pirie, S. E. B. (1996). *What are the data? An exploration of the use of video-recording as a data gathering tool in the mathematics classroom.* Paper presented at the Sixteenth Annual Meeting of the International Group for the Psychology of Mathematics Education, North America, Florida State University, Panama City.

Sensevy, G. Schubauer-Leoni, M., Mercier, A., Ligozat, F., & Perrot, G. (2005). An attempt to model the teacher's action in the mathematics class. *Educational Studies in Mathematics, 59*, 153–181.

Shimizu, Y. (2006). Discrepancies in perceptions of mathematics lessons between the teacher and the students in a Japanese classroom. In D. J. Clarke, C. Keitel, Y. Shimizu (Eds.). *Mathematics classrooms in twelve countries: The insider's perspective* (pp. 183–194). Rotterdam: Sense Publishers.

AFFILIATIONS

Kyungmee Park
Hongik University
Korea

Frederick K. S. Leung
The University of Hong Kong
Hong Kong

MINORU OHTANI

CHAPTER 7

Construction Zone for the Understanding of Simultaneous Equations: An Analysis of One Japanese Teacher's Strategy of Reflecting on a Task in a Lesson Sequence

INTRODUCTION

The purpose of this study was to investigate factors which affect explicit connections among lessons of a Japanese eighth grade mathematics class on simultaneous equations. The data were collected as part of the Learner's Perspective Study (Clarke, 2006), and the class under discussion is the third school in the Japanese LPS data set, referred to as J3 in this chapter.

One specific feature of Japanese classrooms is the explicit connection between lessons (Shimizu, 2007). As already suggested by Sekiguchi (2006), in the J3 class, several lessons have a common theme, and even those with different themes have crucial connections, thus a unit as a whole is well-structured. This study investigated factors affecting student awareness of the explicit connections among lessons.

The paper reports analyses of didactical situations intentionally constituted by the teacher in order to capitalize on students' contributions and promote their progressive understanding of new mathematical concept of simultaneous equations. According to socio-cultural tradition (Vygotskii, 1982), the author has designated such a didactical situation as a "Construction Zone" (Newman, et. al, 1989), in which students with different levels of understanding can interact with each other and have a learning opportunity for deeper understanding. This study analysed the teacher's strategy of constituting a Construction Zone by capitalizing on the students' contributions observed while walking between desks (Kikan-Shidou) and reflecting on a task in a lesson sequence. Specifically, the author focuses on a Construction Zone in which an introductory task is recurrently referred to throughout the topic sequence of ten lessons.

DATA ANALYSIS METHODOLOGY

"Constitutive ethnography" (Mehan, 1979) was adopted to identify patterns in the teacher's strategy for constituting a Construction Zone. This constitutive analysis was used to study both recurrent patterns in the teacher's and the students' interactions and the teacher's strategy for structuring activity that results in these patterns.

F.K.S. Leung et al. (eds.), Algebra Teaching around the World, 113–127.
© *2014 Sense Publishers. All rights reserved.*

A comprehensive analysis of the entire corps of data has generated a provisional structure of interaction which results in the constitution of a Construction Zone. The strategy involves constantly examining discrepant cases until a recursive pattern is identified. Thus, the method can be used to identify a teacher's interactional work of "structuring of the structure" (Bauersfeld, 1995) of the Construction Zone.

In order to ensure that the uncovered recursive pattern or structure converges with that of the participant, the researcher generally adopts a research strategy which consists of observing participants' actions when normal circumstances are disrupted. Patterns in interactions can be difficult to see under normal circumstances.

However, the interactional work becomes visible when normal circumstances are disrupted. In a disruption, people engage in recovery work to re-establish the normal patterns of interaction. This recovery work displays hidden level of interactional work that is normally hidden, but that can be drawn on to inform normal forms of interaction. In other words, studying deviations from normality can reveal normal scenes under normal circumstances. If an expected event does not occur, people will account for its absence.

STRUCTUE OF CONSTRUCTION ZONE

Through the constitutive analysis of transcripts of video-recorded classroom interactions, transcripts of stimulated recall post-lesson interviews with a teacher, and copies of students' written work during lessons, the author has derived a recursive structure in which the teacher constituted a Construction Zone throughout the topic sequence of ten lessons. The following figure illustrates the structure of this Construction Zone for the J3 classroom (Fig. 1).

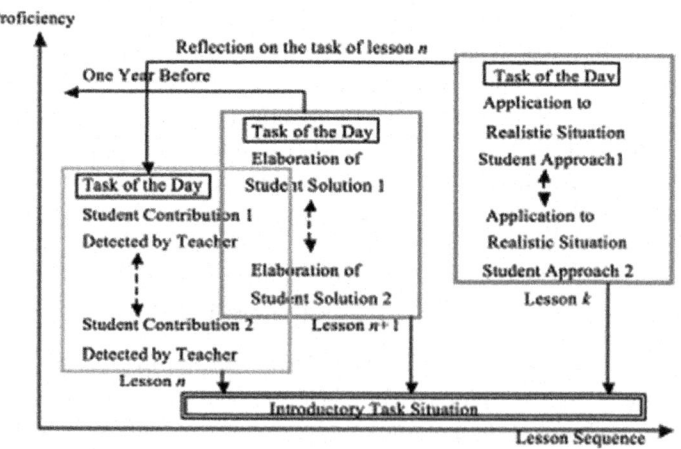

Fig. 1 Structure of Construction Zone in J3 Classroom

In this two-dimensional figure, the horizontal axis represents the lesson sequences and the vertical axis represents the students' levels of proficiency in understanding the mathematical topic. The large rectangular boxes represent the basic lesson activities, which include the main task of the day, and comparisons of the students' solutions or approaches. The first two rectangular boxes represent any two consecutive lessons (lesson n and lesson $n+1$) which have a common overlapping area. Another rectangular box on the right represents a lesson (lesson k) which is temporarily distant in a lesson sequence. Each rectangular box is arranged to the upper right of the preceding one, to represent growth of proficiency over time. The two arrows with broken lines represent comparisons of multiple students' ideas or approaches to the task of the day. The solid-line arrows represent the teacher's strategy of reflecting on a task. In the figure, the introductory task situation is enclosed in double rectangular lines because of its importance. In this figure, the Construction Zone consists of rectangular boxes, an overlapping area and arrows.

There are four key components found in the Construction Zone: (a) Comparison of multiple students' contributions detected and capitalized by the teacher while walking between desks (*Kikan-Shidou*) in a lesson, which corresponds to the rectangular box and arrows of lesson n; (b) Elaborations and generalizations of students' solutions (*Neriage)* in a lesson, which correspond to the rectangular box and arrows of lesson $n+1$; (c) Students' homework as an articulation between lessons, which corresponds to the overlapping area of the two rectangular boxes of lessons n and $n+1$; (d) Reflection on tasks which students worked out before, specifically reflection on the introductory task for conceptual understanding, which corresponds to the arrows from the rectangular boxes of lessons n, $n+1$, and k to the Introductory Task Situation box.

Hereafter, the author describes and interprets episodes in relation to the four components of the Construction Zone (a) to (d) that occurred during the consecutive ten lessons.

ANALYSIS OF CONSTRUCTION ZONE

Analysis of the data shows that, in seven out of the ten consecutive lessons, the teacher intentionally capitalized on the students' contributions, observed while the teacher walked between desks, in order to develop and elaborate new mathematical ideas about simultaneous equations. The following table (Table 1) shows the frequencies of occurrence of various components of the Construction Zone during the ten lessons. In the second row of the table, the plus sign (+) designates the introduction of new mathematical idea and, in the third row, the number designates the number of different solutions.

Tab. 1 Frequencies of Components of Construction Zone in Ten Lessons (Note that video recording of lesson 1 started from the third lesson on simultaneous equations.)

Lesson	1	2	3	4	5	6	7	8	9	10
New Ideas	+	+	+		+		+		+	+
Number of Solutions	2	2	2		2		2	5	4	2
Elaboration and Generalization	*	*	*	*	*	*	*	*	*	
Application to Realistic Situation										**

From the table, we can detect an explicit relationship between introducing a new idea and comparing multiple student solutions in a whole-class discussion. There is evidence of a recursive pattern in which the J3 teacher asked the students to compare two different solutions in order to develop new mathematical idea for themselves. Difference or variation in the student solutions seems to be crucial for understanding mathematical ideas.

Here, we would like to illustrate the teacher's strategy of asking the students to compare two different solutions in order to promote their progressive understanding of the "addition and subtraction method". The episode comes from Lesson 1.

As illustrated by the following transcript, the teacher (abbreviated as T) always began the lesson by reflecting on a task of the previous lesson.

```
T:  Ok, let's start. Well then, we will reconfirm the
    study that we did yesterday and discuss that with
    everyone. And then we'll work out the problem. [He
    writes the question on the chalkboard.]
```

At the beginning of Lesson 1, the teacher wrote the following simultaneous equation (2) on the chalkboard:

$$\begin{cases} 5x+2y=9 \\ -5x+3y=1 \end{cases} \quad ......(2)$$

The task of the previous lesson was to find the solution method of "addition and subtraction". In the previous lesson, the students were also asked to solve the following system of simultaneous equations (1) which was given in the concrete context of purchasing notebooks and pencils:

$$\begin{cases} 4x+3y=840 \\ 2x+3y=540 \end{cases} \quad ......(1)$$

In the previous lesson, the main classroom activity was organized to solve the task (1). The task (2) was left for individual student work. The tasks (1) and (2) could be solved by subtraction and addition methods respectively. During individual work, the teacher walked between the desks and identified interesting examples of students' solutions, to be used for the topic of the next lesson (Lesson 1). The teacher detected a student (KO) who solved the task (2) using subtraction, which was analogous to solving the task (1). However, most students solved the task (2) by using addition. KO's written work is shown below. A closer look at his solution suggests that it is a combined method of "addition" and "substitution".

KO's Redundant Solution

The teacher intentionally nominated KO and asked him to explicate his solution on the chalkboard. In response to his explanation, many students suggested that "There is a much simpler one (solution)". At this point, there were two solutions on the chalkboard. One was the standard solution using the addition method and the other was KO's informal and redundant method. It is interesting that KO himself recommended a simpler solution, saying, "…because during the calculation, there was the fraction, so was difficult and troublesome".

While the teacher drew the students' attention to different solutions and asked them to developing a standard solution method of "addition and subtraction", he also intentionally tried to make an explicit connection to the "substitution" method that would be the objective of the next lesson. In this sense, the comparison of different solution methods functioned not only in illuminating standard solution procedures but also in making a natural linkage between lessons by capitalizing on the students' contributions. Here is an excerpt from a transcript from Lesson 1.

T: Most, actually most students have this opinion [standard solution] that I saw the class [*Kinan-Shido*] that we did yesterday. And in fact, the way which KO did it was different so I wanted him to write it on the chalkboard. Well, the way that is so difficult, but it could work out an answer. **And this is the good way.** (Emphasis is added.)

The teacher gave positive feedback to KO's solution by reflecting on the task at the beginning of the unit.

T: I said this when we studied equations with two
        unknowns first. I told you that there are so many
        answers if you thought only about the simple
        equation with two unknowns. But, when you work out
        the simultaneous equation, there is only one pair.
        As this explanation [KO's informal solution], **this
        is the interesting part of the equation that there
        are two ways to work out.** (Emphasis is added.)

While reflecting on the task, the teacher also asked the students to elaborate on KO's informal solution by using the "Substitution Method".

T: There are some important ideas in this [informal
        solution] process, I think. He subtracted these
        two equations, and about this equation which came
        out after that, he made the equation with the
        'x', then, and substituted that for the original
        equation. **But you don't need to take a roundabout
        way. I said that, for example, you solve this
        [original] equation for 'x' or 'y', and you can
        find the values of 'x' and 'y' as you substitute.**
        (Emphasis is added.)

Thus, the teacher's strategy of reflecting on the tasks of the previous lessons and asking the students to compare different solution methods constituted the Construction Zone, in which the students developed an understanding of the standard solution method as well as an elaborate new solution method.

The teacher posed the task of the day to elaborate on KO's solution to lead to the standard "Substitution Method". The teacher asked the students to work out the original equation, "Either will do, with the 'x' or the 'y' and then you substitute it". While the students engaged in elaborating on KO's method, the teacher was scanning their work and found another important student's [ED's] contribution. ED found that, after solving the equation $5x + 2y = 9$ for 'x' and getting $x = \dfrac{9-2y}{5}$, there were two possible ways to substitute: one way was to substitute 'x' in $5x + 2y = 9$, and the other was to substitute 'x' in $-5x + 3y = 1$. Here is an excerpt from the transcript and his written work.

ED: [To Teacher] Mr. KA, if I substituted here [$5x+2y=9$],
        it would be odd.

T: [To ED] Yeah, it would be odd. It is necessary that you invent a little. You transformed the number one to this, don't you? And you substituted three for one, right? You substituted this for the original equation. But it would be odd [resulting in 9=9], and when you substituted two $[-5x+3y=1]$, it came out $[x=1, y=2]$.

ED: Yes.

T: **You had a good experience. Why was it so?** (Emphasis is added.)

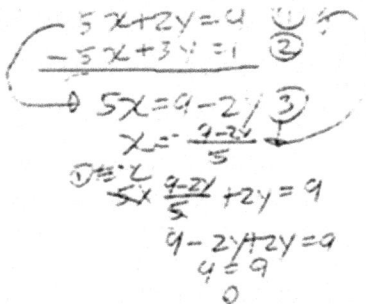

ED's Improper (Odd) Solution

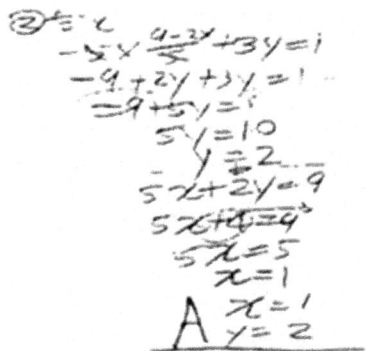

ED's Proper Solution

The Teacher capitalized on ED's work in the whole class activity. He asked ED to write his proper and improper solutions on the chalkboard. There was not enough time left for collective reflection and discussion, so the teacher left it as homework until the next lesson.

T: Today I wanted to make it the main target to
        discuss, but I'm sorry that I couldn't tell you
        my intention clearly. So next class, that will be
        tomorrow, we will discuss here, ok? In this way
        [improper method], as a result of the substitution
        like this, you couldn't work it out, but in that
        way [proper method], you could work it out. Why
        does this happen? [The chimes ring to signal the
        end of the lesson] Please think about it till
        next class. (...) **Now I looked around here roughly;
        before I explained it, about seventy percent of
        the students were having this discussion, I think.**
        Tomorrow we will think about why it happens this
        way. Well, you think about it a bit. Ok? This is
        the homework, all right? (Emphasis is added.)

From the transcript, the teacher assessed the students' awareness of the problem posed by ED. The teacher thought it crucial to let the students think about it, so he asked them to do so for their homework. Thus, ED's contribution, detected by the teacher, served as the mediation for Lessons 1 and 2, and the students' homework functioned as an articulation between the lessons. This kind of linkage between lessons is expressed as the overlapping area of consecutive lessons n and $n+1$ in Figure 1.

The teacher reflected on the student's crucial contribution not only to make connections between successive lessons but also to make connections to individual lessons. For example, in the excerpt of the transcript of Lesson 7, the teacher reflected on ED's contribution to Lesson 1.

T: Ah, do you remember the class we had? Okay, everyone,
        please look at the previous pages of your notebook.
        Actually, ED introduced this way in an earlier
        class. I looked for the date of that class, and
        it was sixty, no. June sixth. Oh, it was continued
        from June fourth to sixth. I think it was Example 1
        we were doing on that day, uh, have you found it?

In this sense, the reflection on the task and the student's contribution was specially and temporally distant.

In sum, we can identify four key components of the Construction Zone and describe the teacher's strategy for constituting it.

(a) The teacher asked the students to compare different solutions that he identified while walking between the students' desks and then capitalized on for his whole-class discussion. In Lesson 1, the students compared two solution methods for solving simultaneous equations. One was the "subtraction method" and the other was KO's redundant informal method. In this case, the teacher had noticed KO's method in the previous lesson. Thus, there was an explicit linkage between the two successive lessons. The following excerpt is from the transcript of the teacher's interview after Lesson 2.

```
INT:   I see. Well, it happens a lot that you take up the
       two or three kinds of the student's solutions in
       regard to the one problem.
T:     Yes.
INT:   It is your typical style, isn't it?
T:     Yes, it is.
INT:   Like your (written) form (for teacher's
       questionnaire).
T:     Well, the position that I think it is the point of
       that.
INT:   Yes.
T:     When I make them think that again, I show several
       solutions.
INT:   Ah, it is on purpose.
T:     Yes, I create the chance to make them think on
       purpose.
T:     To solve the equation in many ways. I want them
       to understand it. And till now, what I have told
       them logically is that there is only one pair of
       solutions for that system of simultaneous equations
       regardless of the way they solve it. So that I want
       them to be aware that it will be the same solution
       if they use the other method to solve it. Now, I
       want them to know that - maybe it will be in future
       because they don't do enough training - they can
       solve this kind of simultaneous equation in the
       most efficient way.
T:     Here well, if they can solve simultaneous equations
       but cannot prove it, it will probably mean that
       they um did not understand the meaning of the
       solution for the equation.
```

(b) The teacher asked the students to elaborate on KO's redundant and inadequate method and compare it to the standard substitution method.

(c) The teacher thought it crucial to let the students think about KO's improper solution and left it for their homework. I He hoped that their thinking about KO's method would promote a deeper understanding of the meaning of "simultaneity" on the part of the students and make an explicit linkage to the next lesson.

(d) The teacher reflected on tasks which the students had worked out previously and/or in former lessons. Reflecting on a task or a student's contribution was crucial for constructing a well-structured knowledge of simultaneous equations. Table 2 shows the frequencies this type of reflection in the lesson sequence.

From the table, we can detect that the reflection on a particular task or student's contribution was specially and temporally distant. As expected, there were constant references in the previous and the next lessons. Except for Lesson 4, the teacher always began by reflecting on a task from the previous lesson. As mentioned earlier, usually the lessons started by reflecting on the homework of the previous lesson. In the J3 class, homework was not just exercise item but a chance to identify the main problems which emerged in the course of elaborating on students' inadequate contributions. So, each lesson ended by formulating an important problem to think about at home, and the next lessen started the with students' ideas about this problem.

Tab. 2 Frequencies of Reflecting on a Task in a Lesson Sequence

Lesson	1	2	3	4	5	6	7	8	9	10
Initial	1	2	2	0	0	0	0	0	0	1
Previous	1	2	3	0	1	3	3	2	2	2
Before	0	1	1	2	0	0	2	0	1	0
Long Before	0	1	4	1	0	0	0	0	0	1
Next	1	1	1	1	3	3	2	2	2	1
Future	1	2	0	0	0	0	0	0	0	0
Total	4	9	11	4	4	6	7	4	5	5

We can detect another classification for reflecting on a task, such as 'before', 'long before', and 'future'. The author has already illustrated a case of 'before', when the teacher reflected on ED's contribution in Lesson 7. By 'long before', the author means that the teacher reflected on a task from a year or a couple of years earlier. For example, the teacher reflected on a linear equation task which was taught in the seventh grade. On the contrary, by 'future', the author means that teacher reflected on a task that would be taught in the future. For example, the necessary and sufficient conditions for a system of linear equations with two unknowns to have solutions are taught at high school.

Hereafter the author focuses on the cases in which the teacher intentionally reflected on the initial task situation. The author hypothesizes that the teacher tried to constitute the Construction Zone when the task of the lesson was difficult or abstract for many students. Reflecting on the initial task situation allowed the students to have concrete references for essential content knowledge and to have a space for interaction and communication.

CONSTITUTE CONSTRUCTION ZONE BY REFLECTING ON
INITIAL TASK SITUATION

In the J3 class, the teacher used a situation from a textbook in order to start the unit on simultaneous equations. The situation came from a school newspaper about a basketball competition, thus providing a realistic context for the students (Fig. 2).

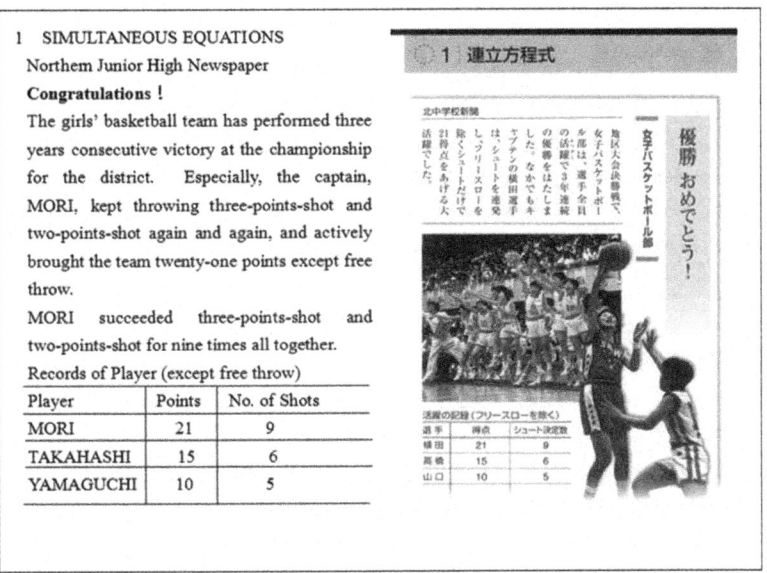

Fig. 2. Excerpt Showing Initial Task Situation

From this realistic situation, the students were introduced to the necessity and meaning of simultaneous equations. In order to find how many three-point shots and two-point shots MORI achieved, we cannot rely on the data about either 'points' or 'number of shots'. We need **both** sets of data to decide the number of successful three-point shots 'x' and two-point shots 'y'. Mathematically speaking, either condition, $3x+2y=21$ or $x+y=9$, has multiple solutions. If we take both conditions into account, we can find $x=3$ and $y=6$.

Analysis of data reveals that the teacher reflected on the initial task situation four times in the unit. In these four occurrences, we can distinguish three distinct cases. These cases are summarized as follows: (a) to clarify the meaning of "simultaneity" when some students tried to solve simultaneous equations by manipulating one indefinite equation with two unknowns; (b) to clarify the meaning of solution of simultaneous equations and to recognize the necessity for substituting the answer into both indefinite equations in order to check the answer; (c) to explain a general cyclic process for solving a real word problem, which consists of "horizontal mathematizing (expressing numerical relations of realistic situation as equations)", "vertical mathematizing (symbolic manipulation to get an answer)", and "reflecting and interpreting" (reflecting on essential aspects of the problem and interpreting the mathematical answer in terms of realistic conditions)".

Here, the author focuses on the two cases (a) and (c) from Lessons 2 and 10.

(a) Lesson 2 was started by reflecting on the homework.

T: All right, so now let's start. So I'll write what we've done so far on the blackboard. We're just going over it. So [writes, $5x + 2y = 1$, $-5x + 3y = 2$ on the blackboard] this is what ED shared with the class, this is how he wrote it for us. What I want to study with you today is, um, the expression number one [$5x+2y=9$] that we've got here, we solved about the x and substitute for one, we got this trivial expression "$0=0$". Moreover, we couldn't find the answer to 'x' and 'y'. When we substituted for two [$-5x+3y=1$], we got the answers for 'x' and 'y'. So did you think about it at home? Can anyone share what they've thought about at home with the class? Any volunteers? I'd really like to hear some of your ideas.

However, none of students could contribute their ideas. This is an illustration of 'the teacher's expectations being disappointed or normal circumstances disrupted'. Then, the strategy he chose was to reflect on the initial task situation.

T: Okay, I'll give you a hint. Um, when you first studied about the simultaneous equations.(Please open that page in your textbooks.) The thing about the basketball goals.

T: How many expressions were you using so far? It's not two. You were using only expression number one. Do you understand? For sure? As I explained before, you can get the solution for the system of equations from the two linear equations with two unknowns. I want you to remember this. That's why I looked back to the part where we studied about Mori. As you can see from this, you have been using only one expression to solve it, although there are two expressions in the problem.

This reflection on the initial task situation played the role of assuring the students to clarify the meaning of 'simultaneity' and 'equality', which is an essential concept in simultaneous equations.

(c) We can illustrate another function in which the teacher's reflection on the initial task situation came into play. The following excerpt from the transcript of

Lesson 10 shows that the teacher tried to develop the student's meta-knowledge of the application of simultaneous equations.

T: So, you have completed this unit of finding the value of simultaneous equations. That means you all should graduate from this topic today. Okay, guys? If you get confused, you can go back to the textbook or come to me to ask questions. All right? And, what we are going to do today is, I want you all to go back to the place where we started to learn about simultaneous equations. Um, page thirty-eight. Ah, the story about basketball from a newspaper.

S: Why are we (going back again?)

The teacher drew a diagram on the blackboard (Fig. 3)

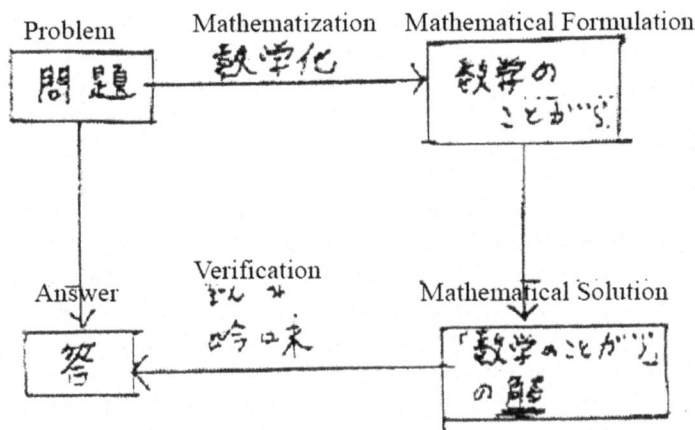

Fig. 3. A Diagram of Application of Mathematics

T: So, you have been doing only calculations of the formula up to now, and maybe you have been wondering why you have to keep doing these kinds of calculations. However, actually, it is not only calculations of the formula. The equation is, in this case for example, it is an article on so-and-so junior high school newspaper, but when you run into situations like this and need to know something, you may come up with the idea of the use of simultaneous equations.

T: I want to teach you some basic form about questions with word problems.

Reflecting on the initial task situation contributed to developing the students' meta-knowledge of the mathematical activity.

CONCLUDING REMARKS

Usually, the primary didactical role of an introductory task is to provide students with a realistic context for a new mathematical structure, to motivate them to learn a new mathematical topic, to suggest new mathematical ideas, to look for new ways of mathematical thinking, and so on.

This chapter has identified one teacher's strategy of reflecting on the task and analysed its function as a construction zone for developing the students' understanding of equations progressively.

In the Japanese J3 class, however, the teacher not only used the initial task situation in the beginning of lessons as usual, but he also reflected recursively on the task situation at strategic points during the unit. Thus, reflecting recursively on the same task situation may have played a role not only in making explicit connections among lessons but also in promoting the students' conceptual understanding. The teacher used the strategy of reflecting on to create a Construction Zone in which students with different levels of understanding could interact with each other and open up a learning opportunity for deeper understanding of simultaneous equations (Ohtani, 2002).

There were different ways in which the teacher utilized reflection. Reflection on multiple students' contributions identified by the teacher while observing their independent work was used to promote the students' conceptual understanding of simultaneous equations. Reflection on the initial task created a zone for interaction between the teacher and students when the students experienced difficulty in understanding essential aspects of simultaneous equations. In addition, reflection on the introductory task situation may have contributed to developing meta-knowledge of mathematical activity: that 'mathematics starts from reality and stays at reality' and that 'one can make sense of abstract procedure and apply it with reality'.

In order to understand these roles of reflection better, two theoretical constructs have been used to explain the analysis further.

First, the act of reflection on a task seems to have something to do with the concept of 'revoicing' (O'Connor, Michaels, 1996). By 'revoicing' we mean a particular kind of re-utterance of one's contribution by another participant in a discussion. Two kinds of revoicing were used extensively and exclusively by the teacher during the classroom interaction. One was 'public revoicing' and the other was 'measured revoicing' (Ohtani, 2008). For public revoicing, the teacher not only replied to nominated individual students, but also addressed all of the students. This means that he capitalized on particular students' contributions to address the whole class in order to promote collective reflection. 'Publicity of revoicing' was obvious during the students' independent work. For 'measured revoicing', the teacher expected a variety of student responses to the assigned task and had a plan to capitalize on their contributions in order to formulate challenging problems and elaborate on their solutions through collective argumentation.

Second, the notion that the same task situation plays many roles for assuring that students understand the essential concept of simultaneous equations as well as developing meta-knowledge of mathematical activity suggests the concept of 'generic task'. The author conceptualizes 'generic task' as mediating tools between students and teacher which constitute a Construction Zone in which people with different levels of understanding can interact with each other and open a learning opportunity for deeper understanding. Data from the teacher's interview and the learners' perspective support these roles that the 'generic task' can play.

REFERENCES

Bakhtin, M. M. (1981). *The dialogic imagination*. M. Holquist (Ed.). Austin, TX: University of Texas Press.

Bauersfeld, H. (1995). The structuring of the structures: Development and function of mathematizing as a social process. In L. P. Steffe, & J. Gale (Eds.), *Constructivism in education* (pp. 137–158). Hillsdale, NJ: Lawrence Erlbaum Associates.

Clarke, D. (2006). The LPS research design. In D. Clarke, C. Keitel, & Y. Shimizu (Eds.), *Mathematics classrooms in twelve countries* (pp. 15–29). Rotterdam, The Netherlands: Sense Publishers.

Mehan, H. (1978). *Learning lessons: Social organization in the classroom*. Harvard University Press.

Newman, D., Griffin, P., & Cole, M. (1989). *The construction zone: Working for cognitive change in school*. New York, NY: Cambridge University Press.

O'Connor, M., & Michaels, S. (1996). Shifting participant frameworks: orchestration thinking practices in group discussion. In D. Hicks (Ed.), *Discourse, learning, and schooling* (pp. 63–103). Cambridge University Press.

Ohtani, M. (2002). *Gakkou Suugaku ni okeru Sugakuteki Katsudou no Shyakaiteki Kusei* (Social Formation of Mathematical Activity in the Classroom). Kazama Shobo.

Ohtani, M. (2008). An analysis of Japanese lessons on linear functions. In O. Figureas et al. (Eds.), *Proceedings of the 32nd conference of the international group for the psychology of mathematics education* (Vol. 1, pp. 97–98). Morelia: PME.

Sekiguchi, Y. (2006). Coherence of mathematics lessons in Japanese eighth-grade classroom. In J. Novotna, H. Moraova, M. Kratka, & N. Stehlikova (Eds.), *Proceedings of the 30th conference of the international group for the psychology of mathematics education* (Vol. 5, pp. 81–88). Prague: PME.

Shimizu, Y. (2007). Explicit linking in the sequence of consecutive lessons in mathematics classroom in Japan. In Jeong-Ho Woo et al. (Eds.), *Proceedings of the 31st conference of the international group for the psychology of mathematics education* (Vol. 4, pp. 177–184). Seoul: PME.

Vygotskii, L. S. (1982). Myshlenie i rech': Psikhologicheskie issredovaniya. *Sobranie sochinenii. Tom vtoroi. Porblemy obshchei pshikhologii* (Thinking and speech: Psychological investigation. *Collected works. Vol. 2. Problems of General Psychology*). c. 5-361. Moskva: Izdatel'stvo Pedagogika.

AFFILIATION

Minoru Ohtani
College of Human and Social Sciences
Kanazawa University
Japan

TOSHIAKIRA FUJII[1]

CHAPTER 8

Understanding the Concept of Variable Through Whole-Class Discussions:
The Community of Inquiry from a Japanese Perspective

INTRODUCTION

Some may be surprised to see that there is no algebra strand and no Japanese word
代数 for 'algebra' in the Japanese Course of Study of elementary and even of lower
secondary school mathematics. This is different from the American curriculum
recently released as the Common Core State Standards which includes 'Operations
and Algebraic Thinking' even from Kindergarten to Grade 5.

The Course of Study in Japan is an official curriculum document that is published
and revised about every ten years by the Ministry of Education, Culture, Sports,
Science, and Technology (hereafter referred to as the Ministry). The textbooks
are published commercially, however they need to be approved officially by the
Ministry to make sure that they are consistent with, or adhere to the Course of
Study. Therefore if there is no algebra strand in the Course of Study, it is likely that
there will not be any unit titled as 'algebra' in the elementary or lower secondary
mathematics textbooks.

Instead of being an independent domain in the curriculum, algebra is included
systematically in various parts of the mathematics curriculum, particularly at the
elementary level. Watanabe (2007) made a list by analyzing Japanese textbooks
through a foreigner's eyes and identified examples to show that much of what is
considered algebra exists in Japanese elementary mathematics textbooks. Even
Japanese teachers may be surprised to see that algebra or algebraic thinking
is embedded in many areas, as they often think of it as an advanced study of
mathematics. Watanabe mentioned that the main focus on it is in the Quantitative
Relations strand in the Course of Study. That strand consists of ideas of functions,
writing and interpreting mathematical expressions, and statistical manipulations.
The contents of the Quantitative Relations strand have strong relationships with the
other three strands, Numbers and Calculations, Quantities and Measurement, and
Geometric Figures (Takahashi, Watanabe, and Yoshida, 2004, p.67). In other words,
these strands also include ingredients of algebra and algebraic thinking. At the lower
secondary level, it is much easier for even Japanese educators to identify what is
considered algebra. However Japanese teachers' perceptions may differ from those
of foreigners.

F.K.S. Leung et al. (eds.), Algebra Teaching around the World, 129–148.
© 2014 Sense Publishers. All rights reserved.

So how do we characterize the Japanese way of seeing school algebra? According to Usiskin (1988), there are three conceptions: (1) Algebra as a study of procedures for solving certain kinds of problems; these procedures include solving equations, where letters are used as unknowns. (2) Algebra as generalized arithmetic where letters are used as pattern generalities. (3) Algebra as the study of relationships among (functions), where letters are used as variables (function arguments), as in the problem: 'What happens to the value of 1/x as x gets larger and larger?' I could say that the Japanese elementary school curriculum may relate to the first two of the three conceptions as algebraic contents. Bednarz, Kieran and Lee (1996) suggested another four perspectives; the Japanese curriculum may relate to the first two of these: (1) A generalization perspective, (2) A problem-solving perspective, (3) A modelling perspective, and (4) A functional perspective. Also C. Kieran (2004) suggested that there are three core activities of algebra: (1) Generational activities (situations, properties, patterns and relationships are represented algebraically and/or interpreted), (2) Transformational activities (algebraic manipulation), and (3) Global/meta-level activities (that is to prove, or solve problems, or to identify structure, and so on). The Japanese lower secondary school curriculum includes part of (1) and (2) but not much of (3).

Although Japanese teachers seem to see functions and algebra to be in different strands in the curriculum, the two are surely related to each other, and I am personally more concerned about activities in functional situations which are rich in learning algebraic expressions and thinking. This paper focuses on lessons on the linear function in which students' conceptions of variable were revealed and reconstructed through whole-class discussions.

The purpose of this paper is to clarify how the students' understanding of variables evolved during the 4th to the 7th lessons of the 10 consecutive lessons of School 1 (J1) in the LPS, focusing on whole-class discussions and the processes leading to them. During these four lessons, the students discussed about the range[2] of independent and dependent variables of linear functions. The teacher considered that the idea of the range of variables is essential, saying at the very last part of the post-lesson interview, "I believe it is very important to make students understand the meaning of the range of variables in teaching linear equations" (Ms. K post-lesson interview, J1-L7). However she underestimated how difficult it would be for her students to learn it, saying, "I thought it was hard to teach them." The difficulty here stemmed not only from the concept of the range of variables but also from the concept of variable itself.

DATA AND METHODOLOGY OF THIS STUDY

The data in this study include the videotaped classroom data and transcripts of both lessons and the post-lesson video-stimulated interviews with the teacher and students, as well as copies of relevant printed or written materials and blackboard writings during the lessons.

The main focus is on the 7th lesson, in which whole-class discussion occurred in order to decide an appropriate range for the independent and dependent variables. The process of how this became the problem for the whole class to consider is described using protocols and the data about blackboard writing. Then the whole-class discussion is analyzed in terms of the understanding of the range of the variables based on the concept of variable. The whole-class discussions are characterized in terms of the community of mathematical inquiry from a Japanese perspective.

BACKGROUND INFORMATION OF SCHOOL ALGEBRA IN JAPAN: ALGEBRAIC EXPRESSIONS, EQUATIONS AND FUNCTIONS

Literal symbols in the curriculum

In the 3rd grade of elementary school, the frame word box (□) used to represent an unknown number is introduced and, in the 4th grade, an additional frame word, such as a circle (○), is introduced. At the 4th grade level, these frame words can be used for variables in a mathematical expression such as □+ ○= 10. In the 6th grade, literal symbols such as 'x' and 'a' are introduced to stand for numbers previously represented by the frame words. However at the 6th grade level there is no place to learn manipulations of literal symbols; this is left until lower secondary school.

In the lower secondary school, in the 7th grade, translations of concrete situations expressed in ordinary language to mathematical expressions using literal symbols and vice versa are emphasized. Calculations of algebraic expressions with one variable required for solving linear equations are studied.

Equations and Functions in the curriculum

In the 7th grade students learn to solve linear equations using attributes of equality, and here the literal symbol 'x' can be used for an unknown number. Proportions as a special case of linear functions are introduced and the definition of variable is given, such as "Letters that take various values are called variables" (Kodaira, 1992, p.97). Also, the definition of the range of the variable is given.

In the 8th grade students are required to develop their abilities further to find quantitative relationships and to express such relationships in formulae by using literal symbols. Computations of simple formulae using literal symbols and the four fundamental operations are emphasized. Simultaneous linear equations in two variables are studied. The linear function is also studied.

In the 9th grade, multiplication of linear expressions and factorizations of simple quadratic trinomials are studied, as well as solving quadratic equations using factorization and formulae of solution. Simple quadratic functions such as $y=ax^2$ and their graphical representations are studied.

FOCUS LESSONS

Phases of problem-solving oriented lessons

This paper focuses on four lessons from the 4th to 7th of 10 consecutive lessons conducted in J1. A Japanese mathematics lesson has a typical flow or structure, particularly when a problem -solving oriented lesson is conducted. Typically, a lesson consists of four phases or components:

Phase 1: Presenting one problem for the day (understanding the problem),
Phase 2: Problem solving by students,
Phase 3: Comparing and discussing (students present solutions),
Phase 4: Summing up by the teacher.

Non-Japanese scholars have already noticed these phases or components of a lesson through observing Japanese lessons (Becker, Silver, Kantowski, Travers & Wilson, 1990; Stigler & Hiebert, 1999).

However, this is not always the case. For the 4th to 7th lessons, these phases were related closely and the four lessons basically tackled the same problem; the distinctions among the four phases were unclear. We could see that the four lessons were aiming to identify independent and dependent variables in the paper-folding problem. From this perspective, Phase 1 happened in the 4th lesson; Phase 2 was conducted up to the first half of the 6th lesson, then Phase 3 happened in the latter half of the 6th lesson and continued to the 7th. From this point of view, I will explain the flow of the lessons, and how and why the range problem has been posed and discussed in the class.

The paper-folding problem

The problem context of the 4th to 7th lessons was folding or bending a rectangular shaped piece of colored paper (12cm×15cm), and considering the perimeter of the figure (See Fig.1).

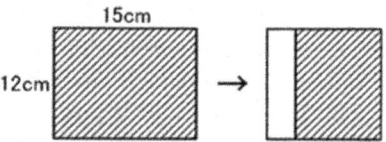

Figure. 1 The paper folding

The students were asked to decide what the independent and dependent variables were and to make a table and graph of the relationship between the variables. In the 4th lesson, two kinds of interpretations or tasks emerged. On Task A, student NO reported that the independent variable was the length of the folded part (the white part in Fig. 2), and the dependent variable was the perimeter of the whole rectangle (See Fig.2). The alternative response (Task B), as reported by student TA, was that the independent variable was the length of the shaded part and the dependent variable was only the perimeter of the shaded part of the rectangle (See Fig.3).

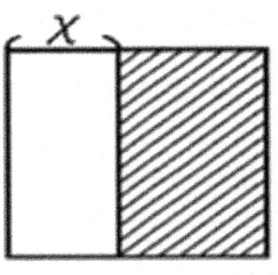
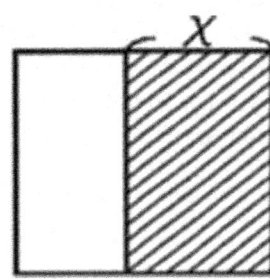

Fig. 2. Task A   *Fig. 3. Task B*

According to the students' interpretations of the paper-folding task, tables for both interpretations were presented and the class was asked to draw graphs of them as homework. The 5th and 6th lessons were basically continuations of the former lesson. In the 6th lesson, Student SH pointed out, "Isn't that a twenty-four for y on the right figure (Task B)? You wrote it as zero" (23:58, J1-L6). In fact, according to the table for Task B on the blackboard, when x is 0, y is 0. Student NO followed this up, saying, "But if there is no width, then the height won't exist, isn't it?" (24:08, J1-L6). This was the moment when the problem of the range of the variable was posed, focusing on Task B. Finally the teacher accepted the two thoughts, saying that there were two ways to think about the problem, and put 24 with parenthesis under the 0 into the table (see Fig.5). In the 7th lesson, another possible value of y, that is y=12, was added (see Fig.6). The activity for the students to do for the 7th lesson was given by the teacher as follows:

```
09:47, L7-J1:
```

```
Okay. Um, yesterday, we had left some parts unfinished and
hadn't got to the answer yet. And, I would like to work on
the graph NI had drawn, and talk further more. So, I will
hand out a new worksheet. Okay? [Handing out a worksheet]
[Putting up a sheet of paper on the blackboard]
```

```
11:15, L7-J1
```

```
Um, if you notice anything, or find something that you
think should be corrected, in the graph in the top, memo,
and the graph on the right, write them down. Write down
anything."
```
In the next section we will see more closely what happened in the 7th lesson according to both the teacher's and the students' comments on the important or significant moments identified during the post-lesson video-stimulated interview.

IMPORTANT MOMENTS IDENTIFIED BY THE TEACHER AND STUDENTS

To facilitate a closer look at the 7th lesson, Table 1 shows what happened not only from the teacher's perspective but also from the students'. It shows the locations in the lesson recording of the moments identified by the teacher and students NI and TA in the post-lesson video-stimulated interview. In total, sixteen events were identified by the teacher and the students as important. These events have been classified into nine groups, from E1 to E9.

Table 1: Important moments identified by the teacher and students

	Events	Teacher	Stud.NI	Stud.TA
E1	Checking homework	2:00	2:38	3:00
	Handing out today's worksheet	11:30		
E2	Monitoring students' working	15:00		
	Demonstration of paper folding		17:25	
	Y=24?	22:00	22:40	
E3	Group discussion y=0 or 24	24:11		23:30
	Voting by students (1) y=0 or 24	25:00*		
	Y=12?	26:00*		
E4	Putting numbers between 0 and1 in the table		26:40	
E5	Voting by students (2) y=0 or 24 or 12	30:00	31:17	
			31:40	
E6	Showing many coordinates	34:30		
	Many coordinates makes a line	37:00	36:25	37:00
E7	Couldn't decide y=0 or 24 or 12	40:00		
E8	Student NO says x is bigger than 0	40:20	40:24	
E9	State the range of y is 24<y≦54	42:00		

25:00*, 26:00* identified by the video data

A discussion about agreements and discrepancies between the teacher and the students has already been discussed by Shimizu (2006). Thirteen events were identified by the teacher, nine by student NI and three by student TA. There were only two moments about which both the teacher and the two students agreed, E1 and the second event of E6; there were four events about which the teacher and one student concurred, the two events of E3 and the single ones of E5 and E8. There were seven moments out of 13 that were only considered as important by the teacher herself. This last fact may imply that the teacher had planned the lesson carefully and that each move or activity had some meaning from her point of view.

In this paper, we describe the analysis of the 7th lesson from the perspective of the teaching and learning of algebra, focusing on the range of variables in the context of function. Since, in total, 13 events have been identified as important moments by the teacher, we can use the data shown in Table 1 to capture the critical moments that happened in the lesson. From the point of view of the understanding of variables, this can be characterised as a lesson that focused on the linear function whose mathematical expression is $y=2x+24$, and students were trying to find the range of the independent and dependent variables.

The 7th lesson seems to have flown in two directions. One was to find an exact value of x and y according to the actual phenomenon, the paper folding or the bending event. When the folding place came to the edge of the paper, students described this as "when x=0." The class tried to find the exact values of y when x=0. This flow started from E2 to E3, then E5.

As well, there were some moments, E4 and E6, dealing with the possible values of the independent and dependent variables. This issue had been considered earlier in the 4th lesson, but only with natural numbers and zero, since the paper folding was introduced by making one-centimetre folds.

In contrast, in the 7th lesson, the teacher discussed the possible values at E4 by putting many numbers into the table, and at E6 by putting many coordinates on the dotted line in the graphical expression of $y=2x+24$.

These two sequences, one from E2, E3, and E5, and the other E4 and E6, eventually integrated into E8 and E9. In the next session, we will see what comments the teacher and students made on the events embedded in these flows.

Finding the exact value of the dependent variable: from E2 to E3, then E5

Three possibilities of the exact value: E2 was basically a kind of opening session: the teacher was handing out the day's worksheet, which she identified as important (Teacher: 11:30, see Table 1), and let the students work on it (Teacher: 15:00, see Table 1). She demonstrated again to make clear what the paper folding meant and which length was to be considered as an independent variable (NI: 17:25, see Table 1).

At E3, the first 'voting by students (1)' happened. During E3, the teacher identified four moments as important, of the students identified two. According to Table 1, Teacher: 22:00 and NI: 22:40 refer to the same event. The teacher, Ms. K, stated at the post-lesson interview that this was because she intentionally asked student SH to make share his opinion with the class, that is y=24, although he did not raise his hand (see interview excerpt below).

Teacher: Ms. K (22:00, J1-L7)

> Here, the students were to think about what y would be when x is zero. I wanted to bring up some of the opinions and examine each of them together with the class. At this point, SH was not raising his hand, but I knew he had 24 as the answer, which is very important. So I brought up his idea on purpose, and started thinking about how to lead them to the conclusion.

The teacher identified SH's idea while monitoring the students' work. This kind of behaviour is considered to be an important and typical one for veteran teachers in Japan.

Although the time is unclear from the post-lesson interview data, the 25:00* event was the 'voting' by the students (1). That is when the teacher wanted to know their thoughts, but not to force them to make decisions.

Teacher: Ms. K (25:00*, J1-L7)

> Like this scene, I think it is important to make them raise their hands when we have some different opinions. It is not for decision making. I do this to see what each student has in his mind.

These intentional moves by the teacher worked effectively at E3 since the students considered it to be important, and they appreciated hearing other students' opinions:

Student NI (22:40, J1-L7)

> Yes. It was nice to hear many other opinions from the class.

Student TA (23:30, J1-L7)

> And, we were to share our opinion with friends. I thought it is twenty-four...
>
> When she said it could not exist, I thought it might be right.

Student NI (31:17, J1-L7)

> And here, we get to hear why it should be twelve, and those who claimed it to be twenty-four,...I realized that there are some other ways of thinking about this. I was also glad to find there are some students who think as I do.

We can say that the teacher and students considered the same events as important, although the teacher the importance arose from the intention or aim of her move, while the students were concerned with how it benefitted them.

The three possible values of the dependent variable were shown on the blackboard: Focusing on the students' expressions sequentially as they were written in the table on the blackboard, we can see their ideas about the value of the dependent variable: 0, 24 and 12.

The first table appeared in the 4th lesson, where y=0 was written. In the 5th lesson, the table was completed by students on the blackboard, so that y=0 when x=0 became obvious again (see Fig.4). It should be noted that this table started with the values of x from larger to smaller numbers, then it was revised in the 6th lesson as shown in Figure 5. Also, in the 6th lesson, y=24 was added under the value of 0 (see Fig. 5). In the 7th lesson, the value 12 was added (see Fig. 6).

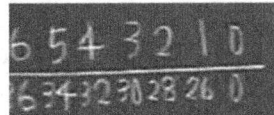

Fig. 4. Table in the 4th, 5th lessons

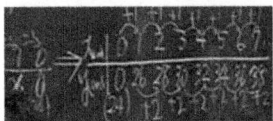

Fig. 5. Table in the 6th lesson

Fig. 6. Table in the 7th lesson

We may characterise the events E2, E3 and E5 as students expressing their conceptions of the value of y when x=0. The teacher intentionally tried to draw out their thoughts and they appreciated hearing other students' ideas. Although the ways in which they said it and the identified time on the video are not exactly the same, the teacher and the students expressed a common feeling about what these important events were in the lesson.

Finding as many numbers or coordinates as possible: E4 and E6

At E4, the teacher Ms. K suggested finding the values of y when x=0.5 and 0.1, as shown in Figure 6. This activity is different from finding the exact values of y when x=0. Rather the activity was intended to lead to the concept of variable. At E4, student NI said the activity helped a lot:

NII (26:40, J1-L7)

```
Here, our teacher put many kinds of numbers, between
zero and one, into x. And that helped a lot.
```

The same thing happened at E6 after the second voting by the students (2). This time it was not concerning the tables but the coordinates in the graphical representation. At E6, the teacher demonstrated the possible values of the variable by using two overhead projector sheets and one graph sheet as shown below (see Fig. 7):

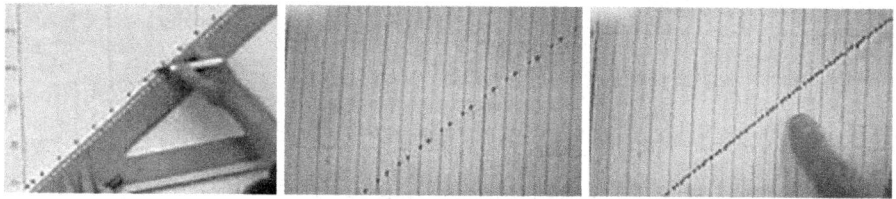

Fig. 7. Teacher's demonstration of making a line by many points.

This activity also impressed student NI:

NI (36:25, J1-L7)

```
INT:   This is when your teacher filled the blank with
       many coordinates, and it finally turned out to be
       a straight line?
NI:    This scene was also good. What she was saying was
       clear to our eyes.
```

Another student, TA, also identified this as an important event:

TA (37:00, J1-L7)

```
INT:   Okay. At thirty seven minutes. Here the teacher
       draws a line connecting the points she found on the
       graph
```

```
TA:    Here, she finds so many points...
INT:   Yes.
TA:    She found a coordinate for every zero point five,
       and showed all the points together make a straight
       line. But she left where you wanted to know blank
       and did not answer here.
```

Ms. K had planned this activity carefully and said that she considered it as an important moment for the lesson.

Teacher (37:00, J1-L7)

```
Ms. K: I made clear the idea of seeing a graph as so many
       points which are put together, and the location
       of the points that get as close to twenty-four as
       possible.
INT:   So, you drew a line which would connect all the
       points with the ruler, right?
Ms. K : Yes.
```

In the 5th lesson, the same activity happened with Task A, in which the class considered the value of y when x is between 7 and 8. One student considered only natural numbers, and the graph became like a trapezoidal shape, as shown below; with rational numbers, it can form a V shape, as shown in Figure 8. This is called the 'seven point five matter' and this event was considered as the climax of the 5th lesson.

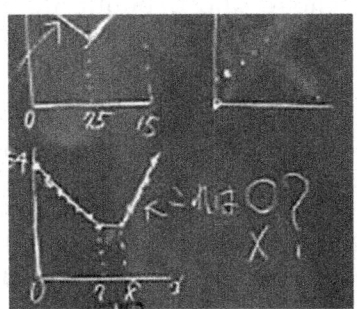

Fig.8 The trapezoid graph

Understanding the range of variable: two sequences integrated into E8 and E9

Two sequences, one from E2, E3, to E5, the other E4 and E6, were eventually integrated into E8 and E9. However, it was difficult to do this. In fact, the two sequences seemed to be stuck at E7, where the students could not decide the value when x=0, as the teacher said in the post-lesson interview:

139

Teacher (40:00, J1-L7)

```
The students were not satisfied with the idea I brought
up. My plan was not to get to the conclusion today,
by then. I thought it couldn't be solved, because it
needs some essence of geometric interpretation. The
students were, as I expected, not satisfied and being
stubborn, so I was thinking, 'What should I do?' But
I had to force my plan considering the time left.
```

However, finally a student brought up an alternative idea to resolve the difficulties, that is x is bigger than 0 (E8). The teacher and one student, NI, believed that this was an important moment. Here all three opinions y=0, 24 and 12 were abandoned, then a new idea came up, that is the value of zero is not included in the range of variable x. In the post-lesson interview, the teacher made two points: one was that she thought the idea of exclusion of the value of zero was difficult for students to understand, and secondly she thanked the student who did bring up the idea to the class.

Teacher (40:20, J1-L7)

```
At this point, a compromise solution had been brought
up. By then, I realized how much the idea 'x should
always be bigger than zero, is hard for them to
understand.

I was pleased by those who brought up such solution. I
think this scene is very special for all the students,
and that is why I thought this is an important stage
of the lesson.
```

At E 8, the class seemed to understand the idea of the range of variable and exclusion of values in the semi-open interval: $0 < x \leqq 15$. This idea could combine two sequences. However it was not so easy. In fact, at E 9 for the range of y, three opinions came up: y=0, 24 and 12; and the students struggled to get the value of y as bigger than 24. Because of the time concern, the teacher decided to give an answer for the range of y.

Teacher (42:00, J1-L7)

```
Some students, like NO, would first write down zero,
and stop for a while and think it over again. At this
point, there was not much time left, so I thought I
shouldn't force them to understand now, but we could
take some time. So I decided to give them the answer
```

```
myself. I would combine all three ideas, and give
them the answer at last. I decided so by then.
```

The 7th lesson concluded by identifying the range of variables through two student voting activities and two demonstrations initially planned by the teacher, and finally one student's idea of exclusion of the value of zero. These events were identified by both the teacher and one or two students as important moments in the lesson. Although the teacher's identification of events was not exactly the same as the students', their considerations of the importance of the lesson seem to be quite consistent and to synchronize with each other.

DISCUSSION

The process of understanding the range of variables

The concept of variable has been discussed for a long time in the mathematics education community. The definition of variable given in the SMSG (School Mathematics Study Group) Student's Text was "the variable is a numeral which represents a definite though unspecified number from a given set of admissible numbers" (School Mathematics Study Group, 1960, p.37). Although the ideas of 'definite' and 'unspecified' appear to be contradictory, the concept of 'variable' needs to include these different aspects (Van Engen, 1961a,b). Based on interviews with Japanese, American and Philippine students, Fujii (2003) identified four levels, from 0 to 3, of understanding of literal symbols: Level 0 is where students have a vague conception of literal symbols. Level 1 is where the 'unspecified' aspect of variable is dominant. Typically students are saying "x can be any number because it's a variable." Level 2 is where the 'definite' aspect of variable appears to become dominant. However, students in Level 2 may have some misconceptions, such as that different letters must stand for different numbers. These students could focus on the 'definite' aspect of variable but they are not able to consider the 'unspecified' aspect at the same time. In Level 3, students are able to attend to both aspects of variable.

Students in the 7th lesson seemed to face these two conflicting aspects, the definite though unspecific aspect of variables, and they needed to integrate them when the difficulty arose. In consideration of the exact values of x and y, that is the first sequence at E2, E3 and E5, the definite aspect was dominant. And in plotting many points on the graph or putting finer numbers in the table, which was the second flow at E4 and E6, the unspecified aspect became dominant.

The concept of variable is related to the concept of the range of variable. In the lesson, when students discussed the value of y when x=15, they seemed to have no problem. Here the definite aspect was dominant, and it was easier for them to grasp the unspecified aspect as well. In other words, the variable x could be any number, but not beyond the value of 15. Generally speaking, the exact limitation makes it easier for us to understand the unspecified aspects. Fifteen is an exact number, definite indeed, so that students find it easier to understand the unspecified aspect of variable. On the other hand, in this particular lesson, the zero value of x was finally abandoned by the whole-class. The range of the variable x did not include the value of zero. Therefore, there was no number which told the students exactly 'not over that'. Variable x can be any number, however the lower limit of the range was unclear. Here the students needed to overcome their difficulties. In other words, it would have been easier them to understand the closed interval as the ranges of the independent and dependent variables as $0 \leq x \leq 15$ and $24 \leq y \leq 54$. However, the lessons dealt with semi-open intervals such as $0 < x \leq 15$ and $24 < y \leq 54$. This fact made it difficult for students to understand the range of a variable.

Refining the expressions of the range of variables: Progressive but a zigzag approach

At E8 and E9 in the 7th lesson, two sequences seemed to integrate or merge into one; in other words two aspects of the concept of variable, the 'definite' and 'unspecified' aspects, were combined. The value of zero as a solution was abandoned and the range of x turned out as $0 < x \leq 15$, then for y as $24 < y \leq 54$. However this sophisticated expression did not come up easily.

The expression concerning the range of the variable appeared in the 6th lesson when Student NO said, "From zero to seven point five, y is decreasing as x is increasing and from seven point five to fifteen, y is increasing as x is increasing". The teacher wrote what the student said on the blackboard, as shown in Figure 9. It is interesting to see that the range of variables was expressed in quite a vague manner as 0~7.5 and 7.5~15. (see Fig. 9)

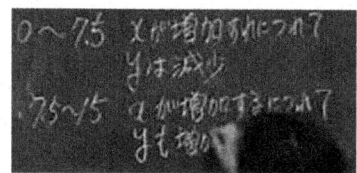

Fig. 9. The vague expression in the 6th lesson

At the beginning of the 7th lesson, the class spent 10 minutes finishing the task of the former lesson: "There is a rectangular parallelepiped which is seventy centimeters in depth, and there is water in it, thirty centimeters from the bottom. You pour water to the water surface at a specific rate (5 centimeters/ minute) every minute. After x minutes, the height of the water surface would be Y centimeters". In the 6th lesson, the class had taken about 7 minutes to identify the mathematical expression as y=5x +30. Then, in the 7th lesson, they tried to find out the variation for x and y and their ranges. These ranges were presented clearly, in a proper mathematical manner, as

$0 \leqq x \leqq 8$, $30 \leqq y \leqq 70$ by the teacher, saying "See, from now on, in this case, we could show it like this but, here, showing x varies from zero to eight by using a sign of inequality. Okay? " (07:56, J1-L7).

However, in the 7th lesson, the vague expression of the range of the variable returned again, when the class discussed the range of $y=2x+24$. In fact, the teacher wrote 0~15 on the blackboard (see Fig. 10). Finally she wrote an appropriate expression, as shown in Figure 12, saying, "Okay? So, he said that x should be bigger than zero. How do you express the variance of x? x is bigger than zero..., like this? [Writing "0<x" on the board]" (40:48, J1-L7)

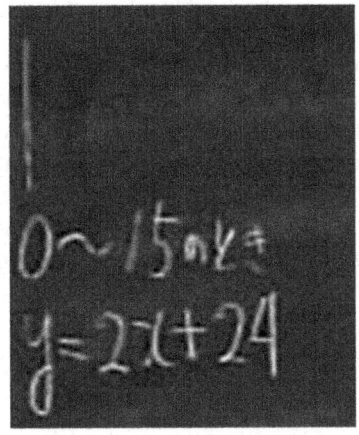

Fig.10

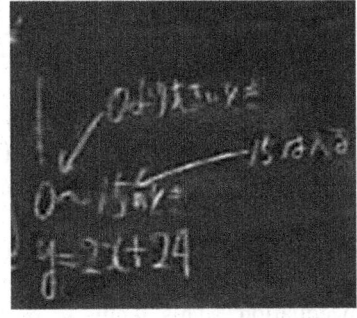

Fig. 11

143

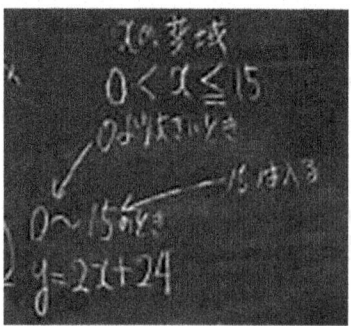

Fig. 12

After starting with a vague expression in the 6th lesson, then moving to a sophisticated one at the very beginning of the 7th lesson, and again a vague one at 40:48 minutes, finally an appropriate one was arrived at. The blackboard of the 7th lesson is shown in Figure 12, focusing on the expression of the range of the variable. The process of getting an appropriate mathematical expression seems to have been a progressive but rather zigzagging move to reach the goal. This fact also supports the notion that the concept of variable and concept of the range of a variable in a functional context is difficult for students to comprehend.

Community of mathematical inquiry

There is widespread agreement in many countries about the critical role played by progressive classroom discourse in whole-class lessons in the generation of new mathematical understandings. This study has analyzed what the teacher said in the post-lesson video-stimulated interview in order to see how she counted on the whole-class discussion as a key to the students' understanding of the teaching content. The whole-class discussion was the context in which the students' understanding was deepened. In order to make that happen, the teacher made particular moves when the students were working individually. For example, after she delivered the worksheet, she walked between the desks and monitored how the students were working; she thought this moment was important (Teacher: 15:00, J1-L7, see Table 1). In the post-lesson interview, the teacher said, "I could see how most of the students were doing by looking from the front of the class. But I could not see all the students, and it was hard to see how those who were most likely to be behind were doing. So I gave them the clear procedure of how to work on such problems, to see the table first because this seems to be the easiest representation; then interpret the graph, or see the table first then think about an equation." This seems to be a typical veteran teacher's behaviour. There is a term that describes this teacher's move in Japanese: *Kikan-*

jyunshi or *Kikan-shido*, translated into English as purposeful scanning or monitoring (Becker et al., 1990; Fujii, 1993).

One of the important roles of the *Kikan-jyunshi* or *Kikan-shido* is to bring individual students' ideas to the whole class. For example, in the 6th lesson, when the students were doing individual work, the teacher was walking between their desks. Then she approached student SH, who suggested the idea of y=24. Then, in the whole-class discussion SH's idea of y=24 came up. In the 7th lesson the teacher pointed out SH's idea again, even though he had not raised his hand. In the interview, the teacher said that she had deliberately pointed out SH's idea because she knew that he had an idea of y=24.

Teacher: (22:00,J1-L7)

```
Here, the students were to think about what y would
be when x is zero. I wanted to bring up some of the
opinions and examine each of them together with the
class. At this point, SH did not raise his hand, but I
knew he had twenty-four as the answer, which was very
important, so I brought up his idea on purpose, and
started thinking how to lead them to the conclusion.
```

Int:

```
So, before this scene, the class had the idea that
when x is zero, y should be zero, too. But you
purposely pulled out the opinion of y being twenty-
four, and made the whole class think this problem
over again. Right?
```

Teacher:

```
Yeah.
```

Kikan-jyunshi or *Kikan-shido* is one of the most important moves done by a teacher while each student is working individually, to elicit students' ideas and bring them forward for whole-class discussion. Bringing rich and potentially advanced ideas to the whole-class is a necessary condition for a rich whole-class discussion.

Another example from this study is concerned with student TA's idea. The teacher identified her idea during *Kikan-jyunshi* and made it open to the whole-class, saying, "Also, I saw that a number of you were having trouble with your graphs when I was going around. ... Wasn't it your group, TA? Could you maybe explain to the class? Yes, come up to the front." (00:32:36, J1-L5)

When the students' ideas were brought to the whole class, all of the students seemed to consider them seriously and to value them. Evidence of valuing others' ideas can also be found also in the teacher's talk, for example: "Well, as we did yesterday, write down someone's opinion in color." (19:14:03, J1-L7) Her purpose in saying this was to recommend writing down others' ideas. Valuing other students' ideas in whole-class lesson could constitute a community of inquiry supported by a prerequisite for whole-class lesson in Japan, as described by Lewis (1995, p.177): "all children, regardless of their academic achievement, are genuinely valued members".

The interpretation of the task offered by TA as Task B was considered continuously and in detail in the 6th and 7th lessons. This is a typical example of the students' ideas being treated with care and even drawn on to affect the content of the following lessons. In other words, sources of mathematical ideas, and the responsibility for learning, are left to the students (Hufferd-Ackles, Fuson, & Sherin, 2004).

Whole-class learning is not intended for individual benefit but to promote the progress of the whole class. The community of inquiry may require a progressive discourse to achieve a common level of whole-class thinking. More generally, to deepen understanding, we need to see "non A" constructing with "A" as "A" is your own idea. The J1 teacher gave an appropriate "non A" to the class, such as student UM's graph, the trapezoidal shape, to lead and create progress in the whole-class discussion about the density of the numbers, as shown by E4 and E6 in the 7th lesson.

Of the four phases of a lesson, the comparing and discussing phase is the most difficult part for a teacher to deal with. This is simply because the teacher may have to orchestrate the whole class properly to create a reflective discourse and to develop the students' mathematical understanding. This process is called *Neriage* in Japanese, which means carefully, meticulously polishing one's thought or creating a progressive discourse in the whole-class. Unsuccessful *Neriage* becomes only 'show and tell'. The post-lesson interview revealed the exact moment when the teacher made a decision, and she did consider that moment as important for the lesson, for example, as illustrated at E3 Ms. K (26:00) and E7 (40:00, J1-L7). The veteran teachers' behavior, which led to a rich and progressive whole-class discussion, was crystallized. In other words, the classroom culture and values were crystallized, such as the importance of moving beyond 'wrong' or 'correct' answers, listening carefully to friends' talk, and avoiding underestimating friends' ideas .

FINAL REMARKS

This paper has aimed to clarify students' understanding of variables focusing on lessons in which whole-class discussions occurred to decide the range of the independent variable in the context of linear function. The lessons focused in this paper were the 4th to 7th of ten consecutive 8th grade mathematics lessons from J1. The analysis has revealed an actual process of exploring the 'what' and 'how' of the students' conceptions of variables were, which were finally reconstructed through whole-class discussion.

It seems that the students' conceptions of variables observed in these lessons were based on the variable range illustrated by an origami paper folding activity. In particular, the definite aspect of the variable emerged in their consideration of the value of x when the folding point comes to the edge of the paper. Understanding the definite aspect of the variable made the unspecified aspect clearer, and this may have helped to lead the students to a deeper understanding of the range of variable. Some of the teacher's behaviors in the lessons are identified, and it seems that these behaviors contributed to the progress of the whole-class discussion. The teacher's behavior, which can be described in Japanese words such as *Kikan-jyunshi* and *Neriage,* played a critical role in deepening the students' understanding about the range of a variable that included both the "definite" and "unspecified" aspects of the variable.

NOTES

[1] The author acknowledges the valuable contribution of Dr. Tad Watanabe, Kennesaw State University, U.S.A. and Prof. Frederick K.S. Leung, The University of Hong Kong, Hong Kong.
[2] In the Japanese lower secondary school mathematics curriculum, technical terms such as 'domain,' 'co-domain,' and 'range' are not used. Rather, the curriculum uses the phrase 'range of a variable' to describe the set of all values a variable may assume. Since the teacher and the students in this study do not use the technical terms, the more general phrase of 'range of a variable' is used in this paper.

REFERENCES

Becker, J. P., Silver, E., Kantowski, M. G., Travers, K. J., & Wilson, J. W. (1990). Some observation of mathematics teaching in Japanese elementary and junior high schools. *Arithmetic Teacher,* 12–21.

Bednarz, N., Kieran, C., & Lee, L. (1996). Approach to algebra: perspectives for research and teaching. In *Approaches to Algebra.* Mathematics Education Library, Kluwer Academic Publishers.

Fujii, T. (1993). Japanese students' understanding of school mathematics focusing on elementary algebra. In G. Bell (Ed.), *Asian perspectives on mathematics education* (pp. 70–89). The Northern Rivers Mathematical Association, Lismore, NSW Australia.

Fujii, T. (2001). American students' understanding of algebraic expressions: focusing on the convention of interpreting literal symbols. *Journal of Science Education in Japan, 25*(3), 167–179.

Fujii, T. (2003). Probing students' understanding of variables through cognitive conflict problems: Is the concept of a variable so difficult for students to understand? *Proceedings of the 2003 Joint Meeting of PME and PMENA, 1,* 49–65.

Groves, S., & Doig, B. (2002). Developing conceptual understanding: The role of the task in communities of mathematical inquiry. In A. D. Cockburn & E. Nardi (Eds.), *Proceedings of the Twenty Sixth Conference of the International Group for the Psychology of Mathematics Education* (Vol. 2, pp. 25–32).

Hufferd-Ackles, K, Fuson, K. C., & Sherin, M. G. (2004). Describing levels and components of a math-talk learning community. *Journal for Research in mathematics Education, 35*(2), 81–116.

Kieran, C. (1992). The learning and teaching of school algebra. In D. Grouws (Ed.), *Handbook of research on mathematics teaching and learning* (pp. 390–419). New York, NY: Macmillan.

Lewis, C. C. (1995). *Educating hearts and minds: Reflection on Japanese preschool and elementary education.* Cambridge: Cambridge University Press.

School Mathematics Study Group. (1960). First Course in Algebra Part I, p.37.

Shimizu, Y.(2006). Discrepancies in perceptions of mathematics lessons between the teacher and the students in a japanese classroom. In *Mathematics Classrooms in Twelve Countries: The Insider's Perspective.* Sense Publishers.

Stigler, J., & Hiebert, J. (1999). *The teaching gap: Best ideas from the world's teachers for improving education in the classroom.* New York, NY: The Free Press.

Takahashi, A., Watanabe, T., & Yoshida, M. (2004). *Elementary school teaching guide for the japanese course of study: Arithmetic (Grade 1-6)*. Madison, NJ: Global Education Recourses.
Usiskin, Z. (1988). Conceptions of school algebra and use of variables. In A. F. Coxford (Ed.), *The Ideas of Algebra, K-12, 1988 Yearbook*. Reston, VA: National Council of Teacher of Mathematics.
Van Engen, H. (1961a). A note on "Variable". *The Mathematics Teacher* March, 172–173.
Van Engen, H. (1961b). On "Variable"_a rebuttal. *The Mathematics Teacher* March, 175–177.
Watanabe, T. (2007). Algebra in elementary school: A Japanese perspective. *Algebra and Algebraic Thinking in School Mathematics, Seventieth Yearbook*, National Council of Teachers of Mathematics.

AFFILIATION

Toshiakira Fujii
Department of Mathematics Education
Tokyo Gakugei University
Japan

ZHONGDAN HUAN, JIANHUA LI, PING MA & LI FU

CHAPTER 9

Understanding the Current Beijing Classrooms Through Linear Inequalities Teaching

INTRODUCTION

The mathematics classroom in Mainland China has been changing dramatically since the end of the last century (Liu & Li, 2010). A new mathematics curriculum was designed based on research studies, including the analysis of the achievements and problems of Chinese mathematics education, and comparisons of the mathematics curriculum and its development with those of other education systems. In July 2001, the China *Mathematics Curriculum Standard for Full-time Compulsory Education (experimental version)* (hereafter *CMCS*) (MOE, 2001) was issued (Ma, Zhao, & Li 2010). All schools have implemented the CMCS since September 2005.

Two surveys collecting feedback on the CMCS from Chinese mathematics teachers were conducted in 2003 and 2005 by the Ministry of Education of China (Ma, Zhao, & Li 2010). From these surveys the level of agreement among the sampled teachers regarding the concept and objectives of the new curriculum was found to be very high (96% in 2003 to 72% in 2005) and the level of disagreement very low (0.1% in 2003 and 3% in 2005). In the 2003 survey, more than 78% of the sample teachers acknowledged the achievability of the concept and the objectives. A later study in one province (Lv & Guo 2008) showed 90% agreement with the concept. There have also been several studies about the conception of the new curriculum, for example, the instructional structure of a mathematics classroom (Tang, 2010), and concept instruction (Wei, 2010). There have also been many articles in local pedagogy journals devoted to teaching design following the requirements in CMCS.

It appears that all of the above studies have been from the viewpoints of teachers and experts, specifically their understanding of the concept of the CMCS and practical experiences or idealized teaching designs according to the CMCS requirements.

In this chapter, we describe our attempts to understand a Beijing Grade 7 classroom, which was videotaped in March and April of 2006 in a prestigious high school in Beijing, when the new CMCS had been in place for about five years. The requirements in the China Mathematics Curriculum Standard were used as the basis for understanding the teaching.

China's primary and secondary education is standards-based. It is compulsory for all Chinese mathematics teachers to adopt the new mathematics curriculum

F.K.S. Leung et al. (eds.), Algebra Teaching around the World, 149–171.
© *2014 Sense Publishers. All rights reserved.*

standards, decreed in July, 2001. In each school, there are mathematics teaching research groups which help every teacher to understand the standards and to exemplify their implementation in each topic (Yang, 2009). Thus, a model that is developed for one classroom, especially in a key school such as the one studied here, can possibly be claimed as representative of the current situation in China.

In this chapter, we will present the teaching in a Beijing Grade 7 classroom in the light of the CMCS requirements. The mathematics content illustrated here is linear inequalities.

The research was based on ten Beijing lessons videotaped in March and April of 2006, when the new CMCS had been in place for about five years. Our study addressed the following two issues in the teaching of linear inequalities:

1. Is the mathematics content aligned well with that of the CMCS? How is the alignment realized? What are the reasons for misalignment?
2. Are the pedagogy and student learning aligned well with those intended in the CMCS? How is the alignment manifested? What are the differences between the intended and implemented curricula, and what are the reasons for these differences?

There were three steps in the study:

Step 1. The ten lesson videotapes were analysed to determine the extent to which the CMCS policies were embodied in the instruction.

Step 2. Based on the analysis in Step 1, the researchers interviewed the teacher to understand her pedagogical concepts, strategies, and routines.

Step 3. The results of the analysis were collated into the Content Alignment Table 1 and the Pedagogical Alignment Table 2 (see appendices).

This chapter is organized into three parts. The first part, including Sections 2 and 3, discusses the alignment of curriculum and pedagogy; the second part, including Section 4, presents the main conclusion and comments; and the last part, consisting of the two alignment tables, includes the main information supporting this study. We have used 'the lesson' to stand for 'the videotaped lessons', for brevity.

ON ALIGNMENT OF MATHEMATICAL CONTENT

For the topic of linear inequalities, the CMCS requires the instructor to achieve the following goals:

1. Students can understand the meaning of inequalities through concrete relations of magnitudes (A1) and explore basic properties of inequalities (A2);
2. Students can solve linear inequalities and locate solution sets on the number axis (B1). They can also determine solution sets of systems of linear inequalities on the number axis (B2);
3. Students can identify linear inequalities in a concrete situation and solve simple problems (C).

We classified the requirements into five items, labelled A1, A2, B1, B2, and C, respectively. The lessons show that all the requirements were met and the levels achieved were higher than expected.

The alignment of the lessons and those of CMCS in content

The content of the lessons was basically consistent with the content required in the CMCS. The ten lessons can be divided into four parts, (1) inequalities and their properties (Lessons 1 and 2); (2) methods of solving a linear inequality (Lessons 3-5); (3) application problems involving linear inequalities (Lessons 6-8); and (4) a system of linear equalities and its applications (Lessons 9-10). The details can be found in Table 1: Curricular Alignment in the appendix.

Modification of some content standards due to students and SHSEE

There were three main modifications made to the lessons.

The CMCS only requires students to be 'able to solve simple linear inequalities'. The teacher raised this to the level of 'being able to solve linear inequalities.' Her reason for doing this was the reality that students have to be able to solve linear inequalities both quickly and correctly in school examinations and the Senior High School Entrance Examination (SHSEE). The teacher strived to develop a conventional stepwise solution method and an acceptable level of routine manipulation in order to achieve high speed and high scores in various examinations.

The content of the LMR (Left Minus Right) method and parametric inequalities is supposed to be taught in senior high school and is not required in the CMCS, which only refers to the years of compulsory schooling. Because of the high level of mathematics proficiency of the students in the school that we studied, this more advanced content was added to the lessons.

The system of linear inequalities and its applications are required content in the CMCS, but not required in the SHSEE. The teacher believed that the topic might help to develop the students' mathematics reading and understanding, which were emphasized in the lessons.

The CMCS is a governmental document, which determines the basic requirements for all students in the country. In Beijing schools, the students are taught well and teachers are allowed to increase contents and requirements. Another reason for doing this is the need to prepare for the various examinations, in particular the SHSEE. Teachers try to train students to solve related problems quickly and correctly.

A well-organized and spiral teaching design

In order to train students to solve linear equalities efficiently, the teacher emphasized normative steps and the format of inequality solving. In each lesson, every discovered error, such as an incorrect sign change, parentheses removal, or a missed multiplication, would be discussed and then compensatory exercises would be assigned as homework. At the beginning of each lesson, the teacher would comment on the students' homework and analyse typical mistakes.

For example, in Lesson 3, the teacher discussed mistakes in the following homework problems: (1) x^2___0; (2) Is "$x>4$" the solution set of "$x+3>6$"? (3) Do "$m>n$" and $a=b$" imply "$am>bn$"? The teacher emphasized that students must be able to distinguish between solutions of an inequality from the solution set of the inequality. In Lesson 5, the errors discussed included: (1) a solution set was not marked on the number axis; (2) the number axis or a segment was drawn without using a ruler; (3) any of three elements of the number axis was missed; (4) the solution of an inequality could not end with $9x - 6 > 9x-7$. Further discussion of these errors was needed.

The teacher considerately designed examples and exercises in class and the students accepted spiral training, so that they had sufficient practice opportunities to understand linear inequalities and their applications. Spiral training is a type of pedagogical progression consisting of several 'similar' connected processes, each of which handles the same topic but with higher and higher task levels. The reader is referred to the examples in Lessons 1 and 2 in both tables in the appendix.

After systematic training of this type, the students were able to utilize mathematics symbols and to write a solution with clear steps, and appeared to have mastery of methods of solving linear inequalities.

ON THE ALIGNMENT IN PEDAGOGY

In relation to pedagogy, the CMCS tells instructors that mathematics teaching is a process of interaction and development between teachers and students. The CMCS requires instructors to:

1. Let students go through processes of formation and application of mathematics knowledge;
2. Encourage students to self-explore and to cooperate with others;
3. Respect students' differences and satisfy a range of students' needs;
4. Pay close attention to necessities, basic processes, and basic methods of proof;
5. Emphasize the connections within mathematical knowledge and improve students' problem-solving abilities; and
6. Utilize information technology wherever possible.

The pedagogical analysis was based on the first two lessons. Similar strategies were employed in the other lessons. The teaching of linear inequalities contains no proofs, so requirement (4) need not be discussed. The question of pedagogical alignment cannot be judged by a simple 'yes' or 'no', it should be demonstrated through examples of real classroom activities. The detailed descriptions are given in Table 2: Pedagogical Alignment in the appendix, in which the six requirements (above) are labelled as D1 to D6.

The pedagogies for students to go through processes of formation and application of mathematics knowledge

The pedagogies took two forms: motivating the concept by real-world examples (in Lesson 1) and producing new knowledge from the old by analogy (in Lesson 2):

The concept of unequal relations was introduced by examples such as the children's seesaw and husking rice mortar and pestle, while the concepts of an inequality and its solution set were illustrated by a distance-velocity problem.

The properties of inequalities were formulated by comparison with those of equalities. The students participated in the process of 'guess and verification'.

Encouragement of student's self-explorations

Self-exploration was initiated either by a challenging problem from the teacher, or an interesting question from a student. After a problem or question was given, the teacher would guide the students to explore step-by-step. She gave them enough time to think about the problem. A student could discuss the problem with other students or within a group. After this, one student was asked to solve the problem in front of the class, others commented on the solution and the teacher assisted the students to achieve better solutions.

Before the concept of an inequality was defined formally, the students were encouraged to formulate their own definitions of inequalities by mimicking the definition of equalities.

In the discussion of 'filling the blank with the appropriate unequal sign', which included $<, >, \leq, \geq$, or $\neq$, in $(-3)^4 \_\_ 3^4$, one student asked if all correct sign should be employed, for example, $3<5$, $3\leq5$, or $3\neq5$. This induced a discussion among students and the teacher.

The discussion was carried out mainly among the whole class. The teacher explained that her main concern was effective cooperation among students. She described an effective instructional method as one in which one student presents a solution and the other students comment, either positively, or interrogatively, so that a modified or new argument is raised. In terms of involvement and effectiveness in the classroom, the teacher expressed the belief that superficial active discussion in randomly selected groups is ineffective, since students feel new to each other, which distracts their attention from the discussion and exploration. Thus she only adopted group discussion for word problems in Lessons 5, 7, and 10.

Respecting students' differences and satisfying a range of students' needs

To fulfil the requirement of respecting students' differences and satisfying various students' needs, the teacher adopted two approaches: (1) providing exercises of tasks arranged in hierarchical levels so that each student could find a starting point; (2) asking students questions designed to reach their ability and understanding levels so that each student was involved in class discussion.

153

After each topic was introduced, the teacher would provide exercises of different difficulty levels. For example, after the inequality properties were set up, she gave the students three groups of exercises. The problems in the first group were direct applications of the properties of inequalities; the problems in the second were designed to move the students towards a general strategy of handling inequalities; and those in the third contained more manipulations.

Group 1. Suppose a<b, then, (1) a-3 ____ b-3; (2) a+4 ____ b+4; (3) 7a ____ 7b; (4) -2a ____ -2b; (5) 7a+6 ____ 7a-6.

Group 2. Suppose a<b then, (1) a-b ____ 0; (2) a+5b ____ b+5b; (3) a/2-b___b/2-b; (4) a+5b ____ 6b; (5) a/2-b ____ -b/2.

Group 3. Suppose x>1, then, (1) 7x ____ 7; (2) 7x ____ 24-2-15; (3) 10x+2-24 ____ 3x-15p; (4) (5x+1)/6-2 ____ (3x-5)/4.

While the students were answering questions, the teacher listened to their answers patiently and commented positively so that they felt confident to be able to achieve a suitable solution. In general, the teacher would ask the slow students first and postpone the participation of the quick students, to encourage the former to think carefully and to avoid simple mistakes.

Emphasizing the connections among mathematics knowledge and raising students' problem-solving abilities Both the concept and the properties of inequalities were established by analogizing the counterpart of equalities. For example, in the establishment of the properties, the teacher listed the properties of equalities with students, namely,

Suppose a=b, then, (1) b=a; (2) a+c=b+c; (3) ac=bc; (4) a/c=b/c, if c≠0;

(5) if b=c, then, a=c.

After listing these, she worked with the students to check if an analogue would hold when the equal sign '=' was replaced by the greater than sign '>'. They finished the discussion by present the properties of > inequalities:

Suppose a>b, then, (1) b<a; (2) a+c>b+c; (3) ac>bc, if c>0;

(4) a/c>b/c, if c>0; (5) if b>c, then, a>c.

To achieve the goal of improving her students' problem-solving abilities, the teacher prepared application, or word problems, which were rather sophisticated and were decomposed into a few sub-problems. It should be clarified here that these sophisticated problems were designed by the teacher and the students had not encountered them in the class before.

Utilization of information technology

The teacher used *PowerPoint (PPT)* and visualizers. *PowerPoint* was used for long statements, such as examples and exercises, and background materials. The visualizer was suitable for presenting students' exercise books and handwritten solutions.

The teacher did not use software (for example Geometer's Sketchpad) to help the students understand the mathematical concepts or display the formation of knowledge. In other words, she used some kind of information technology in the class, but did not use technology to design any specific courseware to enhance the students' understand. In fact, we think she should have used software to improve the teaching and she could have followed the requirement better. However, she did not think the use of software was necessary, and the CMCS leaves the choice about this to individual teachers. The teacher believed that she did well and followed the requirement.

CONCLUSIONS AND COMMENTS

Based on the analysis on the videotape lessons and the interview with the instructor, we can draw the following conclusions.

1. All the requirements regarding content and pedagogy in the CMCS were complied with in the ten Beijing lessons; the teacher strived to follow these requirements strictly.

    The instruction was well-organized and responsive. The lessons usually started with a ten-minute review of the previous lesson, then an evaluation of the graded homework, new content instruction and exercises, summarization, and the assignment of homework.

    After each topic was introduced, a series of hierarchically stratified exercises was given to develop the students' mathematics proficiency; different students started at different points in the hierarchy according to their needs and abilities. This is the way the teacher attempted to accommodate the students' differences and needs.

    The teacher would typically model how to decompose each complicated mathematics object or problem into several sub-problems. This modelled reasoning process was her basic strategy to enable the students to experience the process of forming and applying their mathematics knowledge.

    The connections within mathematics knowledge were revealed mainly by analogizing new knowledge with the old, and the students' problem-solving abilities were developed by using sophisticated word or application problems.

    The systematic training with respect to each mathematics concept, technique, and idea was still central to the instruction in the Beijing lessons; in other words, the instruction still followed the same principles as before.

2. The mathematics content of the lessons generally exceeded the requirements of the CMCS. This was partially due to the tradition of Chinese mathematics education and partially due to the need to prepare for examinations, in particular the SHSEE. All Chinese parents want their children to achieve high scores and to be accepted

into the best senior high schools. In attempting to meet this expectation, Chinese schools and teachers will teach beyond curricular expectations.

3. The CMCS adopted many pedagogical strategies originating from some western cultures. However, teachers in China have not yet built up the experience required to use these strategies effectively, so it is not surprising that their implementation of these strategies are not impressive. For example, in this study, the student's self-exploration and cooperation with others were guided by problems from teacher, which was similar to the traditional exercise in class. The form of cooperation was that one student presented his solution and others commented.

In the interview with the instructor, the instructor told the researchers that she was not confident to carry out these strategies, in particular, how to reveal connections between mathematics knowledge and to raise the student's problem-solving abilities. She thought that she had done well in catering for the students' differences and addressing their various needs, as well as in encouraging them to self-explore and to cooperate with others.

4. Superficially, it appeared that the teacher followed or complied strictly with all of the relevant CMCS requirements. All the CMCS innovations were realized formally in the classroom. The students' participation in the teaching-learning process was impressive - questions and (group) discussion were the main driving force in the classroom. From this point of view, the CMCS was complied with perfectly in the classroom.

On the other hand, the teacher followed the strategies conceptually, and she was not confident about how to realize them. None of the activities were new, but they had new names: self-exploration, cooperation, respecting students' differences and satisfying a range of students' needs. This kind of phenomenon is quite natural since the CMCS was created at this level (Ma, Zhao, & Li, 2010).

Therefore, the lessons described in this article can be considered a comprehensive model of CMCS pedagogy. It is definitely encouraging that the teacher paid conscious attention to the students' esteem and development.

5. Chinese people have a long tradition of accepting the examination as the instrument for social selection. High scores have been the final endpoint of all teaching and learning. In the lessons studied in this article, the senior high school entrance examination played a crucial role. All parents and students are watching the scores achieved by various schools, which means that the achievement of these scores is the life line of teachers as well as of the schools. Thus it is necessary for curriculum standards to be adjusted to take this into account.

REFERENCES

Liu, J., & Li, Y. (2010). Mathematics curriculum reform in the Chinese mainland: Changes and challenges. In F. K. S. Leung, & Y. Li, (Eds.), *Reforms and issues in school mathematics in East Asia*. Rotterdam, The Netherlands: Sense Publishers.

Lv, S., & Guo X. (2008), Survey on the new mathematics curriculum implementation of 7-9 Grade in Gansu Province (in Chinese). *Journal of Mathematics Education, 17*.

Ma, Y., Zhao, D., & Li, Y. (2010). The Mathematics Curriculum Reform of Nine-year Compulsory Education in the Chinese Mainland: Progress and Issues, In Mathematics Education: perspectives and practices in the East and West, *Mathematics Bulletin-a Journal for Educators.*

MOE. (2002). *China Mathematics Curriculum Standards for Full-time Compulsory Education,* (in Chinese) People's Education Publisher.

Tang, Z. (2010). A sketch discussion on the instructional structure of middle school mathematics classroom under the principle of the new curriculum (in Chinese). *China Education Innovation Herald, 33.*

Wei, X. (2010). Research mathematical concept instruction under the principle of the new curriculum (in Chinese), *Mathematics Instruction and Research, 28.*

Yang, Y. (2009). How a Chinese teacher improved classroom teaching in Teaching Research Group: A case study on Pythagoras theorem teaching in Shanghai. *ZDM—The International Journal on Mathematics Education, 41,* 279–296.

AFFILIATIONS

Zhongdan Huan
School of Mathematical Sciences
Beijing Normal University
China

Jianhua Li
School of Mathematical Sciences
Beijing Normal University
China

Ping Ma
The High School affiliated to Renmin University of China
Beijing
China

Li Fu
School of Education
Beijing Normal University
China

APPENDIX: ALIGNMENT TABLES

This appendix includes two "alignment tables," which contain the essential information providing the evidence for the study.

Table 1 provides information on the alignment of the mathematics content and Table 2 provides information on the alignment of pedagogy.

Table 1 consists of four columns. The first shows the requirements listed in the CMCS, the second shows where each requirement was illustrated in the videotaped classes, the third shows the teacher's pedagogical conceptions and the fourth sets out the alignment analyses done by the researchers. The analysis in Table 1 is based on all ten lessons.

In the table, we use the following symbols:

A1: Students can understand the meaning of inequalities through concrete relations of magnitudes;

A2: Explore basic properties of inequalities;

B1: Students can solve linear inequalities and locate solution sets on the number axis.

B2: They can also determine solution sets of systems of linear inequalities on the number axis;

C: Students can identify linear inequalities in a concrete situation and solve simple problems.

Table 2 is based on an analysis of the first two lessons. The table consists of three columns; the first is the requirements listed in CMCS, which are labelled as follows:

D1: Let students go through processes of formation and application of mathematics knowledge;

D2: Encourage students to self-explore and to cooperate with others;

D3: Respect students' differences and satisfy the full range of students' needs;

D4: Pay close attentions to necessities, basic processes, and basic methods of proofs;

D5: Emphasize the connections within mathematics knowledge and improve students' problem-solving abilities;

D6: Use information technology wherever possible.

The second and the third columns contain information drawn from Lessons 1 and 2, respectively.

Each of the last two columns contains three sub-columns:

1. The first sub-column presents the classroom embodiments of each requirement in the CMCS in the videotaped class (Lesson);
2. The second shows the teacher's pedagogical conceptions (Teacher);
3. The third shows the analyses made by the researchers (Analyses).

In Table 2, the reader will see how the teacher showed her conception by a variety of behaviors in the classroom. After interviews with the teacher, the author realized her idea behind her teaching activities, which is given in the 'teacher' columns. The first two lessons are sufficient to show the basic teaching strategy, pedagogical mode, and methods of class control.

Table 1. Curricular Alignment

CMCS	Embodiments	Pedagogical conceptions	Alignment analyses
A1	**Lesson 1** Introduced unequal relations by examples of seesaw and husking rice with mortar and pestle. Attained the concept from a distance-velocity problem.	Obtaining the concept of inequalities from daily examples is a process of mathematization.	The introduction followed A1 and attained the conception from daily examples.
	Asked students to fill the blanks by "<" or ">", such as, $(-3)^4\_\_3^4$; $\|-0.5\|\_\_\|-1000\|$; $6\times(-3)\_\_4\times(-3)$. Did exercises converting word statements to symbolic expressions (three groups of total 22 problems), such as: a is a nonnegative number; 4 times x is not bigger than 7; The difference between $y/2$ and 3 is negative.	The instructional challenge is how to achieve the transformation from words to symbols successfully. The three groups of exercises help students to achieve the transformation step-by-step.	Students' understanding was promoted by systematic training in the completion of problems of increasing degrees of difficulty.
A2	**Lesson 2** The exploration of basic properties of inequalities was initiated using the problem If the equation $(5x+1)/6=(x-5)/4$ is converted to $(5x+1)/6>(x-5)/4$ how can it be solved? First recalled the basic properties of equalities: (1) $a=b$ implies $a+c=b+c$ for any c; (2) $a=b$ implies $ac=bc$ for $c>0$. Imitate properties of equalities to generate those of inequalities: $a>b$ implies $a+c>b+c$ for any c and $ac>bc$ for $c>0$.	The keyword of this part is 'exploration'. Analogy with the properties of equalities assists students to explore those of inequalities.	For basic properties, the teacher used properties of equalities to assist students to explore those of inequalities.
	Based on the properties, do blank-filling exercises such as: When $a<b$, $\tilde{a}-3\_\_\tilde{b}-3$ and $\tilde{a}/2-b\_\_-b/2$(three groups, 14 problems)	Students need a process of exercises and games to understand the basic properties of inequalities.	Students' understanding and mastering of the manipulation of inequalities were enforced by multi-level exercises and self-explorations.

Table 1. Continued

CMCS	Embodiments	Pedagogical conceptions	Alignment analyses
B1	Lesson 1 Concluded with the concept of solution set of an inequality and its representation.	The content of solution sets and their number axis representation is a basis for students' discussion.	The concept of Solution Set is the basis for solving inequalities.
	Lesson 2 After introducing the properties and completing exercises, the teacher asked each student to make up two inequality problems based on the properties.	The requirement B1 that students can solve linear inequalities in everyday problems is not enough. 'Solving correctly' is the key.	The teacher increased the requirement from being able to solve simple linear inequalities to being able to solve linear inequalities in general, in order to ensure that students can solve linear inequalities correctly and thereby obtain high scores in exams.
	Lesson 3 Solved simple inequalities $-3x<0$ and $8x+1\leq5x-3$ by showing students which of the properties were utilized. After analyzing four problems from students, the teacher pointed out the basic steps of solving inequalities and the possible traps in solving. Assigned a take-home test on the solution of inequalities.	To achieve that purpose, students have to master the normative steps of solving linear inequalities. First of all, it is necessary to specify the normative steps and format when teachers show examples to students; Then, students are asked to follow the steps and use the required format when they do exercises and homework. In this way, students will develop a habit of solving problems normatively and reduce the occurrence of mistakes.	

Table 1. Continued

CMCS	Embodiments	Pedagogical conceptions	Alignment analyses
	Lesson 4 Introduced the LMR (Left Minus Right) method and parametric inequalities. Problem 1. If $x<1/2$, compare the magnitude between $2-4x$ and $18x-9$. After asking students to discuss different solutions, the teacher proposed the LMR method.	Although the LMR method and parametric inequalities are not required by the CMCS and SHSEE, they are important when students learn the analogue part in senior high school. The two topics are appropriate to promote mathematical thinking. Learning is a spiral process. It is good for students to see these topics earlier in their education. Another reason for doing this, in this context, is because the students in the school are above the average.	The teacher added the extra topic for high potential students without hesitation.
	Then, she asked students to solve the following two problems individually. Problem 2. If $x>y$, compare the magnitude between $4x+8y$ and $3x+9y$. Problem 3. If $m>2$, solve the inequality $(1-m)x>m-1)$ for x.		
	Lesson 5 Replaced the condition $m>2$ in Problem 3 of Lesson 4 with $m\leq1$, $m>n$ (n is an integer), $m>0.5$, $m<2$, and $m\geq0$ Assigned homework: A set of problems to be solved by LMR. Proposed a general method for solving parametric inequalities; then, asked students to solve the inequality $ax>b$ individually. Assigned a set of parametric inequalities problems (a sheet of problems designed by the teacher).		

Table 1. Continued

CMCS	Embodiments	Pedagogical conceptions	Alignment analyses
B2	Lesson 9 First asked students to solve the following inequalities (1) $2x - 1 > -x$ (2) $0.5x < 3$ (3) $3x - 2 < x + 1$ (4) $x + 5 > 4x + 1$ and systems $\begin{cases} 2x - 1 > -x \\ 0.5x < 3 \end{cases}$ Then suggested that students propose the general steps for solving a system of inequalities. Then asked students to do eight problems of this type. Summarized the steps for solving a system of inequalities. Assigned homework: A set of problems of system of inequalities (a sheet of problems designed by the teacher). Lesson 10 Reviewed the solution steps formulated in Lesson 9 and obtained the solution method: If $a > b$ $\begin{cases} x > a \\ x > b \end{cases} \Rightarrow x > a$ $\begin{cases} x < a \\ x < b \end{cases} \Rightarrow x < b$ $\begin{cases} x < a \\ x > b \end{cases} \Rightarrow b < x < a$ $\begin{cases} x > a \\ x < b \end{cases} \Rightarrow$ Then gave out four rhymes for the four cases of the solution set: Two bigger take bigger; two smaller take smaller; bigger and smaller, or smaller and bigger take sandwich; smaller and smaller, or bigger and bigger take none. Assigned homework of four exercises designed by the teacher.	The students already know linear inequalities rather well so they are able to learn the solution of a system of linear equalities. The focus at this part is to normalize their solution steps.	The teacher emphasized the connection between inequalities and systems and proposed solution steps with plenty of student participation.

Table 1. Continued

CMCS	Embodiments	Pedagogical conceptions	Alignment analyses
C	Lesson 6 Discussed the word problem: There is a kind of commodity on sale in shop A and shop B. If one buys the commodity from shop A, one will get 10% off for the part above 100 dollars; on the other hand, if one buys the commodity from shop B, one will get 5% off for the part above 50 dollars. How should customers choose the shop for their best buy? Students found it difficult to deal with the problem. The teacher formulated four variations: (1) There are four customers, who want to spend 40, 80, 140, and 160 dollars, respectively. How should each customer choose between Shop A and Shop B? (2) If a customer plans to spend more than 100 dollars, should the customer choose Shop A? (3) How much should a customer spend in order for Shop A to be the better choice? (4) Design a table of choices to save more. After the discussion of the solutions of these sub-problems, the teacher formulated a general procedure to approach this kind of problem: (1) set the unknown, (2) formulate equalities, (3) solve the equalities, and (4) explain the answer.	The target in the instruction of word problems or application problems is to develop students' mathematical reading ability, namely, the ability to convert ordinary word language to mathematical symbolic language. The solution of the problem is achieved through its four variations, which become more and more abstract. The normalization of solution steps is still an emphasis.	The requirement in the CMCS for word problems is rather high. On the other hand, the SHSEE and school exams require little about systems of inequalities. How to handle such topics is tricky. The teacher claimed that the word problems in SHSEE possess so much material to read that many students fail to read rather than fail to know how to solve the problems. She believed that word problems relating to linear inequality and its systems can help students to develop their mathematics reading ability and help them to focus attention on the topic.

Table 1. Continued

CMCS	Embodiments	Pedagogical conceptions	Alignment analyses
	Assigned a word problem as homework: Shop A and Shop B sell the same type of teapots and teacups. The prices of the two shops are the same: Teapots are 20 dollars each and teacups are 5 dollars each. If you buy a teapot from Shop A, you will get a teacup for free, while you will get 8% off for the teapots and teacups you buy from Shop B. Now a customer plans to buy 4 teapots and a few, at least 4, teacups; which shop should he choose?		
	Lesson 7 Analysed the errors that appeared in students' homework. Gave students suggestions about solving word problems: (1) Read the problem carefully; and (2) Focus on the background of the problem. Then asked students to present their solutions to the word problem assigned at the end of Lesson 6. Re-emphasized the basic steps and those parts where it is easy to make mistakes.	The normalization of solution steps is the emphasis.	

Table 1. Continued

CMCS	Embodiments	Pedagogical conceptions	Alignment analyses
	Lesson 10		
	Formulated the solution steps to		
	solve word problems:		
	(1) Determine the unknowns		
	(according to the need);		
	(2) Figure out unequal relations;		
	(3) Set up inequalities or system;		
	(4) Solve the inequalities or system;		
	(5) Analyze and explain the result		
	through the word problem		
	Problem 1. A group of traveling		
	boys went to a hotel. If four boys		
	stayed in each room, there would be		
	19 of them with no place to stay; if		
	six boys stayed in each room, there		
	would be one room not occupied		
	fully. What are the possible numbers		
	of rooms and boys?		
	After the discussion, the teacher		
	assigned two other similar problems		
	for students to do in class.		
	Homework was assigned at the end		
	of the class (a sheet of problems		
	designed by the teacher).		

Table 2. Pedagogical Alignment

CMCS	Lesson 1 (Concept of Inequalities)			Lesson2 (Properties of Inequalities)		
	Lesson	*Teacher*	*Analyses*	*Lesson*	*Teacher*	*Analyses*
D1	Recalled child's seesaws together with students; Showed students pictures of mortar- pestle and tools for drawing water from a well; Let students explore a quasi-real problem.	Select less artificial quasi-real problems with math contents.	The math concept was introduced through recalling and exploring quasi-real matters.	Analogized with the solution of equations to assist students in solving inequalities. Furthermore, asked students to infer possible properties of inequalities.	Used students' known knowledge to introduce new knowledge.	The teacher expected that students might progress through the formation of mathematics knowledge (inequalities). The students saw both the connections between equalities and inequalities, and the method of analogical reasoning.
	Gave thirty problems to do successively and interactively. The problems varied from filling blanks to converting a statement to an inequality.	These exercises were designed to develop students' math basics with groups of 3-5 problems.	Develop students' understanding of unequal relations and inequalities by comparison and unequal symbols to unequal relations and their math expressions: inequalities. Train students' to manipulate inequalities.	Gave students three groups of problems (14 in total) to complete and to comment.	Design different groups of problems to develop students' abilities and ways of thinking. The groups of problems with increasing levels were planned to train students to form a strategy for solving inequalities, to prepare them for the later lessons.	The three groups of problems possessed clearly different levels of difficulty, from a few manipulations, such as when a<b, compare 7a with 7b (first group), to compare a+5b and 6b (second group), then to compare (5x+1)/6-2 and (3x-5)/4 (third group). After doing the problems, students experienced the application of new knowledge. Meanwhile, when students were doing the problem a-b__0, the teacher suggested the LMR (Left Minus Right) method.

Table 2. Continued

CMCS	Lesson 1 (Concept of Inequalities)			Lesson2 (Properties of Inequalities)		
	Lesson	*Teacher*	*Analyses*	*Lesson*	*Teacher*	*Analyses*
D2	Gave students word problems and guided them to explore the solution.	Effectiveness is the teacher's main concern for cooperation among students. She believes that an effective way is that one student presents, the other's comment, either positively, or interrogatively, so that a modified or new argument will be raised. She did not adopt the form of randomly selected groups.	Exploration and cooperation were carried out in the whole class.	Asked students to solve (5x+1)/6 -2=(x-5)/4 and to write down each property of equalities. Then asked students how to solve the analogous inequality, say, (5x+1)/6 -2>(x-5)/4.	The expectation is to develop in students a habit of "arguing by reasons" through self-exploration.	The connections between equations and inequalities help students to have more sense of inequalities and to learn "arguing by reasons" consciously by self-exploration.
	Invited students to give definitions of an inequality.		Several students tried to give a definition and to modify each other's definitions. After the teacher's summation, the class reached a proper math definition.	Asked students to propose properties of inequalities by drawing analogies with the properties of equalities.	The students should be able to generate many properties and to rationalize the properties without teacher assistance.	The pedagogical approach was made possible by previous preparation. Students were encouraged to derive properties of inequalities appropriately from those of equalities, which helped students to sharpen their thinking and written abilities.
	In the discussion for filling the blank by a proper unequal sign, which includes <, >, ≤, ≥, or ≠, in (-3)⁴ __ 3⁴, one student asked if all possible correct signs should be filled, for example, 3<5, 3≤5, or 3≠5. This prompted a discussion among students and the teacher.		Students were actively involved in the class, or in the group discussion to determine which sign(s) were correct. The teacher guided the discussion and reached the best result. In the process of discussion, students were getting the meaning of inequalities.	At the end of the lesson, the teacher asked students to design two problems of inequalities at different levels of difficulty on their own and to explain their design ideas and standards for good problems.	The teacher classified the situations proper to group work and cooperation into three types, (1) operational content; (2) very difficult problems; (3) exploration. The assignment of designing problems is in the third type: Allow students to have sufficient imaginary space.	Students' designation of problems put them in the position of an examiner and made them study voluntarily. At the same time they had to go over as many properties of inequalities as they could, which aimed to deepen their understanding of the relevant mathematical knowledge.

Table 2. Continued

CMCS	Lesson 1 (Concept of Inequalities)			Lesson2 (Properties of Inequalities)		
	Lesson	Teacher	Analyses	Lesson	Teacher	Analyses
D3	When students were answering questions, the teacher listened to their answers patiently and commented constructively.	The teacher believed that respecting students' differences meant adopting different instructional methods with different students.	The teacher carried out this principle by asking different levels of questions to different levels of students,	The teacher designed three groups of problems (14 in totals) for students to do and to comment on.	These problems were designed well to match the characteristics of most students, who could either do them fully, or partially. Thus students were diagnosed and promoted through use of the exercises so that they could obtain the basic strategy.	The design is thoughtful, each student may get improved.
	Discussed which sign is proper in filling blank $(-3)^4$ __ 3^4 with students.	The question was unexpected to the teacher (One student asked if all possible correct signs should be filled in the blank "$(-3)^4$ __ 3^4"). The teacher thought the question was understandable to all students and discussed it in front of the whole class to satisfy students' demand.	The teacher guided discussion of an unexpected question to involve the whole class in the exploration and to satisfy different needs among the class.	The Third Group of tasks consisted of: Suppose x>1, then $7x$ __ 7 $7x$ __ $24-2-15$ $10x+2-$ 24 __ $3x-15$ $(5x+1)/6-2$ __ $(3x-5)/4$		The third group of problems aimed to help students to understand the problem type from the viewpoint of the examiner in order to satisfy the needs of promising students.
	The teacher asked slow students first and then quick ones, so that more students would have opportunities to be involved. Thus fewer students would be left behind.	The teacher adopted this pedagogy in order to encourage quick students to think carefully and to avoid simple mistakes as well as to develop the way of questioning. For quick students, previews of textbooks are not encouraged in order to keep the freshness of the lecture. For slow students, previews are meaningful.	The teacher offered both quick students and slow students chances to take part in class discussions. She steered the pace of teaching by asking slow students first and making fast students think deeply.	The teacher asked students to make up two problems of different levels of difficulty by themselves.	Designing their own problems gave students a chance to realize their potential.	Let each student face his or her challenges and make their own judgments.

169

Table 2. Continued

CMCS	Lesson 1 (Concept of Inequalities)			Lesson2 (Properties of Inequalities)		
	Lesson	Teacher	Analyses	Lesson	Teacher	Analyses
D5	The teacher kept emphasizing the analogy, namely, imitating the properties of equalities to obtain those of inequalities.	It takes time and effort to recognize the connections between certain mathematics knowledge. The recognition is constrained by the teachers' abilities. Communication among teachers is crucial.	This analogy is fairly natural to students.	Asked students to discuss properties of inequalities starting from those of equalities and compare the similarities and differences between the types of properties.	To help students understand the relations among the mathematical content, the teacher guided students to read through the text books, and to analyse the remarks so that their understanding was natural and not farfetched.	The teacher guiding students from recalling properties of equalities to finding properties of inequalities helped them to recognize the relationship between equalities and inequalities, and to carry out procedures of reasoning by analogy.
	The teacher gave students a word problem and four sets of manipulation problems to explore.		The teacher introduced the real context of unequal relations through a word problem and asked students to do exercises at different levels at the first lesson.	The teacher designed three groups of problems for students to do and to comment on. The second group: Fill the blanks if we know the relations between a and b: $a+5b\_\_$ $b+5b$; $a/2-b\_\_b/2-b$; $a+5b\_\_6b$; and $a/2-b\_\_-b/2$. The third group: If $x>1$, then $7x\_\_7$ $7x\_\_24-2-15$ $10x+2-24\_\_3x-15$ $(5x+1)/6-2\_\_(3x-5)/4$		The three groups of problems were designed well to both raise students' problem-solving abilities and prepare ideas for the next lesson.

Table 2. Continued

CMCS	Lesson 1 (Concept of Inequalities)			Lesson2 (Properties of Inequalities)		
	Lesson	Teacher	Analyses	Lesson	Teacher	Analyses
D6	The teacher utilized Powerpoint (PPT) to demonstrate pictures, examples, and exercises.	Powerpoint (PPT) and other mathematics software are valuable for long statements, animations, and background materials. The projector is appropriate for displaying students' exercise books and other objects.	PPT was used reasonably well in the lesson.	Utilized PPT to demonstrate examples and exercises.	Writing on the blackboard is still an important part of lessons, since students' thinking follows the rhythm of writing. For a problem with many different solution methods, hyperlinks should be used in PPT to make students think about the problem before seeing any solutions.	The teacher used PPT for electronic blackboard only.

IDA AH CHEE MOK

CHAPTER 10

Teaching the Graphical Method of Solving Equations:
An Example in the Shanghai Lessons

INTRODUCTION: WHY GRAPHS?

The introduction of graphs represents a milestone in the understanding of algebra. The invention of the coordinate system in the 17th century opened a new gateway for the development of new topics and invention in the history of mathematics (Bell, 1953). In the personal learning path prescribed for school students in the curriculum, the experience of this new topic makes it possible to see at a glance the relationship of numbers represented as equations as alternatives for lines and curves in a plane. At this point, students are open to a new representation that transcends their power of visualization. This is certainly a jump in the understanding of algebra and empowerment of the subject. Being able to work with different representations is often seen as a way of understanding the object. Therefore, proficiency in using graphs is a helpful means of enhancing student understanding of functions, lines and curves. Yerushalmy (2000) studied the long-term impact of the functional approach to learning algebra in a technology supported environment. She found that the representation of problem situations evolved from numbers as the only means of modelling, to intensive use of graphs and tables, to the use of more symbolic representations, students also moved from the analysing patterns of numbers to functional relationship between pairs of numbers.

How can a teacher help students acquire the power of the new tool and develop an additional perspective for algebra? In a traditional curriculum when students first learn algebra, they often come across the topic as an extension of arithmetic of numbers by including letters in their list of operating symbols. What they have been doing will hardly go beyond the basic arithmetic operations of addition, subtraction, multiplication, division and exponentiation; a further step is to view equations as a kind of modelling of simple representations of different problem situations; and finally the concept of function.

In the remaining part of this chapter, an analysis of the lessons of a Shanghai teacher is presented to show how the graphical method of solving equations can be taught under the teacher's pedagogical philosophy. It is hoped that this chapter will give a small contribution to understanding how a teacher might possibly ratify his teaching of algebra.

F.K.S. Leung et al. (eds.), Algebra Teaching around the World, 173–190.
© *2014 Sense Publishers. All rights reserved.*

AN EXAMPLE OF TEACHING THE GRAPHICAL METHOD OF SOLVING
EQUATIONS FROM THE SHANGHAI LESSONS

The source of data

The data used in this chapter have been taken from the Shanghai data set of the Learner's Perspective Study (LPS). The teacher was a competent teacher recommended by local researchers. The topic was simultaneous linear equations in two unknowns. In the LPS data were recorded from three Shanghai schools, all on the same topic. In each school, video recordings were made of a sequence of ten consecutive lessons. There was a three- camera setting. Two students were invited for post-lesson interviews after each lesson. The teacher from SH1 was interviewed three times during the data collection period. A stimulated recall method was employed in the interviews. In the interview, the teacher was invited to choose a lesson that he wanted to comment on and evaluate. He was asked to play the video, stop and comment at episodes that he saw as important.

The teacher from SH1 had chosen to comment in detail on two lessons about graphs. This provided a rich set of data to understand his thinking about teaching the topic and triangulation of the findings obtained from analysing the lesson videos. Therefore, the SH1data were selected for use in this chapter.

The teaching and learning of the graphical methods were built upon the students' understanding of other related concepts of solution, equations and coordinate plane. Therefore, it was difficult to look at one standalone lesson. For this reason, the content of nine sequential lessons (L1 to L9) was viewed carefully. The topics and teaching goals are listed in Appendix 1. There were 4 lessons (L2, L3, L4 and L9) about graphs. The lesson video and the teacher's interviews were analysed. In the teacher's interviews, the teacher commented on L2 and L9 in depth. Therefore, the transcripts of these two lessons were also analysed in greater detail for the purpose of triangulation.

Teacher's perspectives of graphs in the learning of algebra

In two of the three interviews, the teacher chose lessons (L2 and L9) about the teaching of graphs to give detailed evaluation. He saw graphs as very important for the learning of algebra. Some of his comments have been translated to illustrate his view.

The teacher saw L2, the first lesson for introducing the Cartesian coordinate plane, as important for several reasons:

An extension for the understanding of numbers. The teacher pointed out that, without this topic, the understanding was about numbers only, whereas the introduction of the topic linked up between numbers and graphs and enriched the understanding of numbers through the empowerment of visualization.

T: It involved a Cartesian coordinate plane, that is
    to say, to relate numbers and graphs. Here we were
    talking about linear equations in two unknowns,
    which mainly show the relationship between numbers
    and numbers. Using Cartesian coordinates, we could
    display the linear equation in two unknowns on the
    Cartesian coordinate plane. Then the students could
    easily understand, by the incorporation of numbers
    and graphs, what the equation would look like on the
    coordinate plane.

A foundation for the graphical methods of solving equations. The learning of any
mathematics topic needs a foundation. The graphical method for solving equations
needs the knowledge of the coordinate plane to serve as a basis. The graphical
method, in turn, serves as a platform for understanding the solution of a system of
linear equations in visual representation (graphs).

T: This served as a condition for the graphical solutions
    of linear equations in two unknowns. At the same
    time it also helped the students to understand the
    topics such as why some systems of equations have
    infinitely many solutions, why some of them have no
    solution. We could see from the graph whether two
    lines were overlapping or parallel. This way I could
    help the students understand the solutions of linear
    equations.

Lesson goals and justification. After explaining why L2 was important, the teacher
continued to explain the goal of the lesson, that was surprisingly simple: a minimum
of the essentials for telling the coordinates of a point on the coordinate plane as
shown in the translated transcript below.

T: The objective of this lesson was that first it
    introduced the x-axis, y-axis, that is, the Cartesian
    coordinate plane. With this concept, then, given
    the position of a point, we could determine the
    coordinates of this point on the Cartesian plane.

Despite the simple goals, the teacher saw this new knowledge, involving visual
representation, as a way to help the students to break through their mechanical
routine for working with equations.

T: That's because, students nowadays, say to solve
    quadratic equations in one unknown, and they solve the
    equations very mechanically. Say if you do this and

that you'll solve the first, second or whatever step. And then when it comes to solve a linear equation in two unknowns, they might try to find a solution using the procedures taught by the teachers. To see from the Cartesian plane, that is to combine numbers and graphs. By using the Cartesian plane, solving linear equations in two unknowns or solving linear functions in the future will be more visual and clear, based on their graphs.

The episodes in Lesson L2 that the teacher saw as important

There were four episodes for which the teacher stopped the video and explained why he saw it as important and his feeling towards the episode. With respect to the content, the episodes were:

1. Why is an ordered-pair necessary?
2. How to find the coordinates of a point.
3. A conclusion for the four quadrants of the coordinate plane.
4. A generalization for the perpendiculars from a point to the axes.

In the following analysis of the teacher's interview and the interactions in the actual lessons, some factors can be found to explain why the teacher saw some episodes as important and worthy to discuss in the interviews. The analysis shows an emphasis on and deep understanding of the content, taking pedagogical strategy into consideration. For example, the teacher saw the ordered-pair as both an extension of previous learning and an important foundation for future learning. He also saw the importance of subtle use of realistic examples to develop different levels of understanding of the concept. With respect to some important questions relating to content, his evaluation showed how he valued the way of guiding students to think, to visualize, to draw conclusions and to make generalizations. These episodes also showed the high cognitive demand associated with acquiring a deep understanding of the concepts with respect to the idea of variable and mathematical generalization within a lesson.

The episode: Why is an ordered-pair necessary?

T: Now think about it, we are now sitting in rows, six rows and eight lines. That means we sit regularly. So think about it, when we are sitting here, each of our seats could be presented on this plane by a point. So let's say, when we present the location of a certain classmate, it is the same as the location of point where the classmate sits. For example, in the first row, if I say, this is the location of the classmate. So think about it, can I indicate the location by telling either a row or a column?

E: No.

T: Can I? Come on? Can I?

E: No.

T: Ah, Why? Tell me, why?

S1: It's because it indicates all the points on this row.

T: Why? Tell me once again.

S1: That is if you tell only the row or the column, you refer to all people of that row or column but not a particular person.

T: Right. We've said that. If I say this classmate belongs to the first row, boys and girls, see how many classmates are there in the first row? There are eight people, eight people, isn't it? So, next, if we say the first column, the second column, the third column, if we say the third column, how many classmates are there?

E: Eight.

E: Six classmates.

T: Six classmates. So it's uncertain. We are not certain of the point at which this classmate sits, are we? So look at this, if we can neither use the row nor the column, what can we do? Think about it. How can we indicate the exact position accurately? Think about it.

S2: Use both the row and the column.

T: Use both the row and the line. That's right. He says using both the row and what? And also the column. So see everybody, it's like we watch a movie in our everyday life. Look at this, you go to watch a movie. This is the movie ticket, how many numbers are there?

E: Two.

T: Ah, which row and which column, how many numbers are there?

E: Two.

T: Right, two numbers. So, look at this again, as these two numbers, say, the fifth row and the fourth column, [teacher writing on the blackboard]

T: The fifth row and the fourth column and the fourth row and the fifth column. See, everyone, do these two

177

pairs of numbers refer to the same position in the cinema?

E: No.

T: No. So in other words, we have to represent it by two numbers and these two numbers have their order, right? In this way, we can use a pair of ordered numbers to refer to a point on a plane. Use a pair of ordered numbers. So we indicate this pair of ordered numbers in this way. That is, here we use a round bracket, round bracket. For these two numbers, one of them comes first and the other comes second. It has an order and we cannot reverse it. Next, in between them, what do we use? We use a comma to separate them. We separate them. So in this way, the coordinates of a point are represented. So in today's class, we are going to talk about, 'The position of point and coordinates on a plane'. [Writing the topic on the blackboard.]

(E: whole class)

A need for foundation and new knowledge: 'Why is an ordered-pair necessary?' This episode refers to the very beginning of the introduction of the new topic, the coordinate plane. The teacher used two realistic examples, the seat arrangement in the class and the seat in a cinema. By explaining the content and the questions-and-answers in the episode, he illustrated how he helped the students to acquire two levels of meaning for why an ordered-pair was necessary. The first level was that two numbers are needed and the second level was that the order cannot be reversed.

T: First, the students needed to clarify that a point on a plane must be represented by an ordered-pair. This was the first concept. Say if I wanted to use the row number to represent a student's seat, or the column number to represent a student's seat. It would not be accurate. That is if I said the second row, everyone in the second row had to stand up, if a student said he was in the third column, then the other six students in the third column had to stand up as well. At this time we could not uniquely identify a student's position. That's why we needed to introduce the idea that a point on a plane needs to be represented by two numbers. This is the first level meaning. The second level meaning is that the order of the two numbers cannot be switched.

> Here we used the numbering of seats in a cinema to give students a more concrete example. We let them know that the fourth seat on the fifth row and the fifth seat on the fourth row were different seats, so it would be more clear if we said the horizontal coordinate and then the vertical coordinate. The order cannot be reversed.

In addition, he thought that the use of realistic examples would help the students to grasp the concept and he thought the episode was good based on his observation that the students' responses were good.

T: At that time I was thinking: First base it on students' everyday life experience. If he can get it correctly, that is to get the ordered pair correctly; it's okay. If he can't get it, then I have to explain it. And let him understand and use horizontal coordinate and vertical coordinate. Here, there is one ordered pair. This was the main purpose.

T: My feeling was that the students' response was good. He could get it clearly, immediately about the seating in a cinema. He could get it clearly that the fourth seat on the fifth row and the fifth seat on the fourth row were different seats. So this student, in his everyday life, can observe these practical examples. It is more or less relevant to mathematics. They can be linked up.

Teacher's perspective of a typical good lesson

When asked to comment on a typical good lesson, the teacher said he would prefer to see the students behave actively and that he was an "inspiring agent" asking questions to guide their thinking instead of telling the conclusion directly.

T: One is that the teacher is the inspiring agent of learning. In this lesson, it shows that the students were the active ones, from the beginning till the end. That is, the teacher's questions led them to answer and, at the end, the students formed a conclusion. Even when we talked about the examples, I did not tell them the conclusion directly. The students had to think and say themselves. I only

> led and guided them. That is, the students were the
> active agents.

Although the teacher's overall comment was that the students were slower in answering questions than they had been in the past, in the teaching episode he did practise what he claimed. The students' answers, despite their brevity, were all probed further by the teacher's questions. For example, the following questions from the episode guided the students gradually to describe the need for using two numbers, both column and row, to tell the position. The realistic example of seating thus became a useful metaphor for understanding the coordinate plane.

T: So think about it, can I indicate the location by
        telling either a row or a column?

T: Ah, Why? Tell me, why?

T: If I say this classmate belongs to the first row,
        boys and girls, see how many classmates are there
        on the first row? There are eight people, eight
        people, isn't it? So, next, if we say the first
        column, the second column, the third column, if we
        say the third column, how many?

T: Six classmates. So it's uncertain. We are not
        certain the point at which this classmate sits,
        are we? So look at this, if we can neither use the
        row nor the column, what can we do? Think about it.
        How can we indicate the exact position accurately?
        Think about it.

It is important to let the students answer: How to find the coordinates of a point?

Below is an episode that occurred after the teacher had finished an elaborated explanation of the coordinate plane. He gave the class a new question. He drew a new plane, marked a point A on the plane and asked, "How can we confirm the coordinates of point A?" A student answered, "Draw a vertical straight line towards the x-axis and another towards the y-axis. Mark the numbers on the x axis and y axis." Picking up the student's answer, the teacher worked out the answer with the whole class. He drew the lines perpendicular to the axes and, at the same time, asked the class questions to enable them to read the coordinates.

The teacher saw this moment as important because this part of the content was important and he wanted the students to answer the question. Also, he was happy with the student's answer. This was shown in his comments in the interview:

T: That's one point that is quite good. He said to draw
        a perpendicular line from point A to the x-axis.
        What is a point where the two perpendicular lines

```
intersect? We have to draw a perpendicular line
from point A to the y-axis, then what is a point
where the two perpendicular lines intersect? This
shows that they had learnt something in geometry
in the pre-junior secondary school grades, and
this language, their language was quite standard.
```

Generalization and working with unknown values

There were two episodes, seen by the teacher as important, that were concerned about generalization involving some unknown values. One episode was about the knowledge of quadrants. The teacher guided the students to look at values not only for a specific point but also for any point in a quadrant. As a result, the students were guided to see a broader perspective of the sign of the coordinates of the points in a quadrant in general. According to the teacher, the episode served multiple functions: conclusion, generalization and revision

```
T:    Why did I do this? On the basis of the example
      before, I gave the coordinates of some points.
      The students had to draw them on a coordinate
      plane. They had a little intuitive knowledge as
      the basis of this. We make a little conclusion. We
      divided the coordinate plane into four quadrants.
      Then, in each quadrant, the horizontal or vertical
      coordinate was bigger or smaller then zero. Then
      through the example before this content, that was
      to locate a point in the four quadrants, to find
      out the general rules. Actually it was to revise
      how to locate the coordinates of a point. After
      that, when the students do similar problems in the
      future, then to determine if a point is drawn in
      the right place on a coordinate plane, they can
      consider whether the x coordinate is bigger than
      zero or smaller than zero and know which quadrant
      it belongs to. This is the way they can locate the
      position of the point.
```

In another episode that was near the end of the lesson, the teacher posed a demanding question:

```
T:    Draw a straight line, draw a straight line. So if
      we draw a straight line which is perpendicular to
      the y-axis. If I draw a straight line here and name
      it L one- so, look at this, what are the features
      of the points on the straight line L one? Come on,
```

181

> this, I choose two points here randomly, one is
> here and the other is here. Oh, think about it.

The question was in fact a very demanding question for the class at this level. However, with the help of the drawings, the scenario became visible and some students could see what the teacher wanted; eventually, so could the whole class, as reflected in their chorused responses later.

S2:   The x-ordinates are the same.
T: What must the x-ordinates be?
E: The same.
T: The x-ordinates must be the same. Sit down please.
        Look at this everybody, is that right?
E: Right.
T: It's because it's parallel to L one and the y-axis.

The discussion then continued under the teacher's guidance to look at more general cases of lines perpendicular to the axes and comparison of the values of the coordinates of the points on these special lines. The discussion was only made possible with the help of the concept of the graphical representations and the visual support of lines and grids on the blackboard. The teacher explained his observation in the interview:

T: I am thinking that one student could tell it clearly,
        because they had not learnt the graphs of linear
        function in two unknowns. Actually, when I drew
        this straight line, I was wondering if the students
        could answer me, if they could answer correctly.
        Then I made use of the blackboard, and the grids,
        like a coordinate plane, so that they could get
        some insight from it.

From his comments, the teacher was aware of the difficulty of the question. He did not let go of the opportunity to continue guiding the whole class with the visual aids even though one student had given a correct answer.

Lessons L4 to L9: Methods of solving a system of linear equations

In the selected 9 lessons, the first was the introduction of the concept of equations and their solutions. In this, the teacher did not talk about graphs. In L2 and L3 the coordinate systems were introduced. These three lessons provided the basis for the students to learn to draw graphs in L4.

The topic of L4 was, in fact, the graphical representation of the solution for one unknown. The teacher guided the students through a list of learning tasks and exercises. This began with a review of transforming linear equations containing two unknowns. The main task was to express one unknown in terms of the other and hence to find the solutions for a single linear equation. Then, representing the solutions of one linear equation as ordered-pairs, they plotted the points and drew the line representing the graph of the equation. With much discussion, they came to a four-part conclusion. (1) "For the ordered pairs to satisfy the linear equation in two unknowns, the ordered pair must be located on the same straight line of the rectangular coordinate plane". (2) "The graph of a linear equation in two unknowns is a straight line". Additional properties are that (3) "every point is the solution of the equation"; and (4) "there is an infinite number of solution and this equation can be extended in infinite length"; were developed in the later part of the lessons. The extended concepts of "infinite number of solutions" and that "every point on the line is a solution" were, in fact, abstract concepts. In this lesson, the use of graphs helped the students visualize these important properties.

L5 to L8 were continuous lessons on the algebraic methods of solving equations. In these lessons, without referring to any graphs, the following were taught:

- The characteristics and forms of a system of linear equations of two unknowns;
- The meaning of solutions of a system of linear equations; and
- The substitution and elimination methods of solving the system of equations.

L9 was the last lesson in the sequence. In this lesson, the teacher resumed the topic of graphs again. He began by asking the class to recall what the graph of a linear equation looked like. The class readily recalled what they had learned in L4 that it was a straight line. Then the teacher started the lesson by asking, "If two straight lines intersect, then how many intersections would there be?" With this probing question, the class readily agreed that they could imagine that the intersection was the solution. In this way, the idea of seeing the solutions in the graphs was triggered off. The other tasks were to provide a platform for the students to learn the skills and strengthening their understanding by the teacher leading a whole-class discussion. Some examples of the tasks are:

1. The teacher asked the class to draw in their own graph paper the graphs of two different equations. Then he gave the ordered-pairs of some points and they had to tell whether the points were solutions or not by working on the graphs.
2. The teacher demonstrated how to solve a system of linear equations with the graphical method step-by-step.
3. Tasks that led the class to see and discuss the different cases of overlapping, parallel and intersecting lines.
4. The generalization of the different cases and the relationship between the coefficients of x and y.

From the examples, one can easily see a dense arrangement of content and strong link between the objectives of the tasks. The flow of information is very visible. The students had to learn some knowledge, concepts or skills in one task in one lesson; and very soon they were asked to apply what they had learned in another task in the same lesson or in other lessons.

I. A. C. MOK

From seeing the graphs to not using the graphs

In the second interview, which took place after this whole sequence of lessons, the teacher started by choosing to comment on the lesson on the algebraic method of elimination. He justified the method of elimination by seeing it as a principle of mathematical thinking.

> T: This is actually a mathematical thinking principle. That is the way of making two unknowns into one unknown in mathematics principles. And then, the students had to see that, by different systems of equations, they can use an algebraic expression in x to represent y or to use algebraic expression in y to represent x. Finally we had to do exercises. Let the students find out the general rule to solve the problems through this example.

After commenting on this lesson, the teacher added that L9, the lesson on the graphical methods, was also important. He referred to two episodes in L9.

Seeing the solutions in the graph.   This was an episode in which the teacher had invited two students to draw the graph. Then he guided the whole class to "see if the intersection is the solution". The emphasis was not only that they could *see* but that they had to explain why.

> T: (in the interview) This intersection is easy to notice. Right, intersection. How to solve it? The students had to see if this intersection was the solution of the system of linear equations in two unknowns. Some students said yes. Then I asked them why: "Think about this problem. What is the purpose of this problem?" One purpose was to let the students draw on their knowledge of solving a system of linear equations in two unknowns, the straight lines of this system. Based on the above discussion, I let them see that their intersection, two straight lines' intersection, and this equation's solution; what relationship they have. This was because some students could find the solution of the equation. I asked why that was the solution. Actually this was one for which the students could incorporate numbers and graphs and could see the solution.

184

From graph to no graph.   Another episode that the teacher saw as important was near the end of the last task in the lesson. The task required the students to draw four lines represented by four given equations. From there, they obtained different pairs (systems) of equations with different situations of overlapping, parallel and intersecting lines. After this, the teacher asked the students to imagine cases without drawing the graphs and to suggest the relationship between the coefficients of the unknowns *x* and *y*; extending the case to generality.

T: Have another look, if we have these few equations and we don't draw the graph, and if we don't solve the linear equations in two unknowns by calculation, then do you think you can determine the situation of the solution of these three systems of linear equations in two unknowns? Can you see it? Let's look at them together. The first equation...what characteristics does it have?

S3:   The two equations are equal.

S4:   Simplify equation two and we get equation two equals two x plus y equals to one, that is equation one. So the two equations are the same. Therefore there are infinitely many solutions.

T: Sit down. Bandson has said to divide each item by two, and it becomes equation one. Now look, the coefficient of x and y, and the constant. What are their relations?

S5:   The multiple of the coefficient of x, y and this constant is the same.

T: The multiple is the same. [Teacher signals the student to sit down]

T: Good. We've learnt about ratios, right? In fact we can write two to...four, coefficient of x to coefficient of y...how many? One to two, is it equal?

E: Equal

T: Equal. Now look at this constant. Is the ratio one to two, is it equal?

E: Equal.

The teacher explained in the interview that it was important that the graphs helped the students see the three situations (overlapping, parallel and intersecting). However, it was also important to find a general rule so that they did not need to draw the graphs in future.

T: In the future when students come to system of
       equations in two unknowns, they will not have to
       draw graphs, and will not have to solve it. They can
       find out directly if the equation has a solution,
       has no solution or infinitely many solutions from
       the coefficient and constant. In this way, through
       this graph observation, find out its general rule.
       Actually this is the purpose.

DISCUSSION

School algebra is an important strand in the mathematics curriculum everywhere in the world. If we search the curricula, we can always find the topic of graphs representing an important part. What is a graph? What role does it play in the understanding and learning of algebra? How can the topic of graphs be taught in the curriculum? There is neither a uniform curriculum nor uniform pedagogical suggestions for these questions. Sometimes, a simple matching of popular topics is not possible. For example, in the small-scale comparative study of the teaching of fractions in Swedish and Hong Kong classrooms, carried out by Runesson and Mok (2005), the first difficulty they encountered was the matching of topics in the curriculum. They found that a topic taught in Grade 4 in Hong Kong was taught in Grades 6 and 7 in Sweden. Even within the same country, such as the United States, there can be 'a tug of war' between the traditional approaches and the reformist (or functional) approaches for school algebra (Kieran, 2007). With so many differences, no wonder the content and approach will be different. Nevertheless, the existence of these differences does not imply that one approach is necessarily better than the other. Embedded within each system, students' understanding of mathematical concepts and their beliefs about the nature of mathematics learning are encultured by their experiences in their mathematics lessons. In these experiences, the teacher plays an influential role, even though this is not necessarily through direct transmission. The teacher, via his personal understanding of the subject, belief in values and pedagogy, contributes significantly to the process of shaping the students' learning (Bishop, 1991). Very often, within an educational system, teaching experimentation and innovation is limited by the cultural assumptions recognized implicitly or explicitly by local authorities. Therefore, the exposure of examples in other places often provides a platform for situated insights into the nature of the teaching practice (Clarke et al., 2006).

In the literature about Chinese pedagogy for mathematics, educators have often highlighted the principle of 'two basics', basic knowledge and basic skills (Zhang, Li and Tang, 2004) Linked to this principle, I have attempted to contribute to the understanding of Chinese pedagogy by documenting a teacher's ratification of the teaching of a topic. This contribution is based on the analysis of a sequence of lessons by a teacher in Shanghai taken from the data of the Learner's Perspective Study. Some characteristics of the teacher's beliefs and practices can be summarised here.

With respect to pedagogical philosophy, first, there was an emphasis on foundation and links between different knowledge points. There was a strong coherent flow between the tasks within a lesson and between the content of different lessons. For example, L1 to L3 can be seen as the most fundamental level. What was taught in these lessons was recalled and applied again and again in later lessons, for example L4 and L5. What was learned was accumulated and was used further in later lessons. As a result, in the final lesson L9, there was a very rapid transcending of cognitive demand in the tasks. The lessons started with simple intuitive observation of the solutions to equations involving the intersection of two straight lines and led to generalization of the relationship of the coefficients of the unknowns in the equations. Second, the teacher expressed a belief that students should be seen as active agents and the teacher's role as asking questions to guide them to think. Also, the interactive pattern of the class discourse showed strong favouring of a three-part IRF pattern: teacher's initiation; student response; teacher's feedback. The student responses were guided closely through the teacher's initiation and feedback (Lenke, 1989).

Finally, with respect to the teaching of the graphical method in algebra, the teacher saw the importance of this method as a mathematical way of thinking, linking between numbers and shapes. This was demonstrated by his very skilful way of orchestrating whole-class discussion to oscillate between arguments based on seeing the graphs and working with the numbers. As a result, we can see a beautiful mutually supportive picture of the two tools helping students to acquire a competent level of understanding of some abstract concepts such as the infinite number of solutions and differentiation of different solution situations.

ACKNOWLEDGEMENTS

The author would like to thank Research Grants Council (Hong Kong SAR, China) and the University of Hong Kong for funding the project.

REFERENCES

Bell, E. T. (1953). *Men of mathematics*. London, UK: Penguin Books.

Bishop, A. J. (1991). *Mathematical enculturation: A cultural perspective on mathematics education*. Dordrecht, the Nether-lands: Kluwer Academic Publishers Groups.

Clarke, D., Emanuelsson, J., Jablonka, E., & Mok, I. A. C. (Eds.). (2006). *Making connections: Comparing mathematics classrooms around the world*. Sense Publishers B.V.

Kieran, C. (2007). *Learning and teaching algebra at the middle school through college levels*. In Jr. K. L. Frank (Ed.), *Second handbook of research on mathematics teaching and learning—A project of the National Council of Mathematics* (pp. 707–762). Reston, VA: NCTM.

Lenke, J. L. (1989). *Using language in the classroom*. Oxford: Oxford University Press.

Runesson, U., & Mok, I. A. C. (2005). The teaching of fractions: A comparative study of a Swedish and a Hong Kong classroom. *Nordic Studies in Mathematics Education, 10*(2), 1–15.

Yerushalmy, M. (2000). Problem solving strategies and mathematical resources: A longitudinal view on problem-solving in a function-based approach to algebra. *Educational Studies in Mathematics, 43,* 125–147.

Zhang, D., Li, S., & Tang, R. (2004). The "Two Basics": Mathematics Teaching and Learning in Mainland China. In L. Fan, N. -Y. Wong, J. Cai & S. Li (Eds.), *How Chinese Learn Mathematics: Perspectives from Insiders* (pp. 189–208). NJ: World Scientific publishing Co.

AFFILIATION

Ida Ah Chee Mok
The University of Hong Kong
Hong Kong

APPENDIX: THE TOPICS AND TEAACHER'S GOALS FOR LESSONS L1 TO L9

L1   Linear equation in two unknowns and its solution: (algebraic / no
     graphs)
     Goals:

   • To understand linear equations in two unknowns and their solutions;
     and the concept of solution sets.
   • To find the parts of solutions that satisfied certain conditions of the
     linear equations in two unknowns solution set.
   • To build the basis for understanding linear equations in two unknowns
     and the concepts concerned; and linear equations in multiple unknowns
     and the concepts concerned.

L2   Rectangular coordinate plane and coordinates (I) (graphs)
     Goals:

   • To give the students a basic concept of the coordinates on the plane
     and the relationship between ordered numbers and inner points on the
     rectangular coordinate plane.
   • To teach the students the correct way to draw an axis and to name the
     coordinates on a rectangular coordinate plane, since this will be used
     in future for learning the graph of linear equation in two unknowns,
     solving the system of linear equation in two unknowns, the graphical
     method, etc.

L3   Rectangular coordinate plane and coordinates (II) (graphs)
     Goals:

   • To draw the points on the rectangular coordinate plane according to the
     coordinates of the point and to calculate the area of the graph.

L4   Graphs of linear equations in two unknowns (graphs)
     Goals:

   • To learn that the graph of the linear equation in two unknowns is a
     straight line and to draw the graph correctly.
   • To learn the relationships between the solution of the linear equation
     in two unknowns, the graph of the equations, and the points on the
     rectangular coordinate plane.
   • To use the above knowledge to solve the system of linear equations in
     two unknowns by the graphical method.

L5   Simultaneous linear equations in two unknowns (Algebraic Methods)
Goals:

- To understand the meaning of systems of linear equations and their solutions.
- To determine whether a given system is a system of linear equations in two unknowns.
- To learn the relationship between the solution of a system and the solution of its individual equations.

L6   Simultaneous linear equations in two unknowns (Algebraic Methods)

- Method of substitution

L7
&
L8   Simultaneous linear equations in two unknowns (Algebraic Methods)

- Method of elimination

L9   Graphical method for solving simultaneous linear equations in two unknowns
Goals:

- To solve the system of linear equations in two unknowns using the graphic method.
- To understand the relationship between two straight lines and the solution of the system of linear equations.
- To help students to form the concept of combining graphs and numbers.

RONGJIN HUANG, IDA AH CHEE MOK &
FREDERICK K. S. LEUNG

CHAPTER 11

Teaching Algebraic Concepts in Chinese Classrooms: A Case Study of
Systems of Linear Equations

INTRODUCTION

"Algebra for everyone" has become a slogan of mathematics education reformers (e.g.,
Edwards, 1990), and the claim that all students will benefit from learning algebra is
bolstered by research findings that those who take algebra courses in high school have
higher chances to enter prestigious universities and get high-salary jobs (Moses &
Cobb, 2001). As recommended by the National Mathematics Advisor Panel in the US
(NMAP, 2008), students "should be able to proceed successfully at least through the
content of Algebra II." Conventionally, the algebra curriculum focused on polynomial
expressions and equations, and relevant algebraic computations. However, with the
wide availability of technology, a function-oriented approach has been promoted
(Bednarz, Kieran, & Lee, 1996). Recently, an effort has been made to integrate
conventional and reform-oriented approaches (e.g., NCTM, 2000, 2009). Multiple
approaches to dealing with school algebra lend variety to algebra texts and, further,
result in the difficulties of teaching and learning algebra (e.g., Kendal & Stacey, 2004).

Studies of algebra learning have documented students' difficulties in understanding
the meaning of letters and equal signs, and in solving equations and so on (e.g.,
Kerian, 2007). It is not uncommon that students manipulate symbols without a
meaningful basis and make non-referential reasoning (Harel, Fuller, & Rabin, 2009).
Thus, making sense of algebra learning has become a crucial and urgent issue under
the context of teaching algebra for all students.

It has been agreed that algebra should be introduced earlier and it is important to
make a smooth transition from arithmetic to algebra (e.g., Creenes & Rubenstein,
2008; Kaput, Carraher, & Blanton, 2008). A comparative study of the introduction
of early algebra in elementary mathematics texts in China, Singapore and the U.S.
showed that the texts in China and Singapore provided a more systematic and
supportive transition from arithmetic to algebra when compared with U.S. texts
(Cai & Mayor, 2008). In addition, Chinese mathematics teachers are perceived to
have sound understanding of mathematics knowledge (An, Kulm, & Wu, 2004; Li,
Huang, & Shin, 2008; Ma, 1999). Thus, it is expected that the teaching of algebra in
China may reveal some interesting features. Existing studies have identified some

F.K.S. Leung et al. (eds.), Algebra Teaching around the World, 191–211.
© *2014 Sense Publishers. All rights reserved.*

characteristics of mathematics classrooms in China, such as the lecture-dominated style, the high cognitive demand of contents, instructional coherence, and practising with interconnected and varied problems covered in the lesson (Huang & Li, 2009; Leung, 1995, 2001). Nevertheless, it is largely unknown how Chinese teachers teach specific algebraic content. In order to examine Chinese teachers' expertise in teaching mathematics, Li, Huang and Yang (2011) investigated five experts' videotaped algebra lessons (with different topics). They found that these teachers demonstrated a profound understanding of the content they taught, skilful treatment of the important and difficult content, and adoption of a problem-based approach to introduce algebra concepts and formulae, with a focus on developing students' computation skills, mathematical thinking and problem-solving abilities.

However, the aforementioned studies of Chinese mathematics classrooms focused mainly on the structure of classroom instruction, and content treatment in general. It should be interesting to understand how Chinese teachers teach a specific algebra concept or algorithm. The Chinese Learners' Perspective Study (LPS) data focus on the teaching of the same topic, introducing the concepts of systems of linear equations and their solutions, over several consecutive lessons. These data provide a unique opportunity to investigate how a concept/algorithm is taught in China. As classroom teaching is complex, there may be many different ways to make observations and interpretations. It is necessary to understand the lessons within a certain theoretical framework to see how an environment conducive to learning can be created. For this purpose, a framework of variation that has been known to be popular in Chinese pedagogy to examine the teaching of concepts was selected (Gu et al., 2004; Wong, Lam, Sun, & Chan, 2009). This study not only contributes to an understanding of how Chinese teachers teach an algebra concept, but also provides an example for international researchers to contrast with other effective ways of teaching algebra.

THEORETICAL CONSIDERATION

Teaching with Variation: A Theory of Classroom Teaching

To identify and interpret the classroom characteristics that are conducive to students learning, the theory of variation espoused by Marton and Booth (1997) was selected; this theory has demonstrated potential to reveal salient features of classroom instruction (Marton & Tsui, 2004). According to Marton and Tsui, learning is a process in which learners develop a certain capability or way of seeing or experiencing. In order to see something in a certain way the learner must discern certain features of the object. Experiencing variation is essential for discernment and is significant for learning. Marton and Tsui (2004) argued that it is important to attend to what varies and what is invariant to a learning situation, which constrains learning and make it possible. Pedagogically, Gu, Huang and Marton (2004) described the fundamental features of teaching with variation, which has been in place in China for several decades. This theory of teaching emphasizes building essential connections between current knowledge and previously learned knowledge through guiding students to experience certain variations focusing on critical features of the object of learning. Two types of variations were suggested to help students learn mathematics meaningfully: *conceptual variation and procedural variation*. Conceptual variation consists of two parts. One is composed of varying embodiments or representations of a concept to form the connotation of the concept. The other is highlighting the substantial features of the concept by providing counterexamples as a contrast. Conceptual variation is meant to provide learners with multiple experiences from different perspectives. Procedural variation refers to the process of forming a concept logically, arriving at solutions to problems and forming knowledge structures. The function of procedural variation is to help learners acquire knowledge step-by-step, enrich their experience in problem solving progressively, and finally obtain well-structured knowledge.

Recently, Wong et al. (2009) developed a further framework to describe different variations in terms of the functions of the problems. This model includes four types of variation (*bianshi*): *inductive, broadening, deepening,* and *applying*. Using '*inductive*' variation, rules and concepts are derived through the inspection of a number of realistic/symbolic situations. These rules are consolidated by systematic introduction of variations into mathematical tasks. In the case of "*broadening*", no new rules and concepts are introduced, and the learners broaden their scope through exploring a variety of problems. At a certain point, by varying the types of mathematical tasks further, the learner is led to mathematics concepts and skills at a deep level. This is called '*deepening*'. Next, mathematics knowledge is applied to a greater variety of realistic/symbolic problems, which can be called '*applying*".

Essentially, the classifications suggested by Gu et al. (2004) and Wong et al. (2009) are related closely. *The inductive* and *broadening* could be roughly grouped into conceptual variation, while *deepening* and *applying* basically fit in with procedural variation. However, since knowledge development is spiral, these categories are all neither static nor exclusive. Thus, the authors regard the classification by Wong et al. (2009) as an extension of the model by Gu et al. (2004).

Teaching and Learning of Algebra

There are different approaches to introducing algebra contents in different curricula (e.g., Bednarz, Kieran, & Lee, 1996). For example, Usiskin (1988) summarized four approaches of dealing with algebra: (1) generalized algorithm; (2) a study of procedures for solving certain kinds of problems; (3) the study of relationships among quantities; and (4) the study of structures. As well, Kieran (2004) synthesized three core activities of conceptualizing algebra, namely, *generational activity, transformational activity, and global/meta-level activity.* The generational activities involve the forming of expressions and equations that are the objects of algebra. The transformational activities include, for instance, collecting like terms, factoring, expanding, substituting, adding and multiplying polynomial expressions, solving equations, simplifying expressions, and working with equivalent expressions and equations. The global/meta-level mathematics activities refer to those for which algebra is used as a tool but which are not exclusive to algebra. They include problem solving, modeling, noticing structure, studying changes, generalizing, analyzing relationships, justifying, proving, and predicting.

The concepts of linear equations and systems of linear equations include representations (tables, graphs, equations, and verbal descriptions), properties, and behaviors of linear relationships and functions as well as elements that comprise them, relationships among them and the situations in which they are used or appear. Researchers have identified several aspects in which students have difficulty with linear relationships (e.g., Herscovics & Linchevski, 1994; Kieren, 1981, 1989; Sleeman, 1984). For example, by investigating middle school students' transformation of equations, Herscovics and Linchevski (1994) found that around half (22 participants at grade 7) were not able to find the solution to the question $4+n-2+5=11+3+5$. Their common mistake was to shorten the left-side expression into $4+n-7$. By studying the methods of solving systems of linear equations, Filloy, Rojano, and Solares (2004) found that students preferred to use the comparison method (e.g., using one unknown to represent the other unknown, and find the other unknown first) rather than the substitution method. They found that it was difficult for students to implement substitution due to insufficient understanding of the equal sign and the complexity of algebraic computation.

In summary, these existing studies focused on the procedural aspect and identified the difficulties of learning these algorithms. Yet, the conceptual aspects of linear equations have not been explored appropriately. This chapter will show how conceptual aspects of equations and solutions might be done in mathematics lessons in China.

Research Questions

In this study, the focus was placed on the formulation and development of the concept of systems of linear equations and their solution in Chinese classrooms. In particular, the aim was to answer the following research questions:

1. What is the process of forming and developing the concepts?
2. Do the activities associated with the development of the concepts help students understand them?

To answer the first question, the activities surrounding the formulation and development of these particular concepts in Chinese mathematics classrooms were identified. The second question was addressed by identifying emerging patterns of teaching the concepts and examining possible learning conditions with regard to the patterns from the perspective of teaching with variations and theories of algebra learning.

METHODS

Data Sources

The data for this study consist of a total of 131 videotaped lessons taken from the Chinese data set of the LPS (Clarke et al., 2006). Forty-six of them are from Hong Kong, 41 are from Macau and 44 are from Shanghai. The backgrounds of these classes are shown in Table 1.

Table 1. Background of the classes

City	School	Class size (no. of students)	The teacher's teaching experience (years)	Duration lesson (minutes)
Hong Kong	HK1	39	20	35
	HK2	39	14	35
	HK3	41	17	38
Macau	MC1	51	3	35
	MC2	58	18	40
	MC3	61	20	45
	SH1	50	27	40
Shanghai	SH2	46	14	40
	SH3	55	23	40

Macau has the largest overall class size, while Hong Kong has the lowest. The Shanghai teachers are the most experienced while the Macau teachers are the least. Shanghai and Macau have the same lesson duration (40 minutes), while Hong Kong's is slightly shorter (35 minutes).

In order to investigate closely how a mathematics concept is constructed in classrooms, we selected all the lessons in which the concept of systems of linear equations and their solution were introduced and consolidated. It was found that, in all cases, this concept was taught within one lesson. Thus, the lesson from each of the nine teachers in which the concept was taught was identified; in total nine lessons were selected.

Data Analysis

A coding system was developed by the authors in order to carry out a deep examination of how the concept of systems of linear equations and their solutions was developed. First, one research assistant (RA) worked with the first author to develop a code system based on the research questions and watching the selected videotaped lessons. Then, the RA coded three lessons (one third of the total sample lessons), and another RA was invited to code the same three lessons independently. The inter-rater reliability was found to be 83%. Through extensive discussion, all the disagreements were resolved. After that, the RA coded all the other six lessons. The codes are explained below:

Introducing a New Concept Directly (ICD). The teacher directly tells the concepts. For example, the teacher wrote systems of linear equations, pointed out the number of unknowns and their indices, and emphasized the relationship between equations with two unknowns and equations with one unknown. The following Hong Kong example is from HK2-L01:

T: Okay. We've looked at two equations; we're looking at two equations. Every equation has some unknowns and we have to find them out.

T: We know that when there are so called 'yuan' we call it 'yuan' in an equation. They are called linear equations in two 'yuans'.

T: Two unknowns and degree is one. We know that there are indefinite solutions.

T: If I want to set the limit this time, I want to group these two equations together; I want [to] constrain the conditions.

T: I want to set the constraint. [The teacher associated the two equations on the blackboard]

T: This is called simultaneous equations. 'Simultaneous' means to associate two unrelated equations together, to set the constraint.

Introducing a New Concept Based on Reviewing (ICR). The teacher first reviews the concept of equations with one unknown including the number of unknowns, indices of the unknowns and meaning of the solution of equations, and then introduces the concept of systems of linear equations with two unknowns and their solution. This method uses the knowledge from the review as a supportive background associated with the new concept. The following is an example from Shanghai (SH1-L05):

T: Today, before we start a new topic, I would like to do some reviews with you. Please look at the slide.

T: Oh, let us look at the first question. Are they linear equations in two unknowns? Put up your hands if you want to say something.

S1: Both of them are not. It is because the index of the unknown is two-

T: The index is two. X is with the index of two.

S1: The second one is not a complete equation.

T: It is not an equation. There is an unknown in the denominator. And because the index of y is not one, good, sit down please.

T: Okay, question two. How many solutions are there in this equation two x plus y equals ten?

S2: Infinite.

T: What's your answer?

S2: The equation that two x plus y equals ten has infinite solutions.

T: It has infinite solutions. In this situation, a linear equation of two unknowns has infinite solutions.

Introducing a New Concept through Drawing Graphs (ICG). The teacher introduces the concept of systems of linear equations with two unknowns and their solution through drawing two straight lines and finding the intersecting point of the two straight lines.

Introducing a New Concept through Solving Word Problems (ICP). The concept of systems of linear equations with two unknowns was introduced through solving word problems, and then the key terms of the concepts, such as the number of unknowns, and their indices are stated, and the relationship with the previous concept (linear equation with one unknown) is referred to. One example from a Hong Kong lesson (HK1-L06) is given below:

T: Okay, before talking about the linear equations in two unknowns, let us try to solve a question first. Please pick up your pen and notebook and think about the problem.

T: Please think while I write the problem slowly on the blackboard. A farmer has some rabbits and some chickens. He does not know the exact number of rabbits and chickens, but in total there are ten heads, remember, ten heads, and there are twenty-six legs.

T: Okay, do you know how many chickens and rabbits the farmer has, so that the total number of heads is ten and the total number of legs is twenty-six? Ha, let's start thinking now. [T writes the question on the blackboard]

Based on discussion about the process of solving this word problem, the concept of systems of linear equations and their solution was explored.

Explaining the Meaning of Systems of Linear Equations (EME). An explanation usually follows the introduction. For example, using a problem about money and one equation in the introduction (ICP) in SH3-L05, the teacher continued to explain the meaning of systems of linear equations by explaining the relevant terms (such as the number of unknowns and the indices) and its relationship with previous knowledge. The following episode in the lesson (SH3-L05) gives an illustration:

T: You can see that one more condition is added into this question, i.e. x plus y equals seven, and the amount is still equal to ten dollars, which remains unchanged.

T: So the values of unknowns x and y not only need to satisfy the first equation, but also need to satisfy the second equation. So, we gather these two equations into one place and use a big bracket to group them together.

T: This is called systems of equations ... that means, if there are some equations formed into one group, we will call it systems of equations. [Show slide]

T: Please observe the system of equations here, how many unknowns are there?

S: Two

T: Two

T: One is x and the other is y

S: y

T: And the index of the unknown is one.

S: Index is one.

T: Index is one. So, we call this system of equations as... system of linear equations in two unknowns.

S: System of linear equations in two unknowns.

T: Very good. [Show slide] That means, if there are two unknowns within systems of equations, and the indices of the unknowns are one, then we will call this system of equations systems of linear equations in two unknowns...

Explaining the Meaning of Solution (EMS). After introducing the concept of the solution of systems of linear equations, the teacher further explains the number (none, only one, infinite) of solutions by using the table method or the graph method. The following excerpt demonstrates this approach (MC2-l01).

T: There are many possibilities in a linear equation system in two variables. Maybe there are infinite solutions, only one solution, or no solution.

T: You should remember the meaning first.

T: Remember one more sentence, a_1, b_1, a_2, b_2 can't both be 0.

T: How can we know the value of the variables? You can think about this. For example, we plug in x=-2, get y=11, is it the solution of this equation system? We only need to plug them into the equations. Both equations should be equal on the left side and right side. We say these are the solutions or roots of this equation system.

T: The one that satisfies only one equation is not a solution to the system of linear equations.

T: We can conclude the definition; the values which satisfy the left side and right side in both equations should be the solution of the system of linear equations in two unknowns.

T: For example the solution of this equation system is x=5, y=6 which can satisfy the left side and right side in both equations.

T: We will explain that in detail; there are many possibilities in the system of linear equations in two unknowns. Maybe there are infinite solutions, only one solution, or no solution. We will explain in detail later. You should know how to plug it into the equations.

Discriminating Systems of Linear Equations (DSE).   After introducing the concept of systems of linear equations with two unknowns, the teacher asks the students to judge whether an equation is a system of linear equations with two unknowns, or give a counterexample. Take the following excerpt from MC2-L01 for example.

T: Ok, let me test you, which one is not a system of linear equations in two unknowns.

T: Some students say C while some students say D. There may not be one correct answer.

S: C, and D

T: Is C wrong? Yes, C is wrong, is D wrong?

S: D is wrong.

T: D is wrong, C and D are wrong. Ok, Only A and B are right. There are two right answers.

T: Can you give another example, which is not a linear equation in two unknowns? Can you think about that?

199

T: Good, try it, give me an example.(Student walked to the blackboard and wrote an equation: $x^3+2x=5$)

T: How many variables are there and what are the powers of the variables? One variable and the power of the variables is three, ok this is not linear equation in two variables.

Discriminating the Solutions of Systems of Equations (DSS). After introducing and explaining the concept of the solution of systems of linear equations, the teacher asks the students to judge whether a pair of ordered numbers is a solution of a system of linear equations. The following episode from a Shanghai lesson (SH3-L05) shows the feature of this category:

T: [show slide] ...Okay, please, based on this concept, do some practices and checking.

T: The values of the two ordered pairs have been given to you. In the first pair, the x is negative two, and y is eight; in the second pair, the x is two, and y is four. Is it the solution of this pair of equations x plus y equals six ...two x plus y equals eight? [Students do practice]...

T: Please try to think about it, how to check whether this ordered pair is a solution of these equations? The first one...[teacher writes something on the blackboard]

T: Let's invite some students to explain, you, how to check..., what's your idea. [Students are thinking]

S: (...)

T: Substitute it into this system of equations...how to substitute...

S: (...) x plus y equals six, two x plus y equals eight, (...) negative two plus eight equals six, then we can substitute it into another one.

T: Substitute it into the second one means we can substitute into each of the two equations, isn't it? Then we can check it, Ok...then we can see...we can follow his thinking.

Self-learning the Concepts through Reading and Discussion (SCR). Students learn the concepts through reading textbooks and discussion in classroom under the guidance of the teacher. Only one Shanghai teacher (SH1-L05) adopted this approach, as follows:

T: Then, today's lesson will be conducted this way. First, I will propose three questions.

T: The first question, what is the definition of systems of linear equations? The second question is how to find out whether this is a system of linear equations in two unknowns or not.

T: The third question is in the following equations, which are from the system of linear equations in two unknowns. How many pairs? But now, I am not going to answer these three questions.

T: Please turn to page twenty-eight. Let us read it. Start from section nine point four - it's about the system of linear equations in two unknowns - and stop at the one with a graph table on the upper side.

T: After you have read it, you can think about the three questions by yourselves. Please read it first.

T: Then, you can discuss it in pairs.

Summarizing (SUM). The key points or critical ideas of the concepts, or the main points (knowledge and method) of the lesson are summarized. Take the following excerpt (SH3-L05) for example:

T: Okay, today we have learned the concept of systems of linear equations in two unknowns. That means, when a pair of equations contains two unknowns and the indices of the unknowns are one, and then we will call it a system of linear equations in two unknowns. The second thing is the concept of solution for systems of equations. This means if a solution is suitable for both [of] the two equations of a pair of equations, we will call it the solution of the system of linear equations in two unknowns.

Introduction of Solving Methods (ISM). Different methods of solving systems of linear equations with two unknowns, such as substitution or elimination, are introduced.

Topic Unrelated (TUN). Some unrelated mathematics learning issues are mentioned, such as talking about public news.

RESULTS

Approaches to Constructing the Concepts

We counted the numbers of teachers who spent times on each of the activities described above. We excluded some least common activities. For example, only one teacher in Hong Kong directly taught the concept (5.8% lesson duration), and only one, another Hong Kong teacher, introduced the concept through graphing the equations (28.5% lesson duration). For another example, only one Shanghai teachers introduced the concept through reading the textbook and discussion (5.8% lesson duration). In addition, one Hong Kong (35% lesson duration), one Macau (12% lesson duration) and one Shanghai teacher (12.8% lesson duration) spent some time on introducing the methods of solving the system of linear equations, and one Hong Kong teacher (3.4% lesson duration) and one Macau teacher (2.1% lesson duration) spent some time on doing topic unrelated things. After excluding these, we displayed, in Table 2, all of the remaining ones, the numbers of teachers who devoted time to them, and the proportions of the lesson time spent on these activities.

Table 2. Distribution of different activities for constructing the concepts

Activities	Hong Kong		Macau		Shanghai	
	No. of teachers	Percent of time	No. of teachers	Percent of time	No. of teachers	Percent of time
ICR	1	7.5	2	1.2	2	10.9
ICP	1	26	2	16.8	2	8.2
EME	2	4	2	16.5	3	7.
EMS	3	17	3	34.8	3	5.3
DSE	0	0	2	5.3	3	11.9
DSS	1	4.7	2	3.7	3	41.7
SUM	2	1.7	3	7.2	3	2.2

Note. ICR-Introducing a new concept based on reviewing; ICP- Introducing a new concept through solving word problems; EME- Explaining the meaning of systems of linear equations; EMS-Explaining the meaning of solution; DSE-Discriminating systems of linear equations; DSS-Discriminating the solutions of systems of equations; SUM-Summarizing.

From Table 2, we can see that the Shanghai teachers showed a tendency to use similar activities. All three Shanghai teachers used explaining the meaning of the concept of systems of linear equations, explaining the meaning of solution, discriminating the concepts (equation and solutions), and summarization. This suggests that explaining the meanings of the concepts (equations and solutions), discriminating the concepts, and summarizing the key points were the most commonly used activities in the Shanghai lessons. The Hong Kong teachers showed the least similarity in their choices of activity. The Macau teachers showed some similarity to the Shanghai teachers. For example, two Macau teachers used activities for discriminating the concepts. All Macau teachers made summarizations.

If we compare these activities between cities, then some characteristics can be identified as follows. First, the most salient feature in Shanghai was to discriminate the concepts from multiple perspectives, while the most noticeable feature in Macau was to explain the meaning of the concepts. The teachers in Macau and Shanghai also emphasized introducing concepts through reviewing and solving word problems. The similarities among these three cities are that the teachers explained concepts clearly and summarized key points in due course.

The diversity in methods of introducing the common concepts is obvious. For example, in one Shanghai lesson (SH1_05), after reviewing the concept of linear equations with one unknown and their solutions, the students were asked to learn the concept of systems of linear equations with two unknowns and their solution through reading the textbook, discussing and doing exercises. In Hong Kong, one teacher (in HK3_06) introduced the same concept through discussing the graphs of linear equations. Another Hong Kong teacher (HK2_01) introduced it through guessing and checking; after reviewing a linear equation with one unknown having one solution, the teacher wrote a linear equation with two unknowns ($2x+y=1$) and asked the students how to solve it. Apart from these differences in methods for introducing the concept, however, one interesting pattern emerged, as described below.

A Pattern of Four Phases

Figure 1 below shows the distribution of the different teachers' activities in the three cities. At first glance, it is too diverse to capture any pattern. However, by

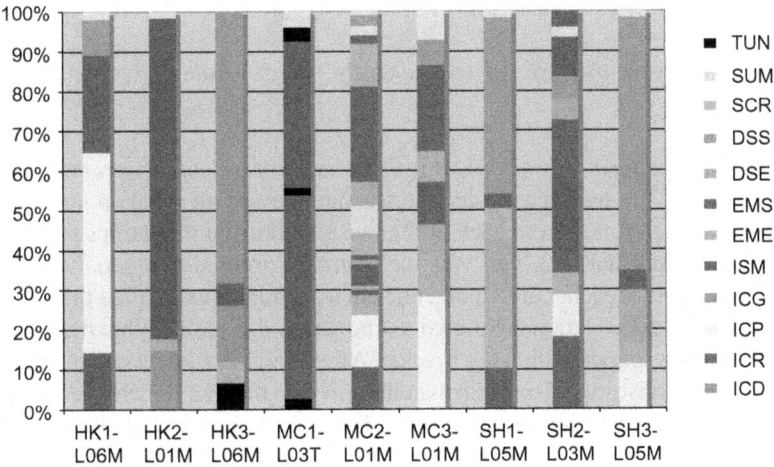

Figure 1. Distribution of different activities in each lesson

focusing on the teachers in Macau and Shanghai, a rough sequence of phases for the development of the concepts can be seen: (1) introducing the concept, (2) explaining the meanings, (3) discriminating the concept with varying exercises, and (4) summarization.

Of course, a particular teacher may just have emphasized some of the four phases. In this section, we use one Shanghai lesson (SH3_05) to demonstrate how the concept was constructed through the typical four phases and also the possible opportunities for students to learn the concepts.

Phase I: Introducing concept through problem solving: At first, the teacher gave a stamps problem with one constraint: "Wang goes to the post office to buy a number of one-dollar and two-dollar stamps. At least one of each type of stamps will be bought. The total amount he spends on buying them is ten dollars. How many stamps of each type does Wang get from the post office?" The class quickly gave the equation $2x+y=10$ and listed four sets of possible solutions. The teacher then added an extra restriction to the question: "The total number of stamps Wang gets is seven." After the teacher got the expected answer ($x + y = 7$), the students were asked to list all possible pairs of solutions for this restriction.

Phase II: Explaining and discriminating the concept of systems of equations. After the students gave the answer, the teacher pointed out that if several equations are associated with a big bracket, it is called a system of equations and if the system consists of two linear equations and both equations share the same two unknowns, this is called a system of equations with two unknowns.

Then students were asked to discriminate whether the following systems of equations are systems of linear equations.

$$\begin{cases} x - 2y = 1 \\ 3x + y = 5 \end{cases}, \text{ or } \begin{cases} x + 8 = 4 \\ 5x - 7y = 2, \text{ or } \end{cases} \begin{cases} xy = 1 \\ 3x + 2y = 1 \end{cases}$$

Once these problems were solved, the teacher made a summarization of the concept.

Phase III: Explaining and discriminating the solution of systems of equations. Based on re-examining the word problems, the teacher showed all whole number ordered pairs that had been found from each of the two equations in the stamps problem, and the students found that $x=3$, $y=4$ was the common ordered pair satisfying the two equations. Then the teacher concluded that such a solution was called the solution of the system of linear equations with two unknowns and explained that the values of x and y should be grouped with a big bracket. After that, the students were asked to do two types of exercises: (1) To decide whether given pairs of numbers are the solution of given systems of linear equations; (2) To identify systems of linear equations that had a given solution; and (3) To construct systems of linear equations with two unknowns that had a given solution set.

Phase IV: Summarization. Based on explanations and discussions, the teacher made the following summary: (1) If systems of equations consisted of two unknowns and their index is one, this system of equations is called a simultaneous system of linear equations with two unknowns; and (2) The common solution for the equations in the system is called the solution of the system of linear equations with two unknowns. Finally, the teacher asked the class to work on the homework.

Learning Opportunities Provided by the Teacher

It was found that the teacher introduced, clarified and deepened the concepts through exploring relevant variations of problems. The following sections illustrate the possible learning opportunities.

Developing the new concepts through exploring inductive/broadening variations of problems. It was evident that the teacher adopted some *inductive problems* (the stamps problems in Phase I) to form the concept of systems of linear equations and their solutions by relating the new concepts to previous knowledge of linear equations and the solution of a linear equation. Meanwhile, the development of this concept was treated as *a way to solve certain kinds of daily life problems* (Usiskin, 1988). In Phase II, based on the students work on the solutions of each linear equation, the teacher clearly explained the concepts and their relationship with previous concepts, as the following excerpt illustrates:

T: Are these six ordered pairs? Then, we can use our own way to write down these solutions. That is, we can show the six ordered pairs like this [shown on slide in tabular form]. Then, all of you can see that one more condition is added to this question, x plus y equals seven, then if the total amount is still equal to ten dollars which is unchanged, so the values of unknowns x and y not only need to satisfy the first equation, but also need to satisfy the second equation. So, we associate these two equations together by using a big bracket. This is called systems of equations - that means, if there are some equations formed into one group, we call it systems of equations.

In Phase III, the teacher again mentioned the word problems, and further developed the concept of solution of systems of linear equations as follows:

T: Okay. We have learned about concepts up to here. Let's go back to the word question. From this question, based on the total expenditure of ten dollars, we can find this equation, then based on this equation [the first equation], we can find out four ordered pairs through the table, based on the total number of stamps is seven, we find x plus y equals seven, then based on this equation [the second question], we can find these six ordered pairs [shows slide]. Therefore, according to this question, the values of these unknowns x, y, not only need to satisfy the first equation x plus two y equals ten, two x plus y equals ten but also need to satisfy the second equation x plus y equals seven. In other words, the values of the unknowns x and y not only need to be one solution to one equation, but also need to be the common solution of two linear equations. Then please find out whether there is such a solution?

S: Yes, there is.
T: Which one?
S: x is three, y is four.
T: Right. Here it is, x is three, y is four, then we will say x is three, y is four, is the solution of this system of equations, solution of the system of equations. We use a big bracket to associate them, and then what is the meaning of the solution for systems of equations? In a pair of linear equations in two unknowns, the solution which satisfies each of the equations is called the solution of this system of linear equations in two unknowns.

Consolidating the concepts through practising with deepening variation of problems. After introducing the concept of systems of linear equations and their solution, the teacher assigned *deepening variations of problems* for students to apply these concepts to deepen their understanding. For example, in Phase III, the students were asked first to solve two basic problems: given systems of linear equations, identify whether a pair of numbers is the solution of the system of equations or not, and given a solution, identify whether systems of linear equations include this solution. A more challenging and open-ended problem was then assigned to the students to solve, as follows:

Given a solution which is x=1 and y=2, find the system of linear equations.

During the sharing session, the teacher encouraged the students to articulate what they knew as follows:

T: Have you finished?
S1: Yes.
T: Okay, let's discuss it. Who wants to try it? Good, S2.

S2:   x plus five equals six, and then x plus two y equals five.

T: Is he correct? Let your classmates judge you.

S1:   Correct.

T: Please sit down.

T: Okay, who will come next? S3.

S3:   Three x plus y over two equals four. I don't have anymore. [Teacher writes notes on the blackboard].

T: You don't have any other equations? Please sit down then. Anybody? Oh, good, S4, please supplement on it.

S4:   Two x minus five y equals eight [teacher writes notes on the blackboard].

T: Please take a look. Is it correct what S4 just said?

Ss: Correct.

T: Okay, good, please sit down, then any other? Oh, S5, this one? Who? S6, you also haven't finished, okay, then who has finished? Please put up your hands. [Some students put up their hands].

T: Good, please put it down. S7.

S7:   Two x plus y equals four, x plus y equals three [teacher writes notes on the blackboard].

T: Good, sit down please. S8, is he correct? Is he correct? Okay, what about yours? [S9 looks at S10's exercises].

S8:   x plus three y equals seven; three x plus five y equals thirteen.

T: S11, is he correct?

S11:   Correct.

In Phases II and III the teacher organized several activities for practising algebraic transformation. Through these the algebraic computation skills were practised extensively.

Reflecting on learning experiences. After introducing the concept of systems of linear equations and their solution, and discriminating between these concepts, the teacher summarized some key points through the use of PowerPoint, as illustrated below:

T: Okay, today we have learned the concepts of systems of linear equations in two unknowns. This means that, when a pair of equations contains two unknowns and the indices of the unknowns are one, then we will call it a system of linear equations in two unknowns. The

> second thing is the concept of solution for systems
> of equations. That means, if a solution is suitable
> for both the two equations of a pair of equations,
> we will call it the solution of this system of linear
> equations in two unknowns [shows slide].

Based on the theory of teaching with variations, in the class, the teacher created possible learning conditions for the students to develop (inducing and broadening variations) and consolidate the concepts (deepening and applying variations), and form an interconnected knowledge structure by summarizing key points as well.

CONCLUSION AND DISCUSSION

Based on the examination of these sample teachers' methods of constructing the particular algebraic concepts, systems *of linear equations with two unknowns and their solution*, the common features have been identified as explaining concepts clearly and summarizing the key points in due course. Although there was diversity in the methods of introducing the concepts, a pattern was identified from these methods: introducing the concepts through reviewing, or solving daily life problems, then explaining the concepts clearly, and finally enhancing the students' understanding of the concepts through discriminating exercises and applying problems, followed by summarization.

Discussion

This study shows that the strategies commonly used in these Chinese classrooms were directly explaining a concept and providing varied practice. These features are accorded to the teacher-dominated teaching style and illustrate further what the teachers actually may have taught in the lessons. On one hand, the "listening-oriented learning" notion (Cortazzi & Jin, 2001) seems to suggest that students can understand a concept to a certain extent through listening. On the other hand, the problem-solving oriented approach that involves introducing a concept through inductive variation of problems, clarifying the concept through discriminating/broadening variations of problems, and consolidating the concept through deepening/applying variations of problems may help students understand the concept progressively and build an interconnected concept system (Gu et al., 2004; Huang, Mok, & Leung, 2006).

With regard to the specificity of learning algebra, the pattern described in this study has demonstrated the feasibility of introducing algebraic concepts as the way to solve certain kinds of contextual problems, and the method to present the relationships among quantities (Usiskin, 1988). In the classes described here, through the whole process of developing and consolidating the concepts, two core algebra activities, *generalization* and *transformation,* were carried out extensively.

Moreover, through the tabular representation and finding the coordinate pairs which fit the equations, the linear functions were explored informally, which paved the way for learning graphical methods of solving systems of linear equations in the subsequent lessons. This approach sheds light on how an integrated approach to learning algebra (function-oriented and algebraic expression- and equation-oriented) may be feasible in the classroom. This observation has important implications for implementing reform-oriented algebra curricula in China.

In addition, although it has been acknowledged widely that the development of conceptual understanding and procedural fluency is important (NCTM, 2000; NMAP, 2008), the ways to achieve this goal are still debated (Rittle-Johnson & Alibali, 1999; Silver, 1986; Star, 2005). The pattern that emerged in the Shanghai and Macau classroom instruction provides an alternative way of developing students' conceptual understanding and procedural fluency, that is to introduce a concept through reviewing and solving word problems, and to explain the definition of the concept clearly, test students' understanding with multiple discriminating practices and finally provide them with problems for application. This strategy of developing new concepts echoes the notion of meaningful learning suggested by Ausubel (1968). It is also conducive to developing students' understanding (Carpenter & Lehrer, 1999). During the whole process of developing the concepts, the generalization and transformation activities fostered the students' development of procedural fluency.

It should be noted, however, that the space of the students' self-exploratory learning may have been constrained, and some learning opportunities may have been lost in such well-designed lessons (Mok, Cai, & Fung, 2008). This could be risky, resulting in students' weakness in solving non-routine problems (Cai & Cifarelli, 2004) and negative attitudes toward mathematics and mathematics learning (Millis et al., 2004; OECD, 2004).

ACKNOWLEDGEMENT

The study was supported partially by a research grant (No. 2566) from the University of Macau, Macau SAR, China. However, any opinions expressed herein are those of the authors and do not necessarily represent the views of the University of Macau.

REFERENCES

An, S., Kulm, G., & Wu, Z. (2004). The pedagogical content knowledge of middle school mathematics teachers in China and the U.S. *Journal of Mathematics Teacher Education, 7,* 145–172.

Ausubel, D. P. (1968). *Educational psychology: A cognitive view.* New York, NY: Holt, Rinehart & Winston.

Bednarz, N., Kieran, C., & Lee, L.(1996). *Approaches to algebra: Perspectives for research and teaching.* Dordrecht: Kluwer.

Cai, J., & Cifarelli, V. (2004). Thinking mathematically by Chinese learners: A cross-national comparative perspective. In L. Fan, N. Y. Wong, J. Cai, & S. Li (Eds.), *How Chinese learn mathematics: Perspectives from insiders* (pp. 71–106). Singapore: World Scientific.

Cai, J., & Moyer, M. (2008). Developing algebraic thinking in earlier grades: Some insights from international comparative studies. In C. E. Greens & R. Rubenstein (Eds.), *Algebra and algebraic thinking in school mathematics* (pp. 169–180). Reston, VA: National Council of Teachers of Mathematics.

Carpenter, T. P., & Lehrer, R. (1999). Teaching and learning mathematics with understanding. In E. Fennema & T. A. Romberg (Eds.), *Mathematics classroom that promote understanding* (pp. 19–32). Mahwah: Lawrence Erlbaum.

Clarke, D. (2006). The LPS research design. In D. J. Clarke, J. Keitel, C., & Y. Shimizu (Eds.), *Mathematics classrooms in twelve countries* (pp. 15–29). Rotterdam, The Netherlands: Sense.

Cortazzi, M., & Jin, L. (2001). Large class in China: "Good" teachers and interaction, In D. A. Watkins & J. B. Biggs (Eds), *Teaching the Chinese learner: Psychological and pedagogical perspectives* (pp. 115–134). Hong Kong/Melbourne: Comparative Education Research Centre, the University of Hong Kong/Australian Council for Education Research.

Edwards, E. L. (Ed.). (1990). *Algebra for everyone*. Reston, VA: National Council of Teachers of Mathematics.

Filloy, E., Rojano, T., & Solares, A. (2003). Two meanings of the "equal" sign and senses of comparison and substitution methods. In N. A. Pateman, B. J. Dougherty, & H. T. Zilliox (Eds.), *Proceedings of the 27th conference of the International Group for the Psychology of Mathematics Education* (Vol. 4, pp. 223–229). Honolulu, HI.

Gu, L. (2000, July). Exploring the middle zone. *Paper presented at the 9th International Congress of Mathematics Education* (Gathering of Chinese scholars), Tokyo/Makuhari, Japan.

Gu, L., Huang, R., & Marton, F. (2004). Teaching with variation: An effective way of mathematics teaching in China. In L. Fan, N. Y. Wong, J. Cai, & S. Li (Eds.), *How Chinese learn mathematics: Perspectives from insiders* (pp. 309–345). Singapore: World Scientific.

Harel, G., Fuller, E., & Rabin, J. M. (2008). Attention to meaning by algebra teachers. *Journal of Mathematical Behavior, 27,* 116–127.

Herscovics, N., & Linchevski, L. (1994). A cognitive gap between arithmetic and algebra, *Educational Studies in Mathematics, 27,* 59–78.

Hiebert, J., & Carpenter, P. P. (1992). Learning and teaching with understanding. In D. A. Grouws (Ed.), *Handbook of research on mathematics teaching and learning* (pp. 65–97). New York, NY: Macmillan.

Huang, R., & Li, Y. (2009). Examining the nature of effective teaching through master teachers' lesson evaluation in China. In J. Cai, G. Kaiser, B. Perry, & N.Y. Wong (Eds.), *Effective mathematics teaching from teachers' perspectives: National and international studies* (pp. 163–182). Rotterdam, The Netherlands: Sense.

Huang, R., Mok, I. A. C., & Leung, F. K. S. (2006). Repetition or Variation: "Practice" in the mathematics classrooms in China. In D. J. Clarke, C. Keitel, & Y. Shimizu (Eds.), *Mathematics classrooms in twelve countries: The insider's perspective* (pp. 263–274). Rotterdam: Sense.

Kaput, J., Carraher, D., & Blanton, M. (2008). (Eds.). *Algebra in the early grades* (pp. 95–132). New York, NY: Erlbaum.

Katz, V. J. (Ed.). (2007). *Algebra: Gateway to a technological future*. Washington, DC: The Mathematical Association of America.

Kendal, M., & Stacey, K. (2004). Algebra: A world of difference. In K. Stacey, C. Helen, & K. Margaret (Eds.), *The future of the teaching and learning of algebra, The 12th ICM Study* (pp. 329–346). Boston, MA: Kluwer.

Kieran, C. (1981). Concepts associated with the equality symbol. *Educational Studies in Mathematics, 12,* 317–326.

Kieran, C. (1989). The early learning of algebra: A structural perspective. In S. Wagner & C. Kieran (Eds.), *Research issues in the learning and teaching of algebra* (pp. 33–56). Reston, VA: National Council of Teachers of Mathematics.

Kieran, C. (2004). The core of algebra: Reflections on its main activities. In K. Stacey, H. Chick, & M. Kendal (Eds.), *The future of the teaching and learning of algebra: The 12th ICMI study* (pp. 21–34). Boston, MA: Kluwer.

Kieran, C. (2007). Learning and teaching algebra at the middle school from college levels: Building meaning for symbols and their manipulation. In F. K. Lester, Jr. (Ed.), *Second handbook of research on mathematics teaching and learning* (pp. 707–762). Charlotte, NC: Information Age.

Leung, F. K. S. (1995). The mathematics classroom in Beijing, Hong Kong and London. *Educational Studies in Mathematics, 29*, 197–325.

Leung, F. K. S. (2001). In search of an East Asian identity in mathematics education. *Educational Studies in Mathematics, 47*, 35–51.

Li, S., Huang, R., & Shin, Y. (2008). Discipline knowledge preparation for prospective secondary mathematics teachers: An East Asian perspective. In P. Sullivan & T. Wood (Eds.), *Knowledge and beliefs in mathematics teaching and teaching development* (pp. 63–86). Rotterdam, The Netherlands: Sense.

Li, Y., Huang, R., & Yang, Y. (2011). Characterizing expert teaching in school mathematics in China: A prototype of expertise in teaching mathematics. In Y. Li & G. Kaiser (Eds.), *Expertise in teaching mathematics: An international perspective* (pp. 168–196). New York, NY: Springer.

Ma, L. (1999). *Knowing and teaching elementary mathematics: Teachers' understanding of fundamental mathematics in China and the United States.* Mahwah, NJ: Erlbaum.

Marton, F., & Booth, S. (1997). *Learning and awareness.* Mahwah, NJ: Erlbaum.

Marton, F., & Tsui, A. B. M. (2004). *Classroom discourse and the space of learning.* Mahwah, NJ: Erlbaum.

Mok, I. A. C., Cai, J., & Fung, A. T. F. (2008). Missing learning opportunities in classroom instruction: Evidence from an analysis of a well-structured lesson on comparing fractions. *The Mathematics Educator, 11*, 111–126.

Moses, R. P., & Cobb, C. E., Jr. (2001). *Radical equations: math literacy and civil rights.* Boston, MA: Beacon.

Mullis, I. V. S., Martin, M. O., Gonzalez, E. J., & Chrostowski, S. J. (2004). *TIMSS 2003 International Mathematics Report: Findings From IEA's Trends in International Mathematics and Science Study at the Fourth and Eighth Grades.* Boston, MA: TIMSS & PIRLS International Study Center, Lynch School of Education, Boston College.

National Council of Teachers of Mathematics. (2009). *Focus in high school mathematics: Reasoning and sense making.* Reston, VA: Author.

National Council of Teachers of Mathematics. (2000). *Principles and standards for school mathematics.* Reston, VA: Author.

National Mathematics Advisory Panel. (2008). *Foundations for success: The final report of the National Mathematics Advisory Panel.* Washington, DC: U.S. Department of Education.

OECD (2004). *Learning for Tomorrow's World: First results from PISA 2003.* France: OECD, Organisation for Economic Co-operation and Development.

Rittle-Johnson, B., & Alibali, M. W. (1999). Conceptual and procedural knowledge of mathematics: Does one lead to the others? *Journal of Educational Psychology, 91*, 175–189.

Silver, E. A. (1986). Using conceptual and procedural knowledge: A focus on relationships. In J. Hiebert (Ed.), *Conceptual and procedural knowledge: The case of mathematics* (pp. 181–198). Hillsdale, NJ: Erlbaum.

Sleeman, D. (1984). An attempt to understand student's understanding of basic algebra. *Cognitive Science, 8*, 387–412.

Star, J. R. (2005). Reconceptualizing procedural knowledge. *Journal for Research in Mathematics Education, 36*, 404–411.

Usiskin, Z. (1988). Conceptions of school algebra and uses of variables. In A. F. Coxford & A. P. Shulte (Eds.), *Algebraic thinking, grades K–12* (pp. 8–19). Reston, VA: National Council of Teachers of Mathematics.

Wong, N. Y., Lam, C. C., Sun, X., & Chan A. M. Y. (2009). From "exploring the middle zone" to "constructing a bridge": Experimenting in the spiral *bianshi* mathematics curriculum. *International Journal of Science and Mathematics Education, 7*, 36–382.

AFFILIATIONS

Rongjin Huang
Middle Tennessee State University
USA

Ida Ah Chee Mok
The University of Hong Kong
Hong Kong

Frederick K. S. Leung
The University of Hong Kong
Hong Kong

RONGJIN HUANG & YEPING LI

CHAPTER 12

*Promoting Mathematical Understanding: An Examination of
Algebra Instruction in Chinese and U.S. Classrooms*

BACKGROUND

It is a paradoxical phenomenon that a seemingly unfavorable learning environment, such as the large-size classrooms dominated with traditional lecture-oriented instruction in China, produces high-achieving students in school mathematics (Fan & Zhu, 2004; Stevenson, Chen, & Lee, 1993). Some researchers have thus examined how Chinese students learn mathematics (Fan, Wong, Cai, & Li, 2004), and what Chinese mathematics classrooms look like (Huang, 2006; Huang & Leung, 2004; Huang & Li, 2009; Li & Huang, 2012; Lopez-Real, Mok, Leung, & Marton, 2004; Stevenson & Lee, 1995). It was found that there were some crucial student-centred elements in these large classrooms in China, such as asking students to explore and share different solutions to variations of problems. In contrast, researchers have reported that the teaching strategies in many U.S. classrooms were still traditional, far from the innovative scenarios that have been advocated in the U.S. (Jacobs, Hiebert, Givvin, Hollingsworth, & Weame, 2006; Wood, Shin, & Doan, 2006).

Underlying these disparities between mathematics classrooms, there may be some fundamental conceptual differences between U.S. and Chinese teachers concerning mathematics instruction. A few studies have focused on teachers' conceptions of 'good teaching' (e.g. Cai & Wang, 2010) and particular teaching strategies (e.g. Huang & Cai, 2011). For example, Huang and Cai (2011) conducted an analysis of pedagogy associated with the use of representations in Chinese and U.S. classrooms in which linear equations were explored extensively. They found that the U.S. teachers tried to develop multiple representations simultaneously over a sequence of lessons through different activities, while the Chinese teachers tried to develop symbolic representations and graphic representations through the use of numerical and tabular representations to solve problems. Cai and Wang (2010) found that the U.S. teachers emphasized developing students' understanding with concrete examples while the Chinese teachers stressed abstract reasoning after using concrete examples. Both groups of teachers agreed that memorization and understanding cannot be separated. However, for U.S. teachers, memorization comes after understanding and, for Chinese teachers, it can occur either before or after understanding. Moreover, Huang and Cai (2010) examined how teachers select and implement mathematical tasks in selected Chinese and U.S. classrooms. The sampled teachers from both countries

F.K.S. Leung et al. (eds.), Algebra Teaching around the World, 213–232.
© *2014 Sense Publishers. All rights reserved.*

provided mathematical tasks with a high cognitive demand for their students to explore. The common strategies that the Chinese and U.S. teachers used to implement mathematical tasks included demonstrating high-level performance, appropriately soliciting and using students' answers, and appropriately organizing exploratory activities. However, compared to the U.S. teacher, the Chinese teacher was better at sustaining the cognitive demand when implementing the mathematics tasks.

These findings help us understand classroom instruction across these two countries from a teachers' perspective, but they give very limited attention to how teachers and students work together around mathematically worthwhile tasks (Martin, 2007; NCTM, 2000). As classroom instruction is a process that involves the participation of teachers and their students, how teachers and students construct classroom events and how they perceive what is happening in classrooms should be indispensable parts of examining classroom instruction.

Classroom instruction is complex, and can be understood better from multiple perspectives (Schoenfeld & Pateman, 2008). In this study, we aimed to go beyond previous studies of Chinese and U.S. classroom instruction that have focused on the use of representations, tasks, and teachers' perceptions. Instead, we focused on how teaching may help to promote students' understanding through a cross-national lens, with the following two considerations: (1). Teaching for understanding is an issue that has been explored for a long time (Baroody, Feil, & Johnson, 2007; Brownell, 1938; NCTM, 2000; Star, 2005), but it is difficult to implement classroom instruction that promotes understanding (Carpenter & Lehrer, 1999; Hiebert & Carpenter, 1992); (2).Cross-cultural studies have found that there are fundamental differences between Chinese and Western teachers in their conceptions of understanding and memorization (Cai & Wang, 2010; Marton, Dall'Alba, & Tse, 1996). For example, through interviews with 20 Chinese teacher educators, Marton and his colleagues (1996) provided a new way of seeing the relationship between memorization and understanding. For Chinese educators, memorization does not necessarily lead to rote learning; instead, it can be used to deepen understanding. This conception is quite different from western notions of the relationship. Thus, a cross-national examination of mathematics classroom instruction in China and the U.S., which have such contrasting cultures, may provide a broader point of view on how we should help students learn and understand mathematics with proficiency.

In particular, we aimed to address this issue of teaching for understanding through exploring the following questions:

1. What are the intended goals Chinese and U.S. teachers wish to achieve in enhancing students' understanding?
2. What perceptions do Chinese and U.S. students have of their classroom instruction with regard to understanding?
3. What are the similarities and differences between Chinese and U.S. classrooms when algebra content is taught?

THEORETICAL CONSIDERATIONS

Teaching and learning mathematics with understanding has long been advocated through educational research (Brownell, 1938; Carpenter & Lehrer, 1999; Hiebert & Carpenter, 1992; Skemp, 1979). The conceptual understanding and procedural proficiency dichotomy is the one used the most to feature students' learning of knowledge (Hiebert & Carpenter, 1992). Some researchers have argued that this kind of dichotomy might not be able to capture students' classroom learning due to the superficial classifications (Star, 2005) and cultural differences (Marton et al., 1996).

On the other hand, Carpenter and Lehrer (1999) put forward a framework describing that students' understanding is rooted in classroom instruction and based on their mental activities. This model suggests that five forms of mental activities are conducive to developing mathematics understanding in classrooms: (a) constructing relationships, (b) extending and applying mathematical knowledge, (c) reflecting on experiences, (d) articulating what one knows, and (e) making mathematical knowledge one's own. In this analysis, 'constructing a relationship' refers to building a relationship between new knowledge and previous knowledge, building internal connections between concepts, and building connections among representations. 'Extending and applying learned knowledge' means to apply knowledge to solve problems and build a foundation for further study. 'Reflection' mainly refers to a summary of and reflection on what students have learned and experienced. 'Articulating' includes group discussions and public sharing. 'Making mathematical knowledge one's own' refers to making mathematics interesting and relating it to daily life, while the students explore the subject matter by themselves.

In particular, classroom instruction consists of interactive activities between the teacher and the students surrounding special contents to achieve some intended goals (Hiebert & Grouws, 2007). A holistic approach to investigating classroom instruction through the lenses of the teacher, the students, and the classroom practice will help us to understand classroom instruction better. Based on the notion of understanding from Carpenter and Lehrer (1999), we examined the connections and relationships among teachers' intentions, classroom practice and students' perceptions.

METHOD

Data Source

The data for this study were part of the Learner's Perspective Study (LPS), which examined the patterns of participation in competently taught seventh or eighth grade mathematics classrooms in sixteen countries in a more integrated and comprehensive fashion than had been attempted in previous international studies (Clarke, 2006a). In this study, we selected one Chinese school data set and one U.S. school data set. The background of the classrooms and the teachers and the main topics taught over 10 consecutive lessons in the Chinese and U.S. classrooms can be found in a previous paper by Huang and Cai (2010).

In particular, one Chinese lesson on the relationship between points and their coordinates in the Cartesian plane and one U.S. lesson consisting of two consecutive sections on judging linear and nonlinear relations, two interviews with each of the two teachers, and two student interviews from each of the classes were taken as the main data for this study. We selected these two lessons for the following reasons. First, during the interviews the teachers themselves described these two lessons as important. Second, the topics are all related to algebra and algebraic representations.

In video-stimulated interviews, the teacher was asked to watch the selected lesson, stop at the moments that he/she believed important, and then talk about what he/she had been doing and feeling at that moment. Specifically, the teacher was prompted by the following questions: (1) What were your goals in that lesson (lesson content/lesson purpose)? (2) In relation to your content goal(s), why do you think this is important for students to learn? (3) In these important moments you identified in the videotaped lesson, what were you doing? How were you feeling? Similarly, the video-stimulated students' interview was guided by the following questions: (1) What did you learn in that lesson? (2) Why do you think that identified moment is important? (3) What were you doing at that moment? How were you feeling?

Data Analysis

Through detailed reading of the interview data, we tried to build a code table based on the five categories suggested by Carpenter and Lehrer (1999). We found it necessary to add two more categories: (1) understanding through listening and seeing, and (2) mentioning understanding in general without specific explanations. The first refers to mentioning directly the importance of listening and seeing for understanding, while the second refers to mentioning students' understanding or lack of it in general terms. Table 1 shows all the categories related to understanding, codes and relevant examples.

One research assistant coded the interview data, and this was re-checked by the authors. Disagreements were resolved through intensive discussions. Moreover, the authors conducted qualitative analyses of the selected lessons using the same framework, through repeatedly watching the videos and reading the transcripts. During the process of data analysis, the authors and the research assistant often discussed how to grasp the meaning as appropriately as possible.

RESULTS

The results were grouped into three sections according to the three research questions, namely the teacher's intention of instruction, the students' perceptions of classroom instruction, and the enactment of classroom instruction.

Table 1. Categories and examples from the teacher interviews

Category	Code	Examples from teacher's interviews
Constructing relationship	CR	So for the arrangement of the contents, by having revision, I will guide the students gently to new materials
Extending and applying	EA	I change the questions systematically, and ask the students to find out the coordinates of various points.
Reflecting	RE	By categorization and summary, the lesson reached its climax
Articulating	AR	That was good for the students to learn from each other, and it could let them clarify the characteristics of the coordinates of the points on the two axes
Making mathematics knowledge student's own	MA	I truly want to make mathematics everybody's business
Understanding through listening and seeing	UL	When we were asking the questions, people were answering and I was seeing like what ... what they were
Understanding or not understanding	UN	You have to fully understand the question in order to solve the question

Teacher's Intention of Instruction

Instructional objectives With regard to the instructional objectives and rationale, the Chinese teacher gave specific descriptions in the first interview as follows:

> This lesson was aimed at letting students know how to determine the location of a certain point based on its coordinates on a Cartesian plane. This would let the students know there's a corresponding relationship between the points on the plane and their coordinates.

> Essentially, the content was about the integration of numbers and figures. For further studies, especially on the topic of functions, the understanding of the graph of linear equations with two unknowns, and the graphical method for solving linear equations with two unknowns, it would be a great help. So from this point of view, this is a tremendous help for the students' further studies. Thus, it is of great significance and importance.

In contrast, the U.S. teacher described more general and ambitious goals of mathematics teaching:

> Teaching mathematics is seeing the forest instead of the trees. Because I think

217

so often [that] people are experiencing math class with a large dose of algebra, but they have no cohesive understanding, no cement to hold all discrete learning together. They have procedures and they have little computations, they solve equations... But they've never had any large conceptual picture of what this may be... It is absolutely important."

Based on the previous descriptions, the Chinese teacher paid more attention to helping students to achieve a concrete and detailed instructional objective for laying the foundation for further study, while the U.S. teacher tended to help her students to build cohesive and connected algebra concepts, with less attention to specific content and skills.

Teachers' preferred instructional approaches Table 2 below displays the teachers' preferences in their attempts to promote mathematical understanding, according to the two interviews conducted with each teacher.

Table 2. Categories of Teacher Interviews

Category	Chinese Teacher	U.S. Teacher
Constructing relationship	9	8
Extending and applying	18	4
Articulating	8	6
Making mathematics one's own	8	4

It is interesting that both teachers expressed the importance of helping students to learn mathematics through constructing relationships between concepts or knowledge (9 and 8 times) and articulating what they think and know (8 and 6 times). For example, the U.S. teacher not only asked the students to draw the graphs of equations, but also to interpret the meanings of the graphs by themselves: "as far as interpreting and creating any meanings around the graph, it was literally pulling teeth to try and get them to write down one logical conclusion from the graph" (US teacher). She also valued her students' ideas and encouraged them to share these; for example, she stated that "to check if I understood this correctly, maybe there's something I've overlooked". Moreover, she showed that she was sensitive to the students' feelings when they made mistakes by saying that "you know we really do learn from our mistakes".

On the other hand, the Chinese teacher emphasized the interrelation between the topic taught and the future topics as follows:

For later studies, especially on the topic of functions, the understanding of the graphs of linear equations with two unknowns and the graphical method in solving the linear equations with two unknowns would be a great help.

He also valued the students' articulation, as indicated by the following excerpts:

From time to time I ask students to have discussions, because discussions are helpful. When the students cannot understand the concepts, or when they find it difficult to learn, discussions can help them to learn from each other.

It seems that the Chinese teacher paid more attention to helping students to learn mathematics through extending and applying learnt knowledge (18 times) than did the U.S. teacher (4 times). The Chinese teacher emphasized classroom exercises with variations, while the U.S. teacher appreciated solving daily-life situation problems. For example, the Chinese teacher put emphasis on searching for different solutions through discussing and sharing as follows:

I asked the students to discuss the question in small groups first, because this question was quite difficult for seventh graders, and there were several ways to solve the question. That means there were two possibilities for the location of the figure. The students usually only considered one solution and they would not consider the other possibility. So they might find it difficult to find solutions.

However, the U.S. teacher emphasized the application of knowledge as follows:

I especially value those - those activities that demonstrate most clearly a starting point, improvement and quizzed understanding. ... We are looking at the waterworks problem that we worked on in the fall.

Furthermore, the Chinese teacher seemed to pay more attention to what is called 'making mathematics one's own' (8 times), when compared with the U.S teacher (4 times). For example, the Chinese teacher put emphasis on motivating students through mathematical explorations:

During this hands-on activity, the students could get to know the concepts. We should cultivate their ability to learn, so I made a daring attempt at this place, I allowed the students to find out the figure on their own."

Meanwhile, the U.S teacher tried to motivate the students' intrinsic interest through exploring the usefulness and elegance of mathematics as follows:

I've been trying to encourage them over the three previous years of the existence of this school to use mathematics ... but I try to convince them of the intrinsic elegance of mathematics.

Students' Perceptions of Classroom Instruction

Table 3 shows how students view or interpret important episodes or events within the existing categories of mathematical understanding.

219

Table 3. Categories and Choices from Student Interviews

Category	Chinese students	U.S. students
Constructing relationships	3	3
Extending and applying	7	4
Articulating	8	11
Making mathematics one's own	3	1
Understanding through listening	3	5
Understanding or not understanding	2	5

Table 3 shows that both the Chinese and the U.S. students found only a few episodes to be of importance in terms of constructing relationships of concepts (3 times). A U.S student recognized an important episode, because, "It was just telling us - there was one equation with - there were four different ways you can show it". On the other hand, a Chinese student paid attention to solving a particular part of a problem, "If you didn't understand the question well, then you would not be able to do the following question?"

With regard to the students' articulation, the U.S. students emphasized expressing what they knew (12 times) more than did the Chinese students (8 times). The U.S. students enjoyed group activities:

> We got into groups, and each group had something to do ... See, this is the part where we're drawing our stuff. We were doing our group thing, that Y equals two ... We talked about it in our groups and we got different ideas.

A Chinese student realized the necessity of discussion:

> Because when the teacher asks us to discuss, if you don't discuss properly, then when the teacher calls on you to elaborate, you will not be able to answer.

In addition, the Chinese students extended their learning through examples and exercises in the classroom more often (7 times) than did the U.S. students (4 times). For example, for the Chinese student, the videotaped lesson was good, because, "It covered all the things in exercise two of the textbook".

A U.S. student showed that she was aware of the importance of assigned group activities by pointing out that:

> She would ask us the questions on the board. ... One [problem is assigned] for the [group] one and the [group] three. And then, another [problem is assigned] for the [group] two and the [group] four.

It was unexpected that the Chinese students put more emphasis on making mathematics one's own. For example, the Chinese students appreciated that the teacher:

Let us learn it by ourselves first. After learning it, we checked to see if there is a way that we can learn by ourselves.

Moreover, both the U.S. students (4 times) and Chinese students (3 times) expressed the belief that learning mathematics through listening and seeing is important. For example, a Chinese student said:

The teacher's speech is also important, because if you simply discuss among yourselves, you won't always get the answer. On the other hand, the teacher can give you a correct answer; tell you what is right and what is wrong.

The U.S. students listened to the teacher and their peers' answers:

When she [the teacher] was asking the questions, people were answering and I was seeing like what ... what they were.

During the interviews, the U.S. students mentioned understanding (5 times) more often than did the Chinese students (2 times). For example, one U.S. student described that, "I understood how to figure out [the graph]", but another student pointed to the difficulties in understanding:

I don't know how to tell if they are curved or not ... when she's just talking to us, it's harder for me to understand.

When comparing the teacher's preferences and students' perceptions, it was found that both the Chinese and U.S. teachers and students emphasized constructing connections and applying learned knowledge to solve problems. In addition, the Chinese teacher and students valued the expression of what students knew and thought. However, the U.S. students seemed to appreciate expressing what they knew. Overall, the Chinese teacher and students emphasized classroom exercise with varying problems more than did the U.S. teacher and students, but the U.S. teacher valued daily-life problem solving.

Enacting Teaching in the Classroom

The aims of the U.S. lessons were to recognize general characteristics of slope and direct variation. The students learnt to move flexibly across the various representations of functions - tables, graphs, verbal descriptions, and equations. At the beginning of the lesson, the class spent around 13 minutes doing warm-up exercises about a number pattern/sequence from which two non-linear functions ($y = 2^x$ and $y = 2^x - 1$) were induced.

After demonstrating how to match the equation $x = 2$ with a relevant table, a graph, and a verbal description of the graph, there was a 'matching activity': The students applied further examples as above. Then, one group member demonstrated the group's work on the blackboard. After that, she distributed two white boards and two markers to each group and had each student label the project 'Ideas *about*

Algebraic Representations'. The students were asked to answer the following five questions in groups on their boards: (1) What are the common features of these graphs? (2) Is $x = 2$ a vertical or horizontal line? (3) Is $y = 2x$ a model of direct variation? (4) Is the slope of this graph positive or negative? (5) Is the point $(0, 2)$ on the x-intercept or the y-intercept?

After completing the above questions, the teacher asked the students to exchange their white boards and gave them the following five new questions to answer: (1) Rename $x + y = 2$ in terms of y. (2) What is the slope of $y = -x + 2$? (3) Are these graphs (parabola, hyperbola) linear or nonlinear? (4) What does non-linear mean? (5) What kind of shape does squaring result in?

In the Chinese lesson, the students were taught 'part two of positions and coordinates of points on a Cartesian plane'. In this lesson, they were expected to learn to draw a point when given its coordinates and vice versa. At the beginning of the class, the teacher reviewed the concept of the Cartesian plane with the class and discussed the way to figure out the coordinates of given points and find the positions of points given their coordinates. Then, they solved some routine problems. The first was to plot five given points on a coordinate plane. After that, one more challenging problem was presented: "Given a straight line segment AB with a length of 4 units. Plot all possible points for C and D so that ABCD is a square." More exercises in the textbook were completed. Finally, a summary was made and some homework was assigned.

Opportunities of Learning with Understanding in the U.S Classroom

In the U.S., the lesson was organized mainly as small-group discussions, which included some cycles of explaining and distributing activities, doing group activities, and sharing their results in class. The teacher highly valued cooperative learning of mathematics. The students were often encouraged to express what they thought. The teacher obviously offered opportunities for them to learn by themselves and to share what they knew. In this section, we closely examine what they were doing during the private and public discussions. Different patterns of interaction between teacher and students may result in different opportunities for students to learn. In the following sections, we describe some types of interaction.

Teacher-led discussions For example, in the first few warm-up activities, the teacher encouraged students to find the patterns of a sequence of numbers, and further to find the function underlying these patterns. The teacher encouraged students to explain their reasoning behind a pattern in one particular set of numbers:

```
T    Um, all right. So, what about this? Who can explain
     it? Let's hear what you've got, um ... Brianne.
Brianne ( ) multiply by ( ). Four times two is eight.
T    Uh-uh. No.
     Brianne  Eight times two is sixteen. Sixteen times two
     is thirty-two. ( ) is sixty four.
```

T   Okay. Times two, times two, times two. That's what I
    was hearing, yes?
Ss Mm-hm.
T   Okay. Anything else? Someone explain it differently.
    Hm, hm, hm, hm. You know what? If I hear times two,
    times two, times two, it sort of suggests to y- me
S   Doubling?
T   Doubling? Yeah. And it sort of suggests to me powers
    of a certain base. I wonder what that base might be?
Ss Square root?
    Heather Square. No, it wouldn't be a square. It would
    be
T   What base? What base number?
Ss Two.
T   Here's a base, here's an exponent [Teacher writes on
    board].
S   Base of two.

Key to symbols used in transcripts in this chapter

A pause of one second or less

*( )   Empty single parentheses represent untranscribed talk. The talk may be
untranscribed because the transcriber could not hear what was said
. . . . Omitted text
[Text] Comments and annotations, often descriptions of non-verbal action
Ss   Students who were not in the focus groups.*

Based on the previous discussion, the students seemed to have some knowledge
about the pattern, yet it is apparent that they were unable to express it in the correct
mathematical terms. However, the teacher did not ask them for more explanations,
nor did she take into account the students' previous discovery, but automatically
made the connection with the equation. She did not give the students any time to
explore the topic further through self-discovery.

T   You told me that Y- all these Y values were powers of
    what?
Ss Two.
T   Two? So, guess where the X is in that equation.
S   Two.
S   The exponent.
T   It's the exponent. It is sure. Two to the first power.
    Two to the second power, two to the third power, two
    to the fourth power.

```
T    So, if I consider these as positions in the line-up,
     these X values ... then these are the Y output values.
     Huh? Everybody see that?
```

Eventually, the teacher commented on the patterns and expressed the function, which may have deprived the students' of the opportunity to explain their ways of solving these problems. For instance, the teacher asked the students what the value of slope m would be in the equation $y = -x + 2$. Although the students did not get the correct answer immediately, she was able to guide them to the correct answer.

```
T         I want to know what the slope is. What is slope
          M? What is the value of M?
Nahoku    Negative X.
Heather   Plus two.
T         Here's the X, what's m? What's implied?
Heather   Plus B. But negative plus a negative should be
          a negative.
T         How many Xs are implied?
Kevin     One.
T         One, and it has to be… I won't tell it. Write it
          down.
T         What's implied? It's not written there but
          what's implied.
Heather   It's negative m because negative times a negative
          equals a positive.
T         White boards up. I don't see your response.
T         (Looking at student's boards) That's true but I
          want to know a number.
T         (Looking at student's boards) Uh, that- that's
          not quite true. It's negative that's part of it.
T         It's negative that's part of it. Negative.
          What's number? (Looking at students' boards)
          Uh-oh, uh-oh, powerhouse, yep, all right.
T         Folks, look over here, it's Sergio and Abraham
          negative what?
Kevin     One.
T         What's implied? How many Xs?
Ss        One.
T         One. Only it's negative one.
```

Teacher's highlighting of key points   For example, the teacher was constructing a relationship between the graph and the equation by showing that both have similar components, such as slope and y-intercept, and 'telling a story about the graph'.

Although the students were familiar with the slope and y-intercept from looking at the equation, the teacher highlighted these features on the graph:

```
T       Okay now. I keep saying these things and this is
        getting more and more mysterious for some of you,
        instead of less and less mysterious.
T       I say graphs tell a story. I say equations tell
        a story, and yet I have just said ... here is a
        general statement of a linear function. A linear
        relationship.
T       And, you know what. What I've written still
        doesn't look like it. But ...
T       Let's transform it. Let's transform this sentence
        one more time and turn it around this way.
T       Okay, all right. Graphs tell a story too. Here
        it is. When we turn this around. Here's our
        Y-intercept of two and the graph is negative.
T       The slope is negative. The slope is negative.
```

By allowing students to come to the conclusion in several smaller steps, the teacher ensures that they know why the answer is correct and helps them make the right connections between the topics.

Students' self-guided discussion   The majority of the U.S. lesson was spent in group discussions between the teacher and students, as well as among students. Therefore, when students did group activities, what they were talking about was crucial. Usually, the students were able to discuss among themselves how a correct solution was to be found. For example, during the white board activity, they were asked the question, "This point zero two is the X-intercept Y-intercept?" Within their group, the students came to the correct answer. One member was confused about which one was the X- and which one was the Y-axis, so a fellow student helped to make the correct distinction. Furthermore, the students were able to clarify small misconceptions during group discussion. For example, when one student working in a group did not know the meaning of a particular term, others of the group helped her/him to figure it out.

```
Heather Does non-linear mean not straight lines, or
        curved?
Kevin   Curved.
Annie   I have no idea what they mean by not straight
        lines.
Kevin   It's curved, that means.
```

When the students were able to discuss the concepts among themselves, they were able to clarify some of their basic misunderstandings. Yet it also seemed that working in a group allowed the students to put less emphasis on learning the basic concepts of mathematics and more on general socializing. The majority of their talks were arrangement-related or trivial, and not so much mathematical. For example, the students were discussing the equation of $x = 2$ and how to draw and describe it.

```
Heather    Can I write the information
Kevin      [Laughing] This is mine.
Heather    Vertical. I am?
Nahoku     Let me borrow it.
Kevin      I'm almost done.
S          Okay what are you doing?
Heather    Are those (big). Oh well here (give me that).
S          The equation?
Heather    Let's go sideways though.
S          I just can't make it in the space (the table).
           Yeah you could do the equation right. Still
           sideways. Oh, you're gonna do the graph?
Heather    Yeah.
S          Alright. There was barely enough room on the
           paper. I think it was kind of silly, I forgot
           to leave- let that one in, but that's okay.
```

During the group discussion, the students did not mention why it was a straight line, how to draw the line effectively, why it was vertical, and so on. Instead, the students were focused primarily on how to arrange the graph, equation, and table visually, rather than explaining the mathematical reasoning behind their answers. Additionally, in the post-lesson video-stimulated interviews, students mentioned they did not know how to differentiate between linear and non-linear by using algebraic equations.

Opportunities for Learning with Understanding in the Chinese Classroom

In the Chinese lesson, the teacher emphasized constructing relationships among concepts through the following: (1) reviewing the previous lesson's concept of the Cartesian plane and introducing the new topic of the relationship between points and their coordinates in the coordinate plane; (2) reflecting on the order of numbered pairs by differentiating the points (3, 4) and (4, 3); and (3) emphasizing the relationships between points and their coordinates through systematic variation. The following episode illustrates the previously mentioned aspect (2) as follows:

```
T:         ...Compare this three, four with the first point A
           four, three. Why aren't they the same point? ...
           Both of them have three and four as the numbers,
           why aren't the two points the same? ... Hong Zhang.
```

Zhang: Because the position of three four is different from four three. That means the positions of the X-coordinate and Y-coordinate are reversed.

T: We've said that there's a pair of ordered numbers in a coordinate, so when you reverse the order of the two numbers, those two points are not the same points.

The Chinese teacher followed a pattern of problem presenting, (extending and applying), problem solving, and sharing (articulating): systematically presenting interconnected mathematics problems for students to solve, by exploring individually or in groups, sharing/explaining answers, and summarizing in due course by the teacher. After the students had solved and discussed a problem, the teacher gave certain praise and comments, and then posed a new problem based on the solved one:

T: Good, that means, point A is negative two, negative three, point B is two, three, point C is two, negative one, point D is negative two, one. Next, I have a question, if I know only the coordinates of points A and B, for this square, I know only points A and B, and I've marked them for you, but how about this square? We haven't finished drawing it, so where are points C and D? What are their coordinates?

Then, the students were separated into groups of four and discussed their solutions. The teacher walked around. Afterwards, the students were encouraged to present and explain their solutions.

T: Let's exchange our ideas together first. We ask... Jing Li please explain a bit. How did you draw it?

Li: The distance between A and B is four units.

T: The distance between A and B is four units.

Li: The four sides of a square are equal. So the distances between the four sides are all four units. The coordinate of point C is one, negative four.

After that, the teacher solicited more solutions from students.

T: So we've got the coordinates of points C and D, right? Good, please sit down. Are there any other methods to draw the square? Gong Wang?

Wang: Our method of drawing is the same as that one, however, its square extending toward the right, while ours are extending toward the left.

T: There is a second square that is extending toward the right.

```
Wang:   Another side of the square, (The side AB, is drawn
        at the right hand side, CD is on the left hand
        side.)
T:      Would you explain how to draw it?
Wang:   We use four as a unit, then from point B, four
        units that is nine zero.
```

After presenting this solution, the teacher concluded that, for this question, these two solutions were correct, that is, there were two figures satisfying the condition of the problem. After several cycles of problem presenting, individual or group solving and solution sharing, the teacher came to the conclusion:

```
T:      Today we've learnt how to use the coordinates to
        find the locations of the points. So, in this
        lesson, we've learnt that, on the Cartesian plane,
        given the location of a point, we can find its
        coordinates that is the content of what we've learnt
        in this lesson.
```

Thus, in the Chinese lesson, the teacher fostered the students' learning of the concept with understanding, according to the selected framework.

CONCLUSION AND DISCUSSION

Conclusion

On the basis of the teacher's intentions, students' perceptions, and classroom enactment of these particular lessons, we conclude that in the Chinese classroom: (1) The teacher had concrete and feasible objectives of teaching which were based on previous knowledge and served for further study. (2) He tried to provide systematically interconnected problems to help students to build a connected concept system. (3) Individual or collaborative problem solving and sharing were encouraged. (4) The students paid much attention to problem solving and sharing. (5) The students paid attention to the teacher's teaching and their peers' explanations.

In the U.S. classroom, the following features were identified: (1) The teacher had a broad and long-term model of the teaching objectives in mind. (2) She greatly emphasized students' collaborative learning and articulation. (3) The students all emphasized the connection of concepts, particularly in relation to different presentations of the algebraic concepts. (4) The students spent a lot of time in making sense of the concept and correcting misunderstandings by themselves. (5) The students paid attention to the teacher's teaching and their peers' articulations.

In summary, both the Chinese and U.S. teachers, as well as their students, emphasized the connection of mathematical concepts, and valued students' expressions, teacher's presentations, and explanations. The essential difference between these two classrooms was the use of problems. The Chinese teacher had a detailed teaching goal. The teacher deliberatively organized a series of interconnected problems to foster the students' progressive understanding. The teacher and students worked on the problems. For the teacher, it was a way to introduce concepts through solving problems. For the students, it was a way to understand the lesson content through solving the problems arranged by the teacher. In this way, the particular teaching goals could be achieved effectively. However, the students may not have grasped the underlying mathematical thinking and, more seriously, they may have lost opportunities to explore these concepts by themselves.

On the other hand, the U.S. teacher held a broad and long-term vision. She organized activities for students' group discussion to explore some 'big' ideas (multiple representations including table, equation, graph, verbal expression presenting the same mathematical object). Through these activities, the students might, have realized the big ideas that the teacher designed for students to pursue. However, some basic concepts and skills might not have been coped with properly. In this particular case, the students might have realized that linear equations, straight lines, T-charts, and verbal descriptions could be used to express the same mathematical object or idea, but some students did not know how to draw a straight line properly, and did not know the meaning of some of the key parameters of a linear equation (slope and y-intercept).

DISCUSSION

The findings in the Chinese classroom of this study, such as emphasizing connections between concepts and systematic variations of problems, are supported by other studies (Huang, Mok, & Leung, 2006; Leung, 2005). Some researchers have argued that the flexible use of interconnected problems to develop, consolidate, and apply new knowledge is a traditional and popular teaching strategy (Gu, Huang, & Marton, 2004; Huang et al., 2006; Li, 2006). However, an inappropriate use of this strategy may also limit students' learning opportunities (Gu et al., 2004). Moreover, innovative features, such as students' self-exploration and sharing, were also noted by some researchers (Huang & Leung, 2004; Mok, 2006), which may reflect the effect of the mathematics curriculum reform since 2001 (Ministry of Education, 2001, 2003).

In the U.S. classroom, the teacher organized a series of group activities to build the connections between different representations with a strong sense of developing students' multiple representations in their minds. Through collaboration and discussion in group activities, students might realize the big idea that the same mathematical object can be represented using different representations. However, the connections might be superficial, because the students did not really experience the importance and usefulness of this big idea. Moreover, the students' attention was not drawn to the underlying concepts and skills. Thus, they might have had difficulty in understanding relevant concepts, such as slope and intercept, and did not grasp the skills needed to draw a straight line.

When comparing these two classroom instructions, on one hand, the Chinese teacher guided the students to achieve pre-determined concrete instructional objectives through exploring a series of deliberatively selected problems and sharing their solutions. This looks very efficient in terms of the intended instructional objectives. However, it is not clear if the teaching helped the students to get a sense of the overarching ideas about the coordinate plane and its roles in mathematics. On the other hand, the U.S. teacher tried her best to let her students explore and discuss. Sometimes, the students got lost; sometimes, they made sense of minor points; sometimes, their discussions did not work and the teacher had to tell them correct answers. This seems to be not so efficient in terms of concrete instructional objectives, but the teacher can learn from the students' expressed thoughts about their difficulties.

At the same time, some crucial questions are left wondering. Is it possible for the Chinese teacher to develop relevant big ideas when pursuing such detailed teaching objectives? On the other hand, is it possible for the U.S. teacher to help students to master basic concepts and skills while also acquiring big ideas about the connection of these concepts? Before answering these questions, it is fundamental to understand how high-quality mathematics instruction is perceived. Although there is no consensus about what constitutes good teaching, it is recognized widely that teachers should be able to select worthwhile mathematical tasks, create challenging and nurturing classroom environments, and facilitate meaningful discourse that leads to a socially negotiated understanding (Henningsen & Stein, 1997; Martin, 2007; NCTM, 2000; NRCIM, 2004). Thus, a desired teaching approach may be reachable by complementing the strengths of the Chinese and U.S. classroom instruction (Clarke, 2006b; Huang & Leung, 2004). For example, teachers should set long-term overarching instructional objectives as well as short-term concrete ones and deliberately select worthwhile interconnected mathematical problems for students to explore individually first, followed by collaborative exchange, and public sharing, with a focus on mastering basic skills and developing problem-solving competence as well.

REFERENCES

Baroody, A. J., Feil, Y., & Johnson, A. R. (2007). An alternative reconceptualization of procedural and conceptual knowledge. *Journal for Research in Mathematics Education, 38*,115–131.

Biggs, J. B., & Watkins, D. A. (1996). The Chinese learner in retrospect. In D. A. Watkins & J. B. Biggs (Eds.), *The Chinese learner: Cultural, psychological, and contextual influences* (pp. 269–285). Hong Kong: Comparative Educational Research Center, The University of Hong Kong.

Brownell, W. A. (1938). Two kinds of learning in arithmetic. *Journal of Educational Research, 31*, 656–664.

Cai, J., & Wang, T. (2010). Conceptions of effective mathematics teaching within a cultural context: perspectives of teachers from China and the United States. *Journal of Mathematics Teacher Education, 13*, 265–287.

Carpenter, T. P., & Lehrer, R. (1999). Teaching and learning mathematics with understanding. In E. Fennema & T. A. Romberg (Eds.), *Mathematics classroom that promote understanding* (pp. 19–32). Mahwah: Lawrence Erlbaum.

Clarke, D. (2006a). The LPS research design. In D. J. Clarke, C. Keitel, & Y. Shimizu (Eds.), *Mathematics classrooms in twelve countries* (pp. 15–29). Rotterdam, The Netherlands: Sense.

Clarke, D. (2006b). Deconstructing dichotomies: Arguing for a more inclusive approach. In D. J. Clarke, J. Emanuelsson, E. Jablonka, & I. A. C. Mok (Eds.), *Making connections: Comparing mathematics classrooms around the world.* Rotterdam, The Netherlands: Sense.

Fan, L., & Zhu, Y. (2004). How have Chinese students performed in mathematics ? A perspective from large-scale international mathematics comparisons. In L. Fan, N. Y. Wong, J. Cai, & S. Li (Eds.), *How Chinese learn mathematics: Perspectives from insiders* (pp. 348–381). Singapore: World Scientific.

Fan, L., Wong, N. Y., Cai, J., & Li, S. (2004). *How Chinese learn mathematics: Perspectives from insiders.* Singapore: World Scientific.

Gu, L., Huang, R., & Marton, F. (2004). Teaching with variation: An effective way of mathematics teaching in China. In L. Fan, N. Y. Wong, J. Cai, & S. Li (Eds.), *How Chinese learn mathematics: Perspectives from insiders* (pp. 309–348). Singapore: World Scientific.

Henningsen, M., & Stein, M. K. (1997). Mathematical tasks and student cognition: Classroom-based factors that support and inhibit high level mathematical thinking and reasoning. *Journal for Research in Mathematics Education, 8,* 524–549.

Hiebert, J., & Carpenter, P. P. (1992). Learning and teaching with understanding. In D. A. Grouws (Ed.), *Handbook of research on mathematics teaching and learning* (pp. 65–97). New York, NY: Macmillan.

Hiebert, J., Carpenter, T. P., Fennema, E., Fuson, K. C., Wearne, D., Murray, H., Olivier, A., & Human, P. (1997). *Making sense: Teaching and learning mathematics with understanding.* Portsmouth: Heinemann.

Hiebert, J., & Grouws, D. A. (2007). The effects of classroom mathematics teaching on students' learning. In F. K. Lester, Jr.(Ed.), *Second handbook of research on mathematics teaching and learning* (pp. 371–404). Charlotte, NC: Information Age.

Huang, R. (2006). Looking into mathematics classroom in Chinese communities. *Journal of Mathematics Education, 2,* 67–70.

Huang, R., & Cai, J. (2011). Pedagogical representations to teach linear relations in Chinese and U.S. classrooms: Parallel or hierarchical. *The Journal of Mathematical Behavior, 30,* 149–165.

Huang, R., & Cai, J. (2010). Implementing mathematics tasks in the U.S. and Chinese classroom. In Y. Shimizu, B. Kaur, R. Huang, & D., Clarke (Eds), *Mathematical tasks in classrooms around the world* (pp. 147–166).Rotterdam, The Netherlands: Sense.

Huang, R., & Leung, F. K. S (2004). Cracking the paradox of the Chinese learners: Looking into the mathematics classrooms in Hong Kong and Shanghai. In L. Fan, N. Y. Wong, J. Cai, & S. Li (Eds.), *How Chinese learn mathematics: Perspectives from insiders* (pp. 348–381). Singapore: World Scientific.

Huang, R., & Li, Y. (2009). Pursuing excellence in mathematics classroom instruction through exemplary lesson development in China: A case study. *ZDM—The International Journal on Mathematics Education, 41,* 297–309.

Huang, R., Mok, I., & Leung, F. K. S. (2006). Repetition or variation: "Practice" in the mathematics classrooms in China. In D. J. Clarke, C. Keitel, & Y. Shimizu (Eds.), *Mathematics classrooms in twelve countries: The insider's perspective* (pp. 263–274). Rotterdam, the Netherlands: Sense.

Jacobs, J., Hiebert, J., Givvin, K., Hollingsworth, H., Garnier, H., & Weame, D. (2006). Does eighth-grade mathematics teaching in the United States align with the NCTM standards? Results from the TIMSS 1995 and 1999 video studies. *Journal for Research in Mathematics Education, 36,* 5–32.

Leung, F. K. S. (2005). The implications of TIMSS 1999 Video Study for Chinese mathematics curriculum reform. *Journal of Mathematics Education, 14*(1), 7–11.

Li, S. (2006). Practice makes perfect: A key belief in China. In F. K. S. Leung, K. D. Graf, & F. J. Lopez-Real (Eds.), *Mathematics education in different cultural traditions: A comparative study of East Asia and the West* (pp. 129–138). New York, NY: Springer.

Li, Y., & Huang, R. (Eds.). (2012). *How Chinese teach mathematics and improve teaching.* New York, NY: Routledge.

Lopez-Real, F., Mok, A. C. I., Leung, F. K. S., & Marton, F. (2004). Identifying a pattern of teaching: An analysis of a Shanghai teacher's lessons. In L. Fan, N. Y. Wong, J. Cai, & S. Li (Eds.), *How Chinese learn mathematics: Perspectives from insiders* (pp. 382–412). Singapore: World Scientific.

Martin, T. S. (2007). *Mathematics teaching today: Improving practice, improving student learning* (2nd). Reston, VA: National Council of Teachers of Mathematics.

Marton, F., Dall'Alba, G., & Tse, L. K. (1996). Memorizing and understanding: The keys to the paradox? In D. A. Watkins & J. B. Biggs (Eds.), *Cultural, psychological and contextual influences* (pp. 69–83). Hong Kong: Comparative Education Research Centre, The University of Hong Kong.

Mok, I. A. C. (2006). Teacher-dominating lessons in Shanghai: The insiders' story. In D. J. Clarke, C. Keitel, & Y. Shimizu (Eds.), *Mathematics classrooms in twelve countries: The insider's perspective* (pp. 87–98). Rotterdam, the Netherlands: Sense.

National Council of Teachers of Mathematics. (2000). *Principles and standards for school mathematics*. Reston, VA: Author.

National Research Council Institute of Medicine (NRCIM). (2004). *Engaging schools: Fostering high school students' motivation to learn*. Washington, DC: National Academies Press.

Schoenfeld, A. H., & Pateman, N. (2008). *A study of teaching multiple lenses, multiple views*. Reston, VA: National Council of Teachers of Mathematics.

Skemp, R. R. (1976). Relational understanding and instrumental understanding. *Mathematics Teaching 77*, 20–26.

Star, J. R. (2005). Reconceptualizing procedural knowledge. *Journal for Research in Mathematics Education, 36*, 404–411.

Stevenson, H. W., & Lee, S. Y. (1995). The East Asian version of whole-class teaching. *Education Policy, 9*, 152–168.

Stevenson, H. W., Chen, C. C., & Lee, S. Y. (1993). Mathematics achievement of Chinese, Japanese, and American children: Ten years later. *Science, 25*, 53–59.

Wood, T., Shin, S. Y., & Doan, P. (2006). Mathematics education reform in three US classrooms. In D. J. Clarke, C. Keitel, & Y. Shimizu (Eds.), *Mathematics classrooms in twelve countries: The insider's perspective* (pp. 75–86). Rotterdam, the Netherlands: Sense.

AFFILIATIONS

Rongjin Huang
Middle Tennessee State University
USA

Yeping Li
Texas A&M University
USA

JOHAN HÄGGSTRÖM

CHAPTER 13

Different Opportunities to Learn: The Case of Simultaneous Equations

INTRODUCTION

This chapter presents a methodology of data analysis as a way to conceptualise the concept 'opportunity to learn'. The examples are taken from a larger comparative study of the teaching of simultaneous equations (Häggström, 2008).

OPPORTUNITY TO LEARN

The term 'opportunity to learn' is a frame used widely by social justice movements in the US in their work to ensure that all children get access to high-quality education in terms of qualified teachers and other resources (see e.g. OTL, 2012).

In the context of mathematics education research the concept 'opportunity to learn' has been used in international comparative studies as a measure to judge whether the student test items will be fair and appropriate, and as a mean to explain differences in performance. In the report of the first IEA study (FIMS) 'opportunity to learn' is related to whether students have been exposed to the topic or problems in question (Husén, 1967). Later Carroll (1989) described 'opportunity to learn' as the time allowed for learning. In their review of research on the effects on classroom mathematics teaching on students' learning Hiebert and Grouws (2007) put forward 'opportunity to learn' as a powerful concept in linking teaching to learning. They, however, expanded the concept beyond 'being exposed to certain content' and 'time allowed for learning'.

> Opportunity to learn as a concept that links teaching and learning is best viewed as something more nuanced and complex than simply exposure to subject matter. Put simply, students who are exposed to a topic obviously have a better chance of learning than students who are not. But, opportunity to learn can mean something more interesting and useful. Consider first graders exposed to a lesson on calculus. Do they have an opportunity to learn calculus? […] So, 'opportunity to learn' is not the same as 'being taught'. (Hiebert & Grouws, 2007, p. 379)

In their review Hiebert and Grouws were not looking for results describing effective teaching in relation to particular goals, such as "solving quadratic equations or

F.K.S. Leung et al. (eds.), Algebra Teaching around the World, 233–242.
© *2014 Sense Publishers. All rights reserved.*

subtracting whole numbers with regrouping" (p. 378). Their aim was to search for outcomes showing more general patterns, for instance what kind of teaching can facilitate students' conceptual understanding of mathematics. On the other hand they also stated that the particularity of the learning goals is vital:

> Researchers must be clear and explicit about the kinds of learning they will study. Talking about teaching, in general terms, as "effective" or "not effective" is no longer helpful. Teaching is effective (or not) for helping students achieve particular kinds of learning goals. Teaching is effective for something and the something must be described and measured as precisely as possible. (Hiebert & Grouws, 2007, p. 393)

It is not only the particular kind of learning that has to be described with precision. The need to describe the classroom interaction in a detailed way, in order to capture students' opportunities to learn, is demonstrated by an example from the analysis of the TIMSS 1999 video data. In the first round of analysis, the problems, which were handled in the grade 8 classrooms in the seven participating countries, were coded. 'Making connection' was one of the categories identified. This kind of problem can provide students with an opportunity to develop their conceptual understanding, as opposed to the problems coded as routine-skills and reciting-fact type of problems. This coding could not explain the poor results in the U.S.

> Results showed that 17% of the problems in an average U.S. lesson indicated intent to make connections; this was within the range of 15% to 24% evident in all other countries except Japan (Japan was an outlier with 54%). (Hiebert & Grouws, 2007, p. 392)

Deepening the analysis, however, changed the picture dramatically.

> A question of special interest is: "What happened to the making connections problems when they were implemented in the classroom?" In all countries except for Australia and the United States, 37% to 52% of these problems were worked on so that the connections implied by the problem statement were made explicit with the students – through examining the problem, comparing solutions methods, justifying why the solution methods worked, and so on. In Australia, 8% of the making connection problems were worked on in this way. In the United States, so few making connection problems were worked on in this way that the percentage rounded to 0%. (Hiebert & Grouws, 2007, p. 393)

The concept 'opportunity to learn' can be useful when comparing teaching in different classrooms. The example from the TIMSS video study, however, shows that high precision and detail are vital in order to utilise the potential of the concept. In the following I will put forward a way to conceptualise 'opportunity to learn' with a high degree of precision in relation to particular learning goals.

AN APPROACH TO STUDY TEACHING OF CERTAIN MATHEMATICS

As pointed out by Hiebert and Grouws, the concept of 'opportunity to learn' can be powerful in describing and comparing teaching if it is taken beyond 'what is taught and for what amount of time'. Being exposed to certain content can be seen as a necessary condition for student learning but, in order to understand differences in the learning of students who have been exposed to the same content, an analysis of *how* the content was handled during instruction is called for. The proposed approach to analysing and comparing teaching will be sensitive to such details regarding the particular mathematics taught. The analytical approach is based on Variation Theory (c.f. Marton & Booth, 1997; Marton, Runesson & Tsui, 2004), which has been developed within the phenomenographic research tradition. Here I will just give a brief description of this development.

The observation that people understand the same phenomena differently can be regarded as a starting point. The 'traditional' phenomenographic research aims at detecting and describing different conceptions of the same phenomena. Different ways of understanding the same thing are categorized by the aspects of the phenomena that are discerned and focused simultaneously.

> Whenever people attend to something, they discern certain aspects of it and by doing so pay more attention to some things, and less attention or none to other things. [...] A particular way of seeing something can be defined by the aspects discerned, that is, the critical features of what is seen. (Marton, et al., 2004, p. 9)

Different conceptions are separated by means of 'critical aspects'. For example, the critical aspects of the concept of 'price' have been found to be 'supply' and 'demand'. The most developed conception of price recognises the simultaneous importance of both of these aspects. Other conceptions include just one or neither of them. Learning within this theoretical frame is thus seen as the discernment of aspects that were not discerned previously. A requirement for discernment of a new aspect of a phenomenon, for example a mathematical concept, is that variation in that respect is experienced. The necessity of variation for learning is at the core of Variation Theory. Features that are invariant – indicating that no variation is experienced – are not possible to discern. This is based on the limitations of the human awareness. Of all the possible things that we can be aware of – for example, every second we receive a large quantity of input from our senses – only a few reach our focal awareness. Variation, however, attracts our attention. An analysis of a mathematics lesson that provides a description of what features are kept invariant and what features are varied has strong implications regarding students' 'opportunity to learn' about the actual object of learning in that particular lesson. The 'object of learning' is used to denote the 'what' aspect of teaching and learning. In the school setting the object of learning is basically what teachers are trying to teach and what students are supposed to learn. This may, of course, be many different things and not necessarily related to the subject matter. A teacher could have many different intentions regarding what students should learn in a lesson or with an activity. For example, the intention could be for the students to develop a capability to work in groups or to speak in front of the whole class. However, in the study discussed here, the objects of learning considered are the ones related to the students' conceptions of the mathematical content. The object of learning must not be confused with the mathematical content itself. The object of learning is a capability, for instance a capability to understand the mathematics in a certain way or a capability to solve certain types of problem.

The attention of the analysis is directed towards the variation and invariance of aspects of the object of learning. A certain aspect cannot be discerned without the experience of variation in that respect. Now, the experience of variation can be accommodated in different ways. A student may experience variation in a certain aspect by comparing what takes place in a situation to his/her pervious experience. For example, a student may compare systems of equations at hand, where only natural numbers are used as coefficients, to the experience of decimal numbers and fractions from previous situations. This comparison can lead to an experienced variation regarding the kind of numbers that can be used in equations. The experience of variation in this case cannot be detected by analysing the interaction in the mathematics classroom – the enacted object of learning – and is of course dependent on the particular experience of the student in question.

The experience of variation may also be connected more directly to the enacted object of learning. For example, students who work, at the same time, with equations where the coefficients are natural numbers, decimal numbers and fractions are provided with an opportunity to experience variation in this respect regardless of their previous experiences. The possible experiences of variation in this case are related directly to the enacted object of learning and to the *Dimensions of Variation* that are opened in the classroom. This establishes a possible link between the variation of an aspect of the object of learning during a mathematics lesson and the discernment of that aspect. Experiencing variation in a certain aspect means experiencing a difference in that Dimension of Variation. "[…] [E]very feature discerned corresponds to a certain Dimension of Variation in which the object is compared with other objects" (Marton & Pong, 2005, p. 336). The concept of Dimension of Variation is used to describe what aspects or features are made possible to discern. The opened Dimensions of Variation during one or more mathematics lessons form the space of learning and provide a detailed description of the students' 'opportunities to learn' in relation to the objects of learning.

The method of analysis requires a close inspection of how the mathematics is handled in order to detect what Dimensions of Variation are opened. In the present study data from six classrooms in which the same mathematical content was taught were analysed and compared. By comparing the teaching of the same content it is possible to detect and describe differences in how the content was handled in terms of which Dimensions of Variation were opened and which were not.

The analytical approach has an explicit focus on the *what* aspect of teaching and learning as it recognises that teaching and learning always involve the teaching and learning of *something*. There are previous studies based on Variation Theory (cf. Runesson, 1999; Runesson & Mok, 2005) that have demonstrated that descriptions of patterns of variation in a mathematics classroom are valuable. This study can be placed in a tradition of 'content oriented' classroom studies conducted at the University of Gothenburg (cf. Emanuelsson, 2001; Kilborn, 1979; Lybeck, 1981; Löwing, 2004; Runesson, 1999) and tries to develop the methodology of classroom analysis further by focusing on differences in how the same mathematics is taught. How to handle the mathematical content is central to mathematics teaching and teachers always have to make decisions concerning what examples and tasks to use, what things to try to draw students attention to and in what way etc. Another aim of the study is to uncover aspects of the particular mathematics that might easily be taken for granted by teachers when teaching and thus 'pass by' undiscerned by students. The practice of mathematics instruction could surely benefit from research in which the focus is on specific mathematical content.

THE CLASSROOM DATA

The empirical data that were analysed consist of sixteen video recorded lessons from six classes in Sweden (SW2) and China (HK1, HK2, SH1, SH2, SH3) and have been collected within the *Learners' Perspective Study* (LPS, 2003). The documentation was done with extensive video recording of three grade 8 mathematics classrooms in each participating country (Clarke, 2000). The classes were video recorded for at least 10 consecutive lessons. The classes in the LPS were selected on the basis of the following criteria. The classes were from government schools in major towns with a demographic diversity, and non-typical student groups were avoided. The teachers were experienced and competent, as locally defined by the community. The classrooms in the LPS could be seen as examples of good mathematics instruction from each country.

In the LPS there were no general agreements regarding the mathematical content in the recorded lessons. Rather, it was perceived preferable to cover many different topics. "It was intended that the lesson sequences should be spread across the academic year in order to gain maximum diversity of local curricular content" (LPS, 2003). However, the research teams in China and Sweden decided to document the teaching of the same topic. The idea was that detected differences, if the content was kept invariant, might be particularly interesting.

FOUR STEPS OF ANALYSIS

In the actual data available, three common objects of learning were identified. These objects of learning were related to students' conceptions of 'simultaneous linear equations in two unknowns', 'a solution to simultaneous linear equations in two

237

unknowns' and 'the method of substitution'. This first step of the analysis reduced the suitable data from the more than 100 lessons in nine classes to 16 lessons in six classes.

The second step involved a repeated close examination of how the mathematics was handled in the 16 lessons. The concept of 'opportunity to learn' was operationalized in terms of which Dimensions of Variation were opened and which were not – an aspect of the objects of learning is either taken for granted in instruction, or the corresponding Dimension of Variation is opened. A Dimension of Variation can be opened more or less explicitly by the tasks and examples used, or by the contribution of possible or hypothetical alternatives. Let me illustrate this step of the analysis by an example. Let us say all instances of simultaneous equations encountered by the students in one class had natural numbers as coefficients, constants and solutions. The kind of numbers used was thus kept invariant and the corresponding Dimension of Variation was not opened. In another class there were examples of simultaneous equations with rational and negative numbers, in addition to the natural numbers. This opened the Dimension of Variation regarding what numbers can be used in simultaneous equations. In yet another class only natural numbers were used, but the teacher, on one occasion, pointed to an example on the blackboard and asked the students, "Can we use other kinds of numbers, for instance fractions, just as well?" In this way, the teacher provided alternatives to the numbers in the examples, which opened the Dimension of Variation. It was also possible that a student opened the Dimension of Variation by asking about the possibility to use other kinds of numbers. A Dimension of Variation is considered opened if there are alternatives or variations provided in the way the content is handled. Differences in how the content is handled in the studied classes were vital in order to detect the Dimensions of Variation. This step generated a set of Dimensions of Variation that were opened in at least one of the classes.

In the third step, the Dimensions of Variation concerning one of the three objects of learning at a time was focused while the data were re-examined. The lessons were divided into shorter episodes and the Dimensions of Variation opened in each episode were noted and finally summed up.

The fourth step was an attempt to verify the findings from the previous steps. This was done by looking at the aspects that were 'taken for granted', that is, the Dimensions of Variation that were not opened. One Dimension of Variation was focused at a time and the data were revisited with questions like, "Was the Dimension of variation concerning what numbers can be used really never opened in Class X?"

DIFFERENCES IN THE TEACHING OF SIMULTANEOUS EQUATIONS

I will exemplify the results from the analysis of the sixteen lessons by discussing differences in one of the three enacted objects of learning. Table 1 summarises the findings regarding the Dimensions of Variation related to the concept of simultaneous

Table 1. Spaces of learning for the concept of system of equations

System of linear equations in two unknowns	SW2	HK1	HK2	SH1	SH2	SH3
Dimensions of variation concerning 'properties'						
1 Number of equations (two or more equations)						
1a two equations, not one	x	x	x	x	x	x
1b more than one equation		x		x		
2 Number of unknowns (two unknowns)						
2a two unknowns not one	x	x	x			
2b two unknowns not three (or more)		x		x	x	x
3 Type of equations (linear equations / first degree unknowns)						
3a xy is not first degree				x	x	x
3b x^2 , $(x + y)^2$, is not first degree				x		
3c $1/y$ is not first degree				x		
4 An unknown represents the *same* number in both equations						
4a unknowns are the same is not taken for granted		x	x	x	x	
5 Constants and coefficients can be different types of numbers						
5a rational numbers not just natural	x	x		x	x	x
5b negative numbers not just natural	x	x	x	x	x	x
5c parameters not just specified numbers				x		
Dimensions of variation concerning 'appearance'						
6 Different letters may be used						
6a the letters x, y are not taken for granted		x	x	x		x
7 A system of equations can be in different formats						
7a format of individual equations not invariant	x	x	x	x	x	x
7b one expression ($ax + by + c = dx + ey + f = g$)		x	x	x		
7c both unknowns not present in both equations	x			x	x	x
Dimension of variation concerning 'use'						
8 A way of representing and solving problems						
8a alternative to use of equation in one unknown		x				
8b alternative to use of guess-and-check method		x				

Note. A grey space indicates that the dimension was opened for variation, and x indicates which alternatives were provided.

equations in two unknowns. The analysis generated eight Dimensions of Variation that were opened in at least one of the classes. There were also different ways to open a Dimension of Variation (for instance by providing different alternatives, but I will not elaborate on this here).

The fourth Dimension of Variation in Table 1, *an unknown representing the same number in both equations*, is probably an aspect that is quite obvious to anyone familiar with the concept of simultaneous equations. It can be manifested in many ways, for example by the simultaneousness of the equations, the values of the unknowns that form the solution, and in the method of substitution where an unknown in one of the equations is exchanged for an expression of the same unknown taken from the other equation. Maybe the idea that unknowns represent the same number in both equations is so 'obvious' to teachers that it is easily taken for granted. On the contrary, it may not be obvious to a novice to this topic. If you have never experienced anything but single equations you may just as well take the opposite for granted – that x in one equation is different from x in the next equation. Why would the two xs in the two equations in a system be the same, when this was hardly ever the case before? The analysis showed that the aspect *an unknown representing the same number in both equations* was taken for granted in two of the six classes. These two teachers, of course, treated the unknowns as being the same, but this was never commented on or elaborated on in a way that opened the Dimension of Variation in these classes. The other teachers did not take this for granted. In one classroom the teacher, on one occasion, pointed to the xs in both equations and made an explicit comparison. He pointed at them in turn and asked, "Are this x and this x the same?" In this way the teacher provided alternatives – the two xs could be the same or they could be different. For a dimension to be opened there need to be at least two potential values at hand. This Dimension of Variation was opened in similar ways in four of the classes and the students were given an opportunity to experience variation regarding one aspect of what the unknowns represented. The 'status' of the unknowns was not taken for granted. In this way the Dimension of Variation was opened in some classes but not in all. In terms of 'opportunity to learn' there was a difference between the classes in which the Dimension of Variation was opened and those in which it was not.

The Dimension of Variation, *the type of equation*, was opened in three of the classes (see Table 1). This was done in an explicit way, with the students given a number of systems of equations and asked to decide which were systems of *linear* equations and which were not. In the exercise, linear equations were contrasted to non-linear equations of different kinds and the exercise in itself opened the Dimension of Variation and made it possible for students to see that there are systems of equations of different kinds and that the system of *linear* equations is just one possibility. The students were given the opportunity to experience variation in respect to the types of equations. In the other classes only systems of *linear* equations were handled and this Dimension of Variation was not opened. Students in the latter classes were not given the opportunity to experience variation in this respect. This made it hard for them to discern that the systems of equations dealt with were of a certain kind and that there are others. To understand the concept of simultaneous linear equations fully, one must know what is *not* a system of this kind. The type of equation is one important aspect to distinguish systems of linear equations from other systems. The analysis of how the content was handled in the six classes showed a difference in students' 'opportunities to learn' in terms of the Dimension of Variation.

OPPORTUNITY TO LEARN

The close attention to the mathematical content within this analytical approach opens the possibility of detecting subtle differences in how teachers handle the same content. These differences – in terms of Dimensions of Variation – can be used to bring the concept of 'opportunity to learn' to a detailed level of how students are exposed to the particular mathematics. The analytical approach is general in the sense that it can be applied to all mathematics teaching, but specific in the sense that, in every case, students' 'opportunities to learn' are related to a particular mathematical content.

In addition, the detailed descriptions of differences in handling the same mathematics in different classroom should be of interest to mathematics teachers (and mathematics teacher educators), as they might point to aspects of the mathematical content that otherwise could be overlooked in teaching. This could be especially true for aspects that are so familiar and natural that they are just taken for granted in teaching (perhaps blocked out by the 'blind spot of the expert').

I hope that the approach to studying teaching that has been outlined in this paper can contribute, to some extent, to the methodological development in the field of research on mathematics teaching and to the development of the concept of 'opportunity to learn' as a powerful tool to analyse and compare mathematics instruction.

ACKNOWLEDGEMENTS

Large parts of the research described in this paper were conducted within the KULT project, funded by the Bank of Sweden Tercentenary Foundation and the ILU project, with funding from the Swedish Research Council.

REFERENCES

Carroll, J. B. (1989). The Carroll model: a 25-year retrospective and prospective view. *Educational Researcher, 18*(1), 26–31.
Clarke, D. (2000). *The Learner's perspective study.* Research design.: University of Melbourne.
Emanuelsson, J. (2001). *En fråga om frågor: hur lärares frågor i klassrummet gör det möjligt att få reda på elevernas sätt att förstå det som undervisningen behandlar i matematik och naturvetenskap [A question about questions. How teachers' questioning makes it possible to learn about the*

students'ways of understanding the content taught in mathematics and science]. Göteborg: Acta Universitatis Gothoburgensis.

Hiebert, J., & Grouws, D. A. (2007). The effects of classroom mathematics teaching on students' learning. In F. K. Lester (Ed.), *Second handbook of research on mathematics teaching and learning* (pp. 371–404). Charlotte, NC: Information Age Pub.

Husén, T. (1967). *International study of achievement in mathematics: A comparison of twelve countries.* New York, NY: Wiley.

Häggström, J. (2008). *Teaching systems of linear equations in Sweden and China: What is made possible to learn? (Ph. D. Thesis).* Gothenburg: Acta Universitatis Gothoburgensis. Retrieved from http://hdl. handle.net/2077/17286%5D

Kilborn, W. (1979). *PUMP-projektet: bakgrund och erfarenheter [The PUMP-project: background and experiences].* Stockholm: LiberLäromedel/Utbildningsförlaget.

LPS. (2003). *The Learner's perspective study.* Retrieved October 29, 2003, from http://extranet.edfac. unimelb.edu.au/DSME/lps/index.shtml

Lybeck, L. (1981). *Arkimedes i klassen: en ämnespedagogisk berättelse [Archimedes in the class: a subject-matter-pedagogical narrative].* Gothenburg: Acta Universitatis Gothoburgensis.

Löwing, M. (2004). *Matematikundervisningens konkreta gestaltning: en studie av kommunikationen lärare—elev och matematiklektionens didaktiska ramar [The concrete formation of mathematics teaching. A study of communication between teachers and pupils and the educational framework of mathematical classrooms.].* Gothenburg: Acta Universitatis Gothoburgensis.

Marton, F., & Booth, S. (1997). *Learning and awareness.* Mahwah: Lawrence Erlbaum.

Marton, F., & Pong, W. Y. (2005). On the unit of description in phenomenography. *Higher Education Research and Development, 24*(4), 335–348.

Marton, F., Runesson, U., & Tsui, A. (2004). The space of learning. In F. Marton & A. Tsui (Eds.), *Classroom discourse and the space of learning* (pp. 3–40). Mahwah, NJ: Lawrence Erlbaum.

OTL. (2012). *National opportunity to learn campaign.* Retrieved October 10, 2012, from http://www. otlcampaign.org/content/about-otl-campaign

Runesson, U. (1999). *Variationens pedagogik: skilda sätt att behandla ett matematiskt innehåll [The pedagogy of variation: Different ways of handling mathematical topic].* Gothenburg: Acta Universitatis Gothoburgensis.

Runesson, U., & Mok, I. A. C. (2005). The teaching of fractions—a comparative study of a Swedish and a Hong Kong classroom. *Nordic Studies in Mathematics Education, 10*(2), 1–15.

AFFILIATION

Johan Häggström
University of Gothenburg
Sweden

DAVID CLARKE

APPENDIX

The LPS Research Design

INTRODUCTION

The originators of the LPS project, Clarke, Keitel and Shimizu, felt that the methodology developed by Clarke and known as complementary accounts (Clarke, 1998), which had already demonstrated its efficacy in a large-scale classroom study (subsequently reported in Clarke, 2001) could be adapted to meet the needs of the Learner's Perspective Study. These needs centered on the recognition that only by seeing classroom situations from the perspectives of all participants can we come to an understanding of the motivations and meanings that underlie their participation. In terms of techniques of data generation, this translated into three key requirements: (i) the recording of interpersonal conversations between focus students during the lesson; (ii) the documentation of sequences of lessons, ideally of an entire mathematics topic; and, (iii) the identification of the intentions and interpretations underlying the participants' statements and actions during the lesson.

Miles and Huberman's text on qualitative data analysis (Miles & Huberman, 2004) focused attention on 'data reduction.'

> Even before data are collected … anticipatory data reduction is occurring as the researcher decides (often without full awareness) which conceptual framework, which cases, which research questions, and which data approaches to use. As data collection proceeds, further episodes of data reduction occur (p. 10).

This process of data reduction pervades any classroom video study. The choice of classroom, the number of cameras used, who is kept in view continuously and who appears only given particular circumstances, all contribute to a process that might better be called 'data construction' or 'data generation' than 'data reduction.' Every decision to zoom in for a closer shot or to pull back for a wide angle view represents a purposeful act by the researcher to selectively construct a data set optimally amenable to the type of analysis anticipated and maximally aligned with the particular research questions of interest to the researcher. The process of data construction does not stop with the video record, since which statements (or whose voices) are transcribed, and which actions, objects or statements are coded, all constitute further decisions made by the researcher, more or less explicitly justified in terms of the project's conceptual framework or the focus of the researcher's interest. The researcher is the principle agent

F.K.S. Leung et al. (eds.), Algebra Teaching around the World, 243–257.
© *2014 Sense Publishers. All rights reserved.*

in this process of data construction. As such, the researcher must accept responsibility for decisions made and data constructed, and place on public record a transparent account of the decisions made in the process of data generation and analysis.

In the case of the Learner's Perspective Study: Research guided by a theory of learning that accords significance to both individual subjectivities and to the constraints of setting and community practice must frame its conclusions (and collect its data) accordingly. Such a theory must accommodate complementarity rather than require convergence and accord both subjectivity and agency to individuals not just to participate in social practice but to shape that practice. The assumption that each social situation is constituted through (and in) the multiple lived realities of the participants in that situation aligns the Learner's Perspective Study with the broad field of interpretivist research.

DATA GENERATION IN THE LEARNER'S PERSPECTIVE STUDY

Data generation in the Learner's Perspective Study (LPS) used a three-camera approach (Teacher camera, Student camera, Whole Class camera) that included the onsite mixing of the Teacher and Student camera images into a picture-in-picture video record (see Figure 1, teacher in top right-hand corner) that was then used in post-lesson interviews to stimulate participant reconstructive accounts of classroom events. These data were generated for sequences of at least ten consecutive lessons occurring in the "well-taught" eighth grade mathematics classrooms of teachers in Australia, the Czech Republic, Germany, Hong Kong and mainland China, Israel, Japan, Korea, The Philippines, Singapore, South Africa, Sweden and the USA. This combination of countries gives good representation to European and Asian educational traditions, affluent and less affluent school systems, and mono-cultural and multi-cultural societies.

Each participating country used the same research design to generate videotaped classroom data for at least ten consecutive mathematics lessons and post-lesson video-stimulated interviews with at least twenty students in each of three participating 8th grade classrooms. The three mathematics teachers in each country were identified for their locally-defined 'teaching competence' and for their situation in demographically diverse government schools in major urban settings. Rather than attempt to apply the same definition of teaching competence across a dozen countries, which would have required teachers in Uppsala and Shanghai, for instance, to meet the same eligibility criteria, teacher selection was made by each local research group according to local criteria. These local criteria included such things as status within the profession, respect of peers or the school community, or visibility in presenting at teacher conferences or contributing to teacher professional development programs. As a result, the diverse enactment of teaching competence is one of the most interesting aspects of the project.

In most countries, the three lesson sequences were spread across the academic year in order to gain maximum diversity within local curricular content. In Sweden,

China and Korea, it was decided to focus specifically on algebra, reflecting the anticipated analytical emphases of those three research groups. Algebra forms a significant part of the 8th grade mathematics curriculum in most participating LPS countries, with some variation regarding the sophistication of the content dealt with at 8th grade. As a result, the data set from most of the LPS countries included at least one algebra lesson sequence.

In the key element of the post-lesson student interviews, in which a picture-in-picture video record was used as stimulus for student reconstructions of classroom events (see Figure 1), students were given control of the video replay and asked to identify and comment upon classroom events of personal importance. The post-lesson student interviews were conducted as individual interviews in all countries except Germany, Israel and South Africa, where student preference for group interviews was sufficiently strong to make that approach essential. Each teacher was interviewed at least three times using a similar protocol.

Figure. 1 Picture-in-picture video display

With regard to both classroom videotaping and the post-lesson interviews, the principles governing data generation were the minimisation of atypical classroom activity (caused by the data generation activity) and the maximisation of respondent control in the interview context. To achieve this, each videotaped lesson sequence was preceded by a one-week familiarisation period in which all aspects of data generation were conducted until the teacher indicated that the class was functioning as normally as might reasonably be expected.

In interviews, the location of control of the video player with the student ensured that the reconstructive accounts focused primarily on the student's parsing of the lesson. Only after the student's selection of significant events had been exhausted did the interviewer ask for reconstructive accounts of other events of interest to the research team. Documentation of the participant's perspective (learner or teacher) remained the priority.

In every facet of this data generation, technical quality was a priority. The technical capacity to visually juxtapose the teacher's actions with the physical and oral responses of the children was matched by the capacity to replay both the public statements by teacher or student and the private conversations of students as they struggled to construct meaning. Students could be confronted, immediately after the lesson, with a video record of their actions and the actions of their classmates.

In the picture-in-picture video record generated on-site in the classroom (Figure 1), students could see both their actions and the actions of those students around them, and, in the inset (top right-hand corner), the actions of the teacher at that time. This combined video record captured the classroom world of the student. The video record captured through the whole-class camera allowed the actions of the focus students to be seen in relation to the actions of the rest of the class.

CLASSROOM DATA GENERATION

Camera Configuration

Data generation employed three cameras in the classroom – a "Teacher Camera," a "Student Camera" and a "Whole Class Camera." The protocol below was written primarily for a single research assistant/videographer, but brief notes were provided suggesting variations possible if a second videographer was available. In order to ensure consistency of data generation across all schools in several countries, the protocol was written as a low inference protocol, requiring as few decisions by the videographer as possible. One or two possible anomalous cases were specifically discussed – such as when a student presents to the entire class. However, the general principles were constant for each camera: The Teacher Camera maintained a continuous record of the teacher's statements and actions. The Student Camera maintained a continuous record of the statements and actions of a group of four students. The Whole Class Camera was set up in the front of the classroom to capture, as far as was possible, the actions of every student – that is, of the "Whole Class." The Whole Class Camera can also be thought of as the "Teacher View Camera." While no teacher can see exactly what every individual student is doing, the teacher will have a sense of the general level of activity and types of behaviors of the whole class at any time – this is what was intended to be captured on the Whole Class Camera.

Camera One: The Teacher Camera

The "Teacher Camera" maintained the teacher in centre screen as large as possible *provided that all gestures and all tools or equipment used could be seen* – if overhead transparencies or boardwork or other visual aids were used then these had to be captured fully at the point at which they were generated or employed in the first instance or subsequently amended – but did not need to be kept in view at the expense of keeping the teacher in frame (provided at least one full image was recorded, this could be retrieved for later analysis – the priority was to keep the teacher in view). The *sole exception* to this protocol occurred when a student worked at the board or presented to the whole class. In this case, the Teacher Camera focused on the "student as teacher." The actions of the Teacher during such occasions should have been recorded by the Whole Class Camera. If the teacher was positioned out of view of the Whole Class Camera (eg front of classroom, at the side), then the Teacher Camera might "zoom out" to keep both the student and teacher on view, but documentation of the gestures, statements, and any written or drawn work by the student at the board should be kept clearly visible. Note: Although the teacher was radio-miked, in the simulated situations we trialled it was not necessary for the teacher to hand the lapel microphone to the student. The student's public statements to the class could be adequately captured on the student microphone connected to the Student Camera. The first few lessons in a particular classroom (during the familiarisation period) provided an opportunity to learn to "read" the teacher's teaching style, level of mobility, types of whole class discussion employed, and so on. A variety of practical decisions about the optimal camera locations could be made during the familiarisation period and as events dictated during videotaping.

Camera Two: The Student Camera

Where only a single videographer was used, the "Student Camera" was set up prior to the commencement of the lesson to include at least two adjacent students and was re-focussed in the first two minutes of the lesson during the teacher's introductory comments – during this time the Teacher Camera could be set up to record a sufficiently wide image to include most likely positions of the teacher during these opening minutes. Once the Student Camera was adequately focussed on the focus students for that lesson, it remained fixed unless student movement necessitated its realignment. After aligning the Student Camera, the videographer returned to the Teacher Camera and maintained focus on the teacher, subject to the above guidelines.

If two research assistants ("videographers") were available (and this was frequently the case), then it became possible for the Student Camera to "zoom in" on each student's written work every five minutes or so, to maintain an on-going record of the student's progress on any written tasks. This "zooming in" was done sufficiently briefly to provide visual cues as to the progress of the student's written work, but any such zooming in had to be done without losing the continuity of the video record of all focus students, since that would be needed for the subsequent interviews. Since it was Learner Practices that were the priority in this study, the continuous documentation of the actions of the focus students and their interactions (including non-verbal interactions) was most important. A copy of the students' written work was obtained at the end of the lesson. The video record generated by this camera served to display each student's activities in relation to the teacher's actions, the tasks assigned, and the activities of their nearby classmates.

Camera Three: The Whole Class Camera

The "Whole Class (or Teacher-View) Camera" was set up to one side of whichever part of the room the teacher spoke from (typically, to one side at the "front" of the classroom). All students should be within the field of view of this camera (it is necessary to use a wide-angle lens). Apart from capturing the "corporate" behavior of the class, this camera provided an approximation to a "teacher's-eye view" of the class. It was also this camera that documented teacher actions during any periods when a student was working at the board or making a presentation to the entire class.

Microphone Position

The teacher was radio-miked to the Teacher Camera. The focus student group was recorded with a microphone placed as centrally as possible in relation to the focus students and recorded through the Student Camera (use of a radio microphone minimized intrusive cables). The Whole Class Camera audio was recorded through that camera's internal microphone.

Fieldnotes

Depending on the available research personnel, fieldnotes were maintained to record the time and type of all *changes* in instructional activity. Such field notes could be very simple, for example:

    00:00 Teacher Introduction
    09:50 Students do Chalkboard Problem
    17:45 Whole Class Discussion
    24:30 Individual Textbook Work
    41:45 Teacher Summation

Specific events of interest to the researcher could be included as annotations to such field notes.

Where a third researcher was available, in addition to the operators of the Teacher and Student cameras, this person was able to take more detailed field notes, including detail of possible moments of significance for the progress of the lesson (eg public or private negotiations of meaning). In such cases, the field notes became a useful aid in the post-lesson interview, and the interviewee could be asked to comment on particular events, if these had not been already identified by the interviewee earlier in the interview.

Student Written Work

All written work produced by the focus students "in camera" during any lesson was photocopied together with any text materials or handouts used during the lesson. Students brought with them to the interview their textbook and all written material produced in class. This material (textbook pages, worksheets, and student written work) was photocopied immediately after the interview and returned to the student.

INTERVIEWS

In this study, students were interviewed after each lesson using the video record as stimulus for their reconstructions of classroom events. It is a feature of this study that students were given control of the video replay and asked to identify and comment upon classroom events of personal importance. Because of the significance of interviews within the study, the validity of students' and teachers' verbal reconstructions of their motivations, feelings and thoughts was given significant thought. The circumstances under which such verbal accounts may provide legitimate data have been detailed in two seminal papers (Ericsson & Simon, 1980; Nisbett & Wilson, 1977).

It is our contention that videotapes of classroom interactions constitute salient stimuli for interviewing purposes, and that individuals' verbal reports of their thoughts and feelings during classroom interactions, when prompted by videos of the particular associated events, can provide useful insights into those individuals' learning behaviour. Videotapes provide a specific and immediate stimulus that optimises the conditions for effective recall of associated feelings and thoughts. Nonetheless, an individual's video-stimulated account will be prone to the same potential for unintentional misrepresentation and deliberate distortion that apply in any social situation in which individuals are obliged to explain their actions. A significant part of the power of video-stimulated recall resides in the juxtaposition of the interviewee's account and the video record to which it is related. Any apparent discrepancies revealed by such a comparison warrant particular scrutiny and careful interpretation by the researcher. Having relinquished the positivist commitment to identifying 'what really happened,' both correspondence and contradiction can be exploited. The interview protocols for student and teacher interviews were prescribed in the LPS Research Design and are reproduced below.

Individual Student Interviews

Prompt One:	Please tell me what you think that lesson was about (lesson content/lesson purpose).
Prompt Two:	How, do you think, you best learn something like that?
Prompt Three:	What were your personal goals for that lesson? What did you hope to achieve? Do you have similar goals for every lesson?

Prompt Four:	Here is the remote control for the videoplayer. Do you understand how it works? (Allow time for a short familiarisation with the control). I would like you to comment on the videotape for me. You do not need to comment on all of the lesson. Fast forward the videotape until you find sections of the lesson that you think were important. Play these sections at normal speed and describe for me what you were doing, thinking and feeling during each of these videotape sequences. You can comment while the videotape is playing, but pause the tape if there is something that you want to talk about in detail.
Prompt Five:	After watching the videotape, is there anything you would like to add to your description of what the lesson was about?
Prompt Six:	What did you learn during that lesson? [Whenever a claim is made to new mathematical knowledge, this should be probed. Suitable probing cues would be a request for examples of tasks or methods of solution that are now understood or the posing by the interviewer of succinct probing questions related to common misconceptions in the content domain.]
Prompt Seven:	Would you describe that lesson as a good* one for you? What has to happen for you to feel that a lesson was a "good" lesson? Did you achieve your goals? What are the important things you should learn in a mathematics lesson? [*"Good" may be not a sufficiently neutral prompt in some countries – the specific term used should be chosen to be as neutral as possible in order to obtain data on those outcomes of the lesson which the student values. It is possible that these valued outcomes may have little connection to "knowing," "learning" or "understanding," and that students may have very localised or personal ways to describe lesson outcomes. These personalised and possibly culturally-specific conceptions of lesson outcomes constitute important data.]
Prompt Eight:	Was this lesson a typical [geometry, algebra, etc.] lesson? What was not typical about it?
Prompt Nine:	How would you generally assess your own achievement in mathematics?
Prompt Ten:	Do you enjoy mathematics and mathematics classes?
Prompt Eleven:	Why do you think you are good [or not so good] at mathematics?
Prompt Twelve:	Do you do very much mathematical work at home? Have you ever had private tutoring in mathematics or attended additional mathematics classes outside normal school hours?

Prompts 9 through 12 could be covered in a student questionnaire – the choice of method may be made locally, provided the data is collected.

Student Group Interviews

Prompt One: Please tell me what you think that lesson was about (lesson content/lesson purpose) (Discuss with the group – identify points of agreement and disagreement – there is NO need to achieve consensus).

Prompt Two: Here is the remote control for the videoplayer. I would like you to comment on the videotape for me. You do not need to comment on all of the lesson. I will fast forward the videotape until anyone tells me to stop. I want you to find sections of the lesson that you think were important. We will play these sections at normal speed and I would like each of you to describe for me what you were doing, thinking and feeling during each of these videotape sequences. You can comment while the videotape is playing, but tell me to pause the tape if there is something that you want to talk about in detail.

Prompt Three: After watching the videotape, is there anything anyone would like to add to the description of what the lesson was about?

Prompt Four: What did you learn during that lesson? (Discuss)
[As for the individual interview protocol, all claims to new mathematical knowledge should be probed. BUT, before probing an individual's responses directly, the interviewer should ask other members of the group to comment.]

Prompt Five: Would you describe that lesson as a good* one for you? (Discuss) What has to happen for you to feel that a lesson was a "good" lesson? (Discuss) What are the important things you should learn in a mathematics lesson?
[*As for the student individual interviews, "good" may be not be a sufficiently neutral prompt in some countries – the specific term used should be chosen to be as neutral as possible in order to obtain data on those outcomes of the lesson which the student values].

Prompt Six: Was this lesson a typical [geometry, algebra, etc] lesson? What was not typical about it?

The Teacher Interview

The goal was to complete one interview per week, according to teacher availability. The Whole Class Camera image was used as the stimulus. In selecting the lesson about which to seek teacher comment, choose either (1) the lesson with the greatest diversity of classroom activities, or (2) the lesson with the most evident student interactions. Should the teacher express a strong preference to discuss a particular lesson, then this lesson should take priority. Tapes of the other lessons should be available in the interview, in case the teacher should indicate an interest in any aspect of a particular lesson.

Prompt One:	Please tell me what were your goals in that lesson (lesson content/lesson purpose).
Prompt Two:	In relation to your content goal(s), why do you think this content is important for students to learn?
	What do you think your students might have answered to this question?
Prompt Three:	Here is the remote control for the videoplayer. Do you understand how it works? (Allow time for a short familiarisation with the control). I would like you to comment on the videotape for me. You do not need to comment on all of the lesson. Fast forward the videotape until you find sections of the lesson that you think were important. Play these sections at normal speed and describe for me what you were doing, thinking and feeling during each of these videotape sequences. You can comment while the videotape is playing, but pause the tape if there is something that you want to talk about in detail.

In particular, I would like you to comment on:

(a) Why you said or did a particular thing (for example, conducting a particular activity, using a particular example, asking a question, or making a statement).

(b) What you were thinking at key points during each video excerpt (for example, I was confused, I was wondering what to do next, I was trying to think of a good example).

(c) How you were feeling? (for example, I was worried that we would not cover all the content)

(d) Students' actions or statements that you consider to be significant and explain why you feel the action or statement was significant.

(e) How typical that lesson was of the sort of lesson you would normally teach? What do you see as the features of that lesson that are most typical of the way you teach? Were there any aspects of your behavior or the students' behavior that were unusual?

Prompt Four:	Would you describe that lesson as a good lesson for you? What has to happen for you to feel that a lesson is a "good" lesson?
Prompt Five:	Do your students work a lot at home? Do they have private tutors?

OTHER SOURCES OF DATA

Student tests were used to situate each student group and each student in relation to student performance on eighth-grade mathematics tasks. Student mathematics achievement was assessed in three ways:

Student written work in class.   Analyses of student written work were undertaken both during and after the period of videotaping. For this purpose, the written work of all "focus students" in each lesson was photocopied, clearly labelled with the student's name, the class, and the date, and filed. Additional data on student achievement was also collected, where this was available. In particular, student scores were obtained on any topic tests administered by the teacher, in relation to mathematical content dealt with in the videotaped lesson sequence.

Student performance to place the class in relation to the national 8th grade population.   In Australia, Japan, Korea, China and the USA, this was done by using the International Benchmark Test for Mathematics (administered immediately after the completion of videotaping). The International Benchmark Test (IBT) was developed by the Australian Council for Educational Research (ACER) by combining a selection of items from the TIMSS Student Achievement test. In the case of this project, the test for Population Two was used, since this was in closest correspondence with the grade level of the students taking part in the LPS project. In administering the IBT, the local research group in each country constructed an equivalent test using the corresponding version of each of the TIMSS items, as administered in that country. In some countries, where this was not possible (Germany, for example), the typical school performance was characterised in relation to other schools by comparison of the senior secondary mathematics performance with national norms.

Student performance in relation to other students in that class.   Since student-student interactions may be influenced by perceptions of peer competence, it was advantageous to collect recent performance data on all students in the class. Two forms of student mathematics achievement at class level were accessed, where available: (a) student scores from recent mathematics tests administered by the teacher, and (b) brief annotated comments by the teacher on a list of all students in the class – commenting on the mathematics achievement and competence of each student.

Teacher Goals and Perceptions

Teacher questionnaires were used to establish teacher beliefs and purposes related to the lesson sequence studied. Three questionnaires were administered to each participating teacher:

— A *preliminary* teacher questionnaire about each teacher's goals in the teaching of mathematics (TQ1);
— A *post-lesson* questionnaire (TQ2 – either the short TQ2S or the long TQ2L version – if the short version was used, the researcher's field notes provided as much as possible of the additional detail sought in the long version);
— A *post-videotaping* questionnaire (TQ3) (also employed by some research groups as the basis of a final teacher interview).

DATA CONFIGURATION AND STORAGE

Transcription and Translation

A detailed Technical Guide was developed to provide guidelines for the transcription and translation of classroom and interview, video and audiotape data. It was essential that all research groups transcribe their own data. Local language variants (e.g., the Berliner dialect) required a "local ear" for accurate transcription. Translation into English was also the responsibility of the local research group. The Technical Guide specified both transcription conventions, such as how to represent pauses or overlapping statements, and translation conventions, such as how to represent colloquialisms. In the case of local colloquial expressions in a language other than English, the translator was presented with a major challenge. A literal English translation of the colloquialism may convey no meaning at all to a reader from another country, while the replacement of the colloquialism by a similar English colloquialism may capture the essence and spirit of the expression, but sacrifice the semantic connotations of the particular words used. And there is a third problem: If no precise English equivalent can be found, then the translation inevitably misrepresents the communicative exchange. In such instances, the original language, as transcribed, was included together with its literal English translation. Any researcher experiencing difficulties of interpretation in analysing the data could contact a member of the research group responsible for the generation of those data and request additional detail.

Data Storage

To carry out serious systematic empirical work in classroom research, there is a need for both close and detailed analysis of selected event sequences, and for more general descriptions of the material from within which the analysed sample has been chosen. To be able to perform this work with good-quality multiple-source video and audio data, video and audio materials have to be compressed and stored in a form accessible by desktop computers. Software tools such as *Final Cut Pro* are essential for the efficient and economical storage of the very large video data files. Compression decisions are dictated by current storage and back-up alternatives and change as these change. For example, when the Learner's Perspective Study was established in 1999, it was anticipated that data would be exchanged between research teams by CD-ROM and compression ratios were set at 20:1 in order to get maximum data quality within a file size that would allow one video record of one lesson to be stored on a single CD. As a result, the complete US data set in 2001 took the form of a set of over fifty separate CDs. Later, it was possible to store all the data related to a single lesson (including four compressed video records) on a single DVD. The contemporary availability of pocket drives with capacities of 60 gigabytes and higher, has made data sharing both more efficient and cheaper. It is possible to store all the data from a single school in compressed form on such a pocket drive, making secure data transfer between international research groups much more cost-effective.

The materials on the database have to be represented in a searchable fashion. In Figure 2, the configuration of the LPS database is displayed as a stratified hierarchy of: Country (column 1), school (column 2), lesson (column 3), data source (column 4), specific file (column 5). Any particular file, such as the teacher camera view of lesson 4 at school 2 in Japan, can then be uniquely located.

Setting up data in this way enables researchers to move between different layers of data, without losing sight of the way they are related to each other. Further, data can be made accessible to other researchers. This is a sharp contrast to more traditional ways of storing video data on tapes, with little or no searchable record available, and with data access limited to very small numbers of people. At the International Centre for Classroom Research (ICCR) at the University of Melbourne, for example, several researchers can simultaneously access the full range of classroom data. This capacity for the simultaneous analysis of a common body of classroom data is the technical realisation of the methodological and theoretical commitment to complementary analyses proposed by Clarke (1998, 2001) as essential to any research attempting to characterise social phenomena as complex as those found in classrooms.

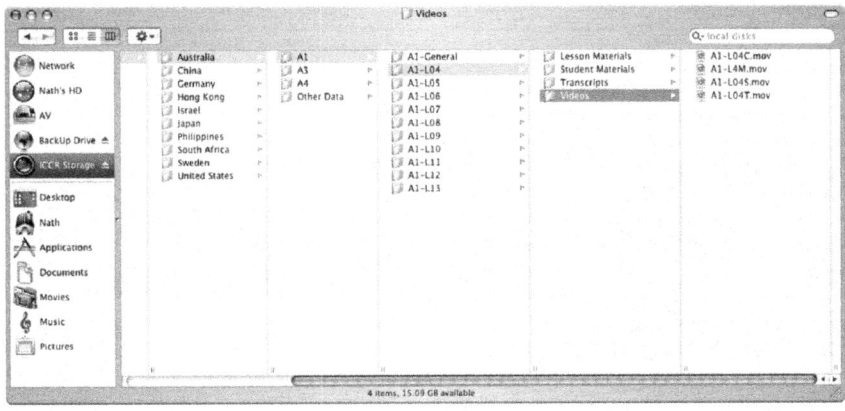

Figure 2. Structure of the LPS database at the ICCR circa 2004

ANALYTICAL TOOLS CAPABLE OF SUPPORTING SOPHISTICATED ANALYSES OF SUCH COMPLEX DATABASES

Research along the lines argued for above requires the development of software tools for analysing video efficiently. The reasons for this are, in short, that video editing software (such as *Final Cut Pro*) is not analytically resourceful enough, whereas qualitative analysis software (such as *Nudist* or *nVivo*) is not well enough adapted to video and audio work. Early examples of video analysis software (such as *vPrism*) have been hampered by problems arising from their project-specific origins, leading to a lack of flexibility in customising the analysis to the demands of each particular project or research focus.

Collaboration with the Australian software company, Sportstec, was carried out to adapt the video analysis software *Studiocode* for use with classroom video data. These adaptations were driven by specific methodological, theoretical and practical needs. For example, the commitment to the capturing and juxtaposition of multiple perspectives on classroom events was partially addressed with the onsite capture of the picture-in-picture display shown in Figure 1, but the need to 'calibrate' the actions of the focus students against the actions of the rest of the class required multiple viewing windows.

Figure 3 displays the key analytical elements provided within *Studiocode*: video window, time-line, transcript window, and coding scheme. The researcher has the option of analysing and coding the events shown in the video window, or the utterances shown in the transcript window, or both. The resultant codes can be displayed in timelines (as shown in Figure 3) or in frequency tables. Once coded, single lessons, events within single lessons, or combinations of lessons can be merged into a single analysis.

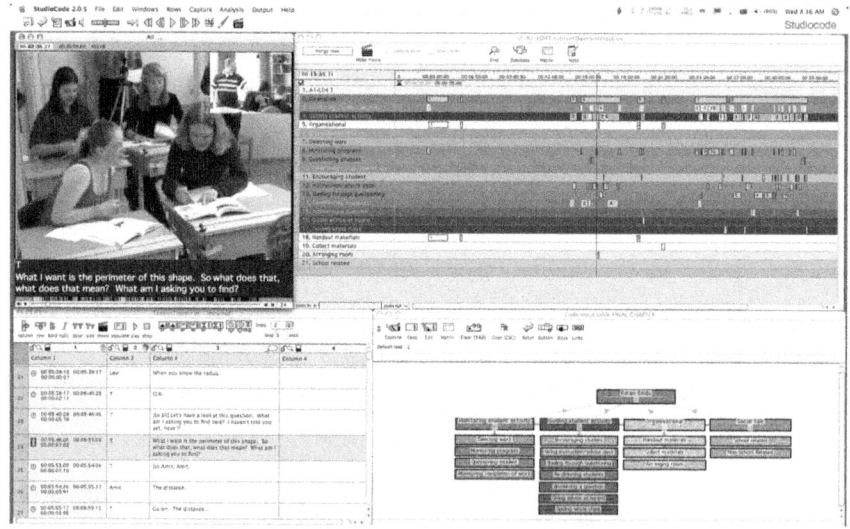

Figure 3. Sample analytical display (Studiocode) – video window (top left), time-line (top right), transcript window (bottom-left) and coding facility (bottom-right)

The continual addition of new countries to the Learner's Perspective Study community required that video data already coded should not need to be recoded when additional data (eg from a different country) were incrementally added to the database. Only the new data should require coding and the newly-coded data should be accessible for analysis as part of the growing pool of classroom data. This flexibility is ideally suited to a project such as the Learner's Perspective Study, with many collaborating researchers adopting a wide range of different analytical approaches to a commonly held body of classroom data.

The *Studiocode* software described above is only one of the many analytical tools available to the classroom researcher. Increasingly sophisticated public access software tools are being developed continually. Most of the chapters in this book and in the companion volume (Clarke, Keitel, & Shimizu, 2006) report specific analyses of different subsets of the large body of LPS classroom data. Each analysis is distinctive and interrogates and interprets the data consistent with the purpose of the authoring researcher(s). Analytical tools such as *nVivo* and *Studiocode* can support the researcher's analysis but ideally should not constrain the consequent interpretation of the data. In reality, all such tools, including statistical procedures, constrain the researcher's possible interpretations by limiting the type of data compatible with the analytical tool being used, by restricting the variety of codes, categories or values that can be managed, and by constraining the range of possible results able to be generated by the particular analytical tool.

REFERENCES

Clarke, D. J. (1998). Studying the classroom negotiation of meaning: Complementary accounts methodology. In A. Teppo (Ed.), *Qualitative research methods in mathematics education*, monograph number 9 of the *Journal for Research in Mathematics Education* (pp. 98–111). Reston, VA: NCTM.

Clarke, D. J. (Ed.). (2001). *Perspectives on practice and meaning in mathematics and science classrooms*. Dordrecht, The Netherlands: Kluwer Academic Press.

Clarke, D. J., Keitel, C., & Shimizu, Y. (Eds.). (2006). *Mathematics classrooms in twelve countries: The insider's perspective*. Rotterdam: Sense Publishers.

Ericsson, K. A., & Simon, H. A. (1980). Verbal reports as data. *Psychological Review, 87*(3), 215–251.

Miles, M. B., & Huberman, A. M. (2004). *Qualitative data analysis* (2nd ed.). Thousand Oaks, CA: Sage Publications.

Nisbett, R. E., & Wilson, T. D. (1977). Telling more than we can know: Verbal reports on mental processes. *Psychological Review, 84*(3), 231–259.

AFFILIATION

David Clarke
International Centre for Classroom Research
University of Melbourne
Australia

SUBJECT INDEX

A

Achievement, 12, 43, 146, 156, 250, 252, 253
Activity, 2, 23, 32, 42, 51, 74, 81, 96, 97, 100, 113, 116, 119, 126, 127, 133, 135, 138, 139, 146, 193, 202, 214, 219, 221, 225, 229, 236, 245, 246, 248, 252
  exploratory, 214
  group, 220, 222, 225, 229
  instructional, 18, 248
  interactivity, 6, 167, 187, 215
  mathematical theory, 51, 100, 126, 127
Algebraic competence, 60
Alignment, 12, 150–155, 158, 160–171, 247
  Curriculum, 151, 160–166
  Pedagogy, 150, 152–155, 167–171
Articulating, articulation, 115, 120, 215, 217–220, 227, 228
Asia, Asian, 10, 244
Assessment, 44, 83, 88, 89, 94, 95, 97

B

Balance model, 2, 6, 19, 20, 22, 23, 26–33, 35, 51, 53
Basic skills, 186, 230
Beijing, 3–6, 8, 9, 149–171
Big ideas, 33, 229, 230
Blended Model, 8–10

C

China, Chinese, 3, 4, 6, 7, 11, 149–230, 237, 244, 245, 253
Chinese pedagogy, 186, 192
Classroom
  discourse, 8, 93, 94, 144

practice, v, 5, 8, 11, 12, 42, 59, 215
research, v, 101, 254, 255, 257
Class size, 195
Coherence, 4, 9, 43, 192
Cognitive, 6, 18, 19, 41, 96, 176, 187, 192, 214
  engagement, 10, 82
Collaboration, 6, 63, 65, 71, 229, 256
Collaborative problem solving, 228
CMCS [China Mathematics Curriculum Standard for Full-time Compulsory Education (experimental version)], 149–152, 155, 156, 158–171
Communication, 102, 122, 170
Community of inquiry, 12, 129, 146
Competence, 3, 60, 61, 62, 78, 111, 230, 244, 253
Complementarity, 1, 101, 244
Confucian-Heritage Culture (CHC), 4
Conceptual understanding, 6–10, 19, 115, 126, 209, 234
Connection of concepts, 228
Constructivism, 127
Cultural differences, 4, 215
Culture, 12, 43, 129, 146, 156, 186, 214,

D

Dialogue, 127
Didactic relationship, 99
Didactical, 12, 54, 113, 126
  contract, 10
  theory of didactical situations, 113
Discourse, 8, 35, 93, 94, 144, 146, 187, 230
  teachers' orientations of, 35

259

Lightning Source UK Ltd.
Milton Keynes UK
UKOW01f1950291017

311847UK00004B/47/P

9 789462 097056